NORVAL BARO

# DANCING WITH DeBEAUVOIR

# DANCING WITH
# De BEAUVOIR

### JAZZ AND THE FRENCH

**Colin Nettelbeck**

MELBOURNE UNIVERSITY PRESS

Melbourne University Publishing Ltd (MUP Ltd)
PO Box 1167, Carlton, Victoria 3053, Australia
mup-info@unimelb.edu.au
www.mup.com.au

First published 2004
Text © Colin W. Nettelbeck © 2004
Design and typography © Melbourne University Publishing Ltd 2004
Edited by L. Elaine Miller of Otmar Miller Consultancy Pty Ltd, Melbourne

Typeset in Janson Text 10.25/14 point, by Syarikat Seng Teik Sdn. Bhd., Malaysia
Printed in Australia by McPherson's Printing Group
Designed by Phil Campbell

National Library of Australia Cataloguing-in-Publication entry

Nettelbeck, Colin W.
  Dancing with De Beauvoir: jazz and the French.
  Bibliography.
  Includes index.
  ISBN 0 522 85113 4.
  1. Jazz—France. I. Title.
781.650944

# Contents

# List of photographs

**Facing Part One Title Page:** The Berry Brothers, New York Cotton Club review at the Moulin Rouge, Paris, 1937: X, Collection of C. W. Nettelbeck.

**Facing Part Two Title Page:** Duke Ellington with, from left to right, Boris Vian, Juliette Gréco and Anne-Marie Cazalis at the Club Saint-Germain, at a gala organised in his honour on 19 July 1948: Keystone—France

James Reese Europe's military band at the Chambéry train station, February 1918: X, kindly provided by 'Connaissance de Challes-les-Eaux'.

Poster advertising *La Revue Nègre*, Paris, 1925: Paul Colin/ADAGP. Licensed by VISCOPY, Sydney 2003. Image from Bibliothèque nationale de France, Paris.

Django Reinhardt and Stéphane Grappelli, 6 December 1935: X, Bibliothèque nationale de France.

Whyte's Hopping Maniacs performing the 'Lindy Hop', Cotton Club review: Brucken, Collection of C. W. Nettelbeck.

Jungle dance, Cotton Club review, 1937: Brucken, Collection of C. W. Nettelbeck.

Tramp Band, Cotton Club review, 1937: Brucken, Collection of C. W. Nettelbeck.

Charles Delaunay presents Sidney Bechet with a gold disc celebrating the sale of his millionth record with Vogue at the concert held at the Olympia on 19 October 1955. Behind, from left to right: Claude Philippe (banjo) Benny Vasseur (trombone): Jean-Pierre Leloir.

Count Basie and Hugues Panassié at the Salle Pleyel, October 1963: Jean-Pierre Leloir.

Jazz club Caveau de la Huchette, Paris, 1957: Chenz (c)Mephisto.

Miles Davis and Juliette Gréco, Club Saint-Germain, Paris: André Sas/Rapho.

Anne-Marie Cazalis and Raymond Queneau, 1948: Keystone–France.

Jean-Paul Sartre, Boris Vian, Michelle Vian and Simone de Beauvoir, Café Procope, Saint-Germain-des-Prés: Yves Manciet/Rapho.

Boris Vian and André Hodeir, Charles Cros Academy, 1958: Jean-Pierre Leloir.

Jean Cocteau, Francis Crémieux and Norbert Gamsbon and Jean Wiéner recording memoirs of *Boeuf sur le toit*, summer 1958: Jean Mainbourg/Rapho.

Louis-Ferdinand Céline, 1932: X, Collection of C. W. Nettelbeck.

Book covers, courtesy of Editions Robert Laffont and Editions de Minuit.

On the set of Jacques Becker's *Rendez-vous de juillet* (1949). Nicole Courcel, Brigitte Auber, Pierre Merlin, Claude Rabanit and Claude Luter: Masour, Bibliothèque nationale de France.

Sidney Bechet in a bistro near Notre-Dame-De-Lorette Church, Paris, 1960: Edouard Boubat/TOP–Rapho.

Pianist Martial Solal, winner of the Jazz Academy's Django Reinhardt award, with Honorary President Jean Cocteau, June 1955: Jean-Pierre Leloir.

Martial Solal at the celebration of the donation of the Delaunay Collection to the National Library of France, May 1986: André Clergeat, Bibliothèque nationale de France.

Michel Portal and Henri Texier, January 1985: Jean-Pierre Leloir.

Benny Carter and Charles Delaunay at the celebration of the donation of the Delaunay Collection to the National Library of France, Paris, May 1986: André Clergeat, Bibliothèque nationale de France.

Michel Petrucciani, Nevers 1994: Mephisto (c) Mephisto.

The graves of Frédéric Chopin and Michel Petrucciani, Père-Lachaise cemetery, 2003: Johnny Fogg.

Joachim Kühn, Ornette Coleman and Jacques Derrida, La Villette Jazz Festival, July 1997: Christian Ducasse.

# Acknowledgements

The research for this project was funded by a three-year grant from the Australian Research Council, and I thank the ARC for this generous support. I am deeply grateful for the research assistance provided by a number of people: David Bancroft and the CPEDERF team in Paris, especially Alistair Rolls and Julia M<sup>c</sup>Laren; Sarah Potaznic for her successful prospecting in Nantes; Jacqueline Dutton, Julia Martin and Emily Street for their invaluable library and archival work; Roger Dumollard and the group Connaissance de Challes-Les-Eaux; Richard Miller for his work on *Jazz Hot*; Anne Legrand for facilitating access to the resources of the Bibliothèque de France; Kirsten Newitt, Jane Nethercote and Emily Street for their help preparing the manuscript. Photographers Christian Ducasse, Jean-Pierre Leloir, André Clergeat and Johnny Fogg were personally accommodating as well as professionally helpful. Thanks, too, to the colleagues and friends who made suggestions on draft material, especially Rosemary Lloyd, Jaynie Anderson and Charles Sowerwine. Melbourne University Press has been wonderfully supportive, and I especially thank Sybil Nolan, copy editor Elaine Miller and designer Phil Campbell for their contributions.

The acquisition of the rights to publish illustrative material was assisted by a publication grant from the University of Melbourne. Early versions of some parts of this study have appeared in *Australian Journal of French Studies*, *Nottingham French Studies*, *Modern and Contemporary France*, and *French Cultural Studies*.

**For Carol**

# Introduction

**Jazz . . . arguably America's outstanding contribution to the world of music . . . European audiences are far more receptive to jazz, and thus many American musicians have become expatriates.**
**'Jazz',** *The Columbia Encyclopedia*[1]

At the New York Library for the Performing Arts in 1998, when I told a librarian at the reference desk that I was researching the impact of jazz in France, she responded as if it were a matter of common knowledge: 'Well, they're the ones who have preserved it.' The impression that jazz has had a better reception in Europe—and in France in particular—than in its own country of origin is a pervasive one, among historians and critics and also among many musicians themselves. Jazz's positive experience of France is as notable as France's positive experience of jazz. The steady increase in passionate audiences, the emergence of a considerable number of first-rate French jazz musicians, the use of jazz as a source of creative inspiration and transformation by artists of all kinds—all of these things point to a climate of overwhelming congeniality.

Without jazz, French culture would not have developed in the same way. While its impact on the 'high' music tradition in France has been marginal (without being negligible), it has been an essential ingredient in the development of popular music forms. Beyond music, jazz has been a stimulus for other forms of creation, both visual and literary, and has informed the work of significant numbers of key artists. In other words, the passage of jazz through French cultural history is not simply a story of influence or appropriation. France has derived a great deal from jazz, and in doing so, it has been nourished by it and has used jazz as the basis for new creations, which have in turn enriched the artistic culture of the world.

Live jazz arrived in France towards the end of World War I. From the very start, it was received not only as a new form of music but as a fertile symbol of many other things. As its sounds were being picked up and emulated with varying degrees of success by young French musicians, commentators sought to explain it in broader terms. Jazz was music, certainly, but it was also an embodiment of artistic freedom, it was modernism, it was America (both as promise and menace), it was African primitivism, sexual liberation, social decadence and moral decay. This heterogeneous collection of intermingled and conflicting associations helped to produce one of the most potent and exciting explosions in French cultural history.

The whole phenomenon was, and remains, contentious. In fact, no uncontroversial statements can be made about the birth of jazz or about its arrival in France, because there has never been general agreement about what jazz itself is. Dispute about what kinds of music the term 'jazz' can cover has simmered, and sometimes raged, since the word first began to gain currency during the Great War. It is rare to find any study of the music that does not at some point engage in the polemic of what distinguishes 'true' jazz from forms of music that fall outside a particular commentator's canonical definition.

Many die-hard traditionalists, for instance, recognise as jazz only that music developed by African-Americans in New Orleans in the early twentieth century. They might accept the respectful performance of that style by white Americans—the Chicago trumpeter Bix Beiderbecke is almost universally cited as a paragon in this regard. But they are unable to include developments such as the be-bop revolution led by the likes of Thelonious Monk and Charlie Parker, let alone free jazz, or even the rhythmic experiments of a Dave Brubeck, who dared in the 1950s to challenge the 4/4 time signature of traditional jazz and write tunes in 5/4 or even 9/8 time. Conversely, people who have come to jazz later in its evolution often have difficulty taking seriously—other than in a museum-visit spirit—even some of the great masters of early jazz, such as Louis Armstrong or Jelly Roll Morton.

The word itself reflects this turmoil. From very early on, various etymologies have been offered, based on wild and unverifiable theories. Some saw it as deriving from the name of a person, Jasbo Brown (whose real first name was James, unless it was Charles—'Jas' or 'Chas'). Others have believed the word to be of African origin (perhaps coming through Arabic) and meaning to 'speed things up': to 'jazz' a tune would mean to play it more quickly. A number of historians have taken the position that it is a Creole variant of the French word 'jaser' (meaning to 'chatter', 'warble', 'gossip'). Yet another view suggests that it was originally a slang word, believed sometimes to be specifically black, sometimes more broadly popular, for sex.[2]

All of these theories, whatever their historical validity, are linked to other connotations that give them a culturally marked and sometimes an ideological dimension. The Jasbo Brown story is in the lineage of many foundational myths that seek to establish the idea of a single foundational moment: Gutenberg for the invention of printing, for instance, or the Lumière brothers for the creation of cinema. In this respect, reflections about jazz are affected by the age-old human tendency to seek simple, single answers about what happened 'in the beginning'. The suggested African/Arabic etymology enlarges on this idea, but it also carries a strong claim for a set of exclusive ethnic territorial rights in the ownership of the term.

The French connection, giving precedence to a white European origin over the African one, has persuasive phonological and contextual aspects: the pronunciation of 'jaser' in French is 'jazz', and the musicological links between early jazz and the French quadrille—a popular nineteenth-century dance and its accompanying music—are well documented. But, obviously, this approach also contains resonances of colonialist nostalgia or neo-colonialist appropriation. As for the sexual connotations, the ambiguity is a nice one: if taken as a product of a white honky-tonk background, whether that be the dance halls of San Francisco or the speakeasies of New Orleans, the word 'jazz' carries all of the wild and sleazy vulgarity that would become the permanent target of its conservative critics. As a black term, it both wilfully transgresses dominant cultural taboos (analogous to the musical activity of 'playing dirty'—distorting and slurring notes and phrases), and celebrates cultural uniqueness and authenticity.

Within ten years of the first appearance of the word 'jazz' in print,[3] all of these etymologies surfaced and found their share of believers. There is no real basis for choosing among them, and indeed, any such choice is unnecessarily limiting. It makes more sense to treat them as a complex of elements in dynamic tension with one another, and as an example of how difficult it is to trace the birth of jazz—as of any art—to a single source. We can be reasonably confident that the word 'jazz', as a musical term, was in existence around the beginning of the twentieth century (even if we are sceptical of Ferdinand 'Jelly Roll' Morton's claim to have 'originated' it in New Orleans around 1902!)[4] but it is unlikely that we will ever be sure of anything more precise.

One intriguing piece of ultimately apocryphal evidence dates the word's existence as far back as the 1870s. In 1917, a New York journalist, with tantalising vagueness, stated that 'jazz' was referred to in a text by that eternal expatriate, Lafcadio Hearn.[5] One of modern literature's most gifted interpreters of other cultures, Hearn's authority in this issue, repeated by many subsequent commentators after the 1917 allusion, is not to be ignored. The problem is that exhaustive searches of Hearn's works have failed to find the text in question.[6] Pertinently, there is no entry for 'jazz' in Hearn's dictionary of New Orleans Creole, where we might most readily have expected to find it.

However, Hearn's presence in the jazz debate is far from being without foundation. Any reader of the articles and letters that Hearn produced during his decade in New Orleans (1877–87) will find extraordinarily rich testimony of the tumultuous social, cultural and artistic forces in that post-Civil War city. The French influence was enduring, not just in the crumbling elegance of the architecture, or in the daily life and language of the large Creole population, but in Hearn's weekly newspaper translations of contemporary French authors such as Flaubert, Zola, Baudclaire and Loti. There was also a strong Spanish-speaking presence, including a sizeable and boisterous Mexican community. The mix of ethnicities contained a vigorous African-American population, and a Creole community that itself was very diverse, being both white and of mixed blood. With his highly cultivated interest in music, Hearn is a prize witness of the musical potpourri that characterised New Orleans during the gestation of jazz. He wrote excitedly about the weird melodies and rhythms of Creole songs, the fierce merriment of guitar-playing Mexicans who accompanied themselves by banging on upturned glasses with spoons, and sounds produced by black pianists to echo the chords and note-picking of the banjo.

Given Hearn's unwavering commitment to high culture aestheticism and art, his views on Creole music are highly relevant. Writing to his musicologist friend H.E. Krehbiel[7] in Cincinnati in 1878, he observed:

I am writing you a detailed account of the Creoles of Louisiana, and their blending with Creole immigrants from the Canaries, Martinique and San Domingo; but it is a subject of great latitude, and I can only outline it for you. Their characteristics offer an interesting topic, and the bastard off-spring of the miscegenated French and African, or Spanish and African, dialects, called Creole, offer pretty peculiarities worth a volume. I will try to give you an entertaining sketch of the subject. I must tell you, however, that Creole music is mostly Negro music, although often remodelled by French composers. There could neither have been Creole patois, nor Creole melodies, but for the French and Spanish blooded slaves of Louisiana and the Antilles. The melancholy, quavering beauty and weird-ness of the Negro chant are lightened by the French influence, or subdued and deepened by the Spanish.[8]

A few years later, in 1885, Hearn's knowledge, derived from both his con-tinuing extensive reading and his growing experience of local life, had greatly expanded, and he raised with Krehbiel the possibility of writing an introduc-tion to African-American music. He linked the African-American aptitude for improvisation back to the Griot tradition, and in fact his understanding of the music's specificities, and of its origins, had become quite precise:

I have never yet met a person here able to reproduce on paper those frac-tional tones we used to talk about, which lend such weirdness to those songs. The naked melody robbed of these has absolutely no national charac-teristic. The other day a couple of darkeys from the country passed my corner, singing—not a Creole song, but a plain negro ditty—with a re-current burthen consisting of the cry:
    Oh! Jee-roo-sa-le-e-em!
    I can't describe to you the manner in which the syllable lem was broken up into four tiny notes, the utterance of which did not occupy one second —all in a very low but powerful key. The rest of the song was in a regular descending scale: the oh being very much prolonged and the other notes very quick and sudden. I think all the original negro-Creole songs were characterized by similar eccentricities.[9]

Less a professional ethnomusicologist than a passionate amateur, Hearn was nonetheless an impressive researcher. In the light of his vast knowledge, which embraced not only the modern Western tradition, but also ancient and contemporary music from all over the world (Egypt, Greece, Africa, China, Japan), his view that the African ingredient was crucial to the newly emerging music adds weight to that core tenet of the jazz tradition. At the same time, Hearn's work does remind us that trying to settle the question of the origins of jazz—in the sense of providing some simple, singular, linear account—is bound to be futile. We would do better to concentrate on the immense diversity of the circumstances surrounding its birth, on the fundamental importance of the African and New Orleans dimensions of that diversity, and on the sheer excitement and energy that brought the new music into being.

There are no recordings or written transcriptions of the music that began to take form in New Orleans in the last decade of the nineteenth century—only stories. The musical elements have often been repeated: the minstrel music, the blues and work songs, the spirituals, the rags, the airs of the French quadrilles and gigues, the Spanish guitar rhythms, the local and Caribbean Creole music. Well before emancipation, the African slaves had turned their Sunday recreation in Congo Square into a weekly rite of drumming, singing and dancing. Hearn witnessed later manifestations of the Congo Square phenomenon:

> Yes, I have seen them dance; but they danced the Congo, and sang a purely African song to the accompaniment of a dry-goods box beaten with sticks or bones and a drum made by stretching a skin over a flour-barrel . . . There are no harmonies—only a furious contretemps. As for the dance,— in which the women do not take their feet off the ground,—it is as lascivious as possible. The men dance very differently, like savages, leaping in the air . . .
>
> The Creole songs, which I have heard sung in the city, are Frenchy in construction, but possess a few African characteristics of method. The darker the singer the more marked the oddities of intonation.[10]

Described by one contemporary as 'uncontrolled frenzy',[11] the Congo Square activities were distinguished by their intense physicality. They were also an important crucible for future musicians. The grandfather of Sidney

Bechet, Omar, who was emancipated as a child, was a regular participant in the Congo Square rituals in the 1870s.[12] And Rudy Blesh speculates that many of the future members of the marching bands that led the legendary parades and funeral processions in the New Orleans of the 1890s must have had their apprenticeship in Congo Square, before its decline in the 1880s.[13]

One enduring myth about the spread of jazz from New Orleans grew out of the famous closure of Storyville, the New Orleans pleasure district. Military ordinances prohibiting prostitution within five miles of army or naval establishments effectively shut down all brothels in New Orleans in 1917. By November of that year, the military action allegedly provoked an exodus of major musicians and band leaders: the jazz emigration went north and east to Memphis, St Louis, Chicago and New York and west to California.[14] More recent scholarship tells a rather different story. It shows that the spread of jazz, via the boat traffic on the Mississippi and through the peregrinations of individual musicians, was more gradual and complex, following the migration of large numbers of African-Americans who left the South in search of better lives. For instance, Jelly Roll Morton, who did play in Storyville, left New Orleans for the West Coast around 1908 and spent the war in Chicago. Also, most of the great New Orleans bands were not associated with the city's brothel culture at all, and while many of them did travel it was not because they were forced out, but rather because the north seemed to offer better opportunities.[15]

Jazz in its early days developed and spread through existing patterns of vaudeville, novelty music, ragtime and a succession of society dance crazes. It also merged with the appearance of a generation of classically trained African-American musicians, such as Will Marion Cook and James Reese Europe, who would both play important roles in the future development of jazz. The progressive legitimisation of home-grown American music is also important: it had already begun in the 1890s with the establishment of the National Conservatory of Music of America, with Antonin Dvořák as its founding director. Dvořák's contribution to America's awakening consciousness of its cultural worth was considerable, and for many African-American musicians, 'high culture' music became a well-trodden path in their attempt to achieve successful social and artistic integration into mainstream America. However, they often failed. Formidable racial barriers led to widespread segregation of African-American musical activities from white music venues, and it was only through popular music channels and commercial entertainment (musical theatre, dance and comedy shows, nightclub acts and so on) that most black musicians were able to develop viable professional careers.

The year 1917 was a watershed. In January, in New York, The Original Dixieland Jazz Band made the first recordings explicitly linking the word 'jazz' to a particular form of music. This group, made up of white New Orleans musicians, had been recruited to play in Chicago a year earlier. Reid Badger, in his biography of James Reese Europe, points to this event, together with the death of the master ragtime composer and pianist, Scott Joplin, on 1 April, and the US entry into World War I on 6 April as being symbolic of the end of an era.[16] It was also the beginning of another.

The connection between jazz and America's assumption of a major role in the Great War is critical. The war accelerated the spread of jazz across the United States and it was through American troops abroad that jazz established its first foothold in Europe. More portentously, May 1917 marked the expedition to Puerto Rico by the young James Europe, to recruit musicians for the band of the 15th Infantry Regiment (Colored Americans) of the New York National Guard. This band—later to be known as the 'Hellfighters'—would in the following winter bring France one of its first major experiences of jazz.

The sounds of jazz were not altogether new to French ears; forerunners of the new music had been around for three-quarters of a century. In the 1840s, Louis Moreau Gottschalk, a New Orleans Creole musician, was celebrated as both an inventive composer and a virtuoso pianist. He has since been styled (with some exaggeration) as 'the granddaddy of all jazz musicians'.[17] Gottschalk's mixed family background and his upbringing are in the image of a new world. His businessman father was an English Jew of German origin; his mother, of French extraction and a Catholic, was a descendant of the exodus from the French Caribbean after the great slave rebellion of the 1790s. Gottschalk senior had a mulatto free woman as a long-term mistress with whom he shared many business dealings, including the trading of slaves.[18] His son's childhood was immersed in all the ambiguities of multilingualism, blurred ethnic origins, and mixed religious heritage. His music, too, grew out of similarly heterogeneous roots.

Trained with classical rigour by French teachers, Moreau Gottschalk quickly revealed himself as a child prodigy, and in 1841, at the age of twelve, he was sent to Paris. Many of his compositions—'Bamboula (Danse de nègres)', 'Le Bananier (Chanson nègre)', 'The Banjo (Fantaisie grotesque)', 'Pasquinade (Caprice)'—reflect the variety of melodies and rhythms of the composer's New Orleans childhood. While clearly adapted to the romantic mode dominant in Paris at the time, the music draws on many of the different traditions from the New Orleans melting pot: the opulence of grand opera, of which New Orleans was the New World capital; the formality of old French dances; the sensual choreography of African-American syncopation; the sweet melancholy of Creole songs; the jerky sprightliness of street and folk musicians.

The sound is still fresh and exotic today, and for the European audiences of the 1840s, Gottschalk became a veritable cult figure. Accepted, indeed acclaimed by the most prominent musicians of the day—Berlioz, Bizet, Chopin, Liszt—he was also the object of attentive praise from great writers such as Théophile Gautier and Victor Hugo.[19] Whether or not one accepts Gottschalk as a forefather of jazz,[20] his story certainly tells us a lot about the conditions of its birth. The New Orleans that produced this extraordinary adaptor of Creole rhythms and melodies offered an astonishingly rich musical experience to all of its inhabitants. It even welcomed black slaves into its many opera houses (albeit in segregated sections). In reflecting on the diversity of ingredients that feed into the origins of jazz, it is worth remembering that Italian operatic arias were among the tunes that these workers were heard to reproduce.[21]

In the course of the late nineteenth century, other forms of African-American music and culture found their way into France. Minstrel shows were common and John Philip Sousa included a lot of ragtime in the repertoire of his 1900 French tour. Ragtime, which had attracted wide attention at the Chicago World Fair in 1893,[22] had also begun to circulate freely in sheet music form. In the opening years of the new century, the cakewalk (originally developed by black slaves to mock the stilted manners of European dance style[23] through exaggerated back-arching and high-stepping) became a dance craze in modish Paris. It even provoked a flurry of shocked reactions, with stern warnings about the threat that this imported syncopated rhythm posed to the integrity of French culture.[24] Such worries did not prevent the women's fashion magazine *Femina* from engaging African-American dancers to demonstrate the cakewalk and other steps as the centre-piece of its annual garden party in 1904.[25] For his part, Claude Debussy enjoyed ragtime. He knew Gottschalk's work, and indeed was connected to him through his own teacher, Ernest Guiraud, another native of New Orleans and a protégé of Gottschalk's. Debussy celebrated the pleasure that he found in ragtime by including it, playfully but respectfully, in his own work. The best known example of this is 'Golliwog's Cake-Walk' in *The Children's Corner* suite, composed in 1908.

France's readiness for the arrival of jazz is neatly symbolised in the 1917 show *Parade*. Combining the talents of Cocteau, Picasso and Satie together with Diaghilev's Russian ballet company, Ballets russes, this scandal-producing performance has become identified as one of the milestones in the development of avant-garde art.[26] It was in the program for *Parade* that Apollinaire coined the word 'surrealism', and while the spectacle contained traditional circus and music-hall elements, its deliberately fragmented forms, rowdy sound effects, Cubist sets and complete narrative incoherence turned it into an entirely new experience for Paris audiences. Based on 'acts' supposedly designed to attract an audience into the main event, an event that in fact never occurs, *Parade* develops an aesthetic of non-resolution and unfulfilled expectation. There is a curious American motif, represented by a Manager, and a Little American Girl who enacts such modern experiences as catching a train, driving an automobile and being a movie-star. Satie's music for this section is called 'Ragtime du paquebot' ('Steamboat ragtime'). The steamboat image, with its connotations of jazz in movement and the transat-lantic setting, represents an almost eerie prefiguration of the landing, barely a month later, of Americans in France—the first big contingents of American soldiers. The exact contemporaneity of the performance of *Parade* in Paris and the formation of James Reese Europe's Infantry Band in New York is no doubt a coincidence, but it heralded the historic meeting that was about to take place.

The French have not been slow to assert a special role in the development of jazz as a legitimate art form. In the editorial of the legendary magazine *Jazz Hot* in 1945, the claim was undisguised:

We know that jazz was born in the United States, but it was in Europe that it gained its artistic legitimacy. Well before the Yankees became aware of its importance, intellectuals of the old world had taken an interest in the new music. They were followed by the real enthusiasts who devoted themselves to the study and diffusion of jazz.[27]

Hugues Panassié, known in France as 'the pope of jazz', was voicing, with his typical arrogance, a view widely held by Europeans and Americans alike. It is a view that has been contested by the American historian James Lincoln Collier,[28] who argues that the whole jazz phenomenon in America, including jazz history and criticism, has been much vaster than anything that happened in Europe, thereby making statements like Panassié's appear, quite simply, silly. In a nationalistic reclaiming of the whole jazz phenomenon as American, Collier concludes:

> For jazz, I believe, represents much that is best about America: the frankness and generosity that have always been thought to be characteristic of its people; the freedom of expression that is built into its Constitution; and the spontaneity that is so crucial a part of the music. In sum, what is essential to jazz is precisely the Americanism that lies at its heart: and what is typical of America is this jazz music that is produced and nurtured.[29]

Panassié, too, was flaunting his nationalism in asserting that French artists and intellectuals had been quicker than their American counterparts to take up the cause of jazz and to articulate its artistic specificities. Moreover, in the process, there was some hegemonic blurring of national boundaries. Neither Panassié nor any other French commentator had any qualms about treating as part of the French jazz tradition such texts as the famous and canonical article by Ernest Ansermet (who was Swiss),[30] or the commentaries of the Belgian poet Robert Goffin.[31] But such quibbles aside, early French commentaries on jazz were numerous. They appeared in books (Coeuroy and Schaeffner's *Le Jazz* is acknowledged as the first monograph on jazz), in the most highly respected musical publications (such as *La Revue musicale*), in an enormous range of other journals devoted to art and culture, and above all, in *Jazz Hot* itself, which, when launched in May 1935, had a reasonable claim to being the first magazine in the world devoted exclusively to jazz.

For the cultural historian, it matters less that French jazz enthusiasts were first to express themselves in this way than that their willingness to treat jazz seriously laid the foundations of a rich and permanent tradition of thoughtful jazz commentary, which became and has remained an integral dimension of an identifiable French jazz culture. To be sure, much of the content of the early jazz histories and commentaries in France is of debatable quality, as often based on personal taste and ideological bias as on reliable research. Nonetheless, the wave of interest was sufficiently substantial to create its own momentum, and it has drawn behind it a steady flow of more systematic and authoritative work.

Legitimisation in French culture is still powerfully shaped by the written word. The unbroken stream of writing about jazz was accompanied by increasing dissemination of the art form through other means: radio and television programs, specialist magazines,[32] the steady spread of jazz festivals across France, and the formal inclusion of jazz as part of accepted music education in the nation's conservatoriums.

France can even be said to have anticipated, albeit in a modest and embryonic way, the epic televised history of jazz produced in America (and broadcast worldwide) by Ken Burns in 2000. In 1993, Jean-Christophe Averty, with Pierre Bouteiller, created a three-part television series for channels France 3 and Canal +, entitled *Jazzband: Une histoire du jazz français*. As its name suggests, the series was concerned entirely with the French experience, although in adopting this focus, it inevitably included footage of some pivotal American musicians—one can see performances of the James Europe Band, for instance, in 1918, Cab Calloway at the Salle Pleyel at the time when the jitterbug was introduced in 1934, and long-term residents Bud Powell and Kenny Clark from the 1960s on.

The French historian Ludovic Tournès has referred to the mysterious 'alchemy' through which jazz was assimilated so readily into French culture.[33] It is true that the process was extremely complex and multifaceted, cutting both simultaneously and differently through the richly layered fabric of French cultural life. Building on work done by Tyler Stovall's groundbreaking study of African-Americans in France,[34] on Jody Blake's explorations of jazz in relation to artistic modernism,[35] and on other recent studies including that of Tournès,[36] Jeffrey Jackson's study of the diffusion of jazz in interwar France[37] rightly affirms that for puzzled French musicians, critics and audiences trying to make sense of it, jazz, above all, 'represented something transformative'.[38] As such, it could be perceived either as attractive or threatening, depending on perspective and the moment in time. When observed over the whole period of its history in France, however, the jazz story is overwhelmingly positive, and to grasp the impact of jazz and the reasons for its happy assimilation, we need to look *through* the music to a whole array of French cultural creation.

PART 1 | **NEW SOUNDS FROM AMERICA**

# CHAPTER 1

# A DIFFERENT MUSIC
## Jazz Comes to France

**I have to be continually on the lookout to cut out the result of musicians' originality.**
**James Reese Europe[1]**

In the Théâtre Graslin in Nantes on 12 February 1918, the atmosphere is one of curious expectancy, tinged with impatience. It is winter, and nobody is aware that the Great War has entered its last year, though with the arrival of massive numbers of reinforcements from North America, hopes are rising. The members of the full-house audience have paid to participate in a celebration of Lincoln's Birthday, organised in collaboration with the American Army. The women are dressed in their best ceremonial finery, the men in dinner suits or uniforms. They are waiting for the arrival of the official party, already thirty minutes late. On the stage, the musicians of James Reese Europe's regimental band also wait, sitting silently and neatly in accordance with the discipline imposed by their military training and their leader.

The group of dignitaries finally enters, led by the mayor, who, unperturbed by his own lateness, proceeds to deliver a stirring ten-minute oration. After the applause dies down, the American band—the core and the major part of the evening's entertainment—begins its concert with the popular

French march '*Sambre et Meuse*', which brings mumurs of enthusiastic recognition from the public. Much of the rest of the concert, however, is filled with music, and song and dance performances, that are completely new to the people of Nantes. Never before have they heard tunes like 'Negromance' or 'Memphis Blues'; above all, they have never heard playing like that produced by this group of all black musicians. They are delighted, dazzled. But how could they be aware of the historical significance of the event in which they are participating?

Most jazz historians acknowledge the performances of James Reese Europe's band in France in early 1918 as foundational for the French experience of jazz.[2] Several other black American military bands were also active in France during this time, often led by musicians whose pedigrees were almost as good as those of Europe. They were considered to be of paramount value to troop morale.[3] But James Europe's band was not only the first to give performances outside the purely military arena; it also captured the imagination of its French audiences in ways that others were unable to do.

Formed in Harlem in June 1916, the 15th New York Infantry Regiment was mustered into active service in the summer of 1917 and arrived in France in late December that year. The US military establishment was endemically racist, with interdictions to prohibit black and white troops serving in the same units and institutional discouragement of any combat training for black soldiers. So, like many other African-American units, the 15th began its service in France in stevedoring and port service in Saint-Nazaire, where the American army had been building up massive installations since June 1917.[4] Its eventual participation at the battle front—from 9 April 1918 until the end of September—was made possible only by its integration into the French army, where it was renamed the 369th. This service was deemed to be extremely distinguished, earning the regiment a collective citation and the Croix-de-Guerre.[5]

The regimental band was formed early in the unit's existence, and James Reese Europe was recruited as its leader by the enterprising Colonel William Hayward. Europe was already a major figure in the New York popular music scene, as a performer, composer and band leader, with a long list of successes in clubs and musical theatre. Europe recruited his close friend and colleague Noble Sissle, and secured the services of Francis Eugene

Mikell, another experienced and well-trained professional. By the time the 15th reached France, the band was a finely tuned ensemble with an extensive repertoire that included anthems and military marches, but also traditional African-American songs (performed with vocals), original compositions by Mikell and Europe himself, and ragtime and blues. Performances were highly syncopated, and included segments where the musicians were released from the constraints of their scores, and—under the close scrutiny of their leader—allowed to improvise.

The concert in Nantes[6] marked the beginning of a tour that would take the band across France to Aix-les-Bains, where it spent several weeks entertaining the troops and the local population. The Nantes performance was also part of a local charity drive for the war effort, one of many events organised to demonstrate Franco-American friendship. The streets of Saint-Nazaire and Nantes were often festooned with French and American flags, and large crowds turned out to watch the 'Sammies' march to the accompaniment of their military bands.[7]

From the point of view of the regiment, the Théâtre Graslin performance was a great success. The commander, Captain Arthur Little, recorded the enthusiastic reception:

> I doubt if any first night or special performance at the Metropolitan Opera House in New York ever had, relatively, a more brilliant audience. The French people knew no color line. All they seemed to want to know, was that a great national holiday of their ally was being celebrated—and that made the celebration one of their own. The spirit of emotional enthusiasm had got into the blood of our men; and they played as I have never heard them play before.[8]

The perceived absence of a 'color line' was a central factor in the sense of triumph experienced by members of the band. Tyler Stovall draws attention to the myth of a 'color-blind France', proposing that 'the idea of France as a refuge from American racism had far more to do with conditions in the United States than conditions in Paris'.[9] However, there is no doubt that the musicians had a genuine impression of being accepted and praised for their artistry and originality, a perception integral to their 'emotional enthusiasm'. Noble Sissle half-humorously reached the conclusion that the band's performance brought the French something more important than military aid:

Colonel Hayward has brought his band over here and started 'ragtimitis' in France; ain't this an awful thing to visit upon a nation with so many burdens? But when the band had finished and people were roaring with laughter, their faces wreathed in smiles, I was forced to say that this is just what France needs at this critical time.[10]

These American assessments of the event, based as they are on feelings of shared patriotic and artistic values, are no doubt accurate enough. However, when one turns to how the French themselves experienced the occasion,[11] it becomes apparent that the reception of the music by the audience in Nantes was rather more complex.

In 1918, the city of Nantes boasted a population of around 150 000 and a lively daily press, notably *Le Populaire* and *Le Phare de la Loire*. Both papers ran announcements of the concert for some days beforehand, under the heading 'Manifestation franco-américaine'. The publicity build-up was handled with an eye to ensuring the concert's success. On 9 February, both papers included a full program.[12] The next day they concentrated on the attraction of the music (although describing it as being 'in some ways analogous to that of the naval bands in France'), and the reputation of the musicians (with Europe and Mikell described as 'two eminent artists'). On the 11th, *Le Populaire* stressed the significance of honouring the memory of President Lincoln, and the planned presence, at the event, of the notables of Nantes, various allied generals, and the Consul-General of the United States: what had seemed originally to be an entertainment for charity purposes had begun to take on a greater political dimension. This article ends on a couple of intriguing notations:

An American band, led by an American conductor, with a considerable reputation on the other side of the Atlantic will perform a representative program made up of American pieces and songs.
    All the musicians of the 'New York Infantry Band' are 'color gentleman' [*sic*] whom the citizens of Nantes will make a point of honour of hearing, acclaiming and applauding.[13]

This is the only reference, in the entire reporting of the event, to the fact that the musicians were black. Given the emphasis on the American character of the orchestra, the conductor and the music, the reference to 'color gentleman' seems bizarre. Is it simply a bit of novelty and exoticism for publicity purposes? Could it be that the writer is transmitting information provided by the band itself, the members taking pride, as African-Americans, in its national ambassadorial role? Certainly there is no suggestion of any real 'colour consciousness', or anything that would invalidate Captain Little's observation that the French 'knew no color line'. For *Le Populaire*, James Europe's orchestra and music were as American as Lincoln's birthday.

The celebration of Lincoln's birthday began with an all-male gala banquet hosted by the Mayor, Paul Bellamy, at the Hôtel de France. Among the sixty guests at the lavishly decorated tables were the Prefect, the French military and naval chiefs stationed in the region, the civic and business leaders of Nantes, and the Consuls of Britain, Italy and Belgium. On the American side, the guests of honour were General Walsh, commander of the American base in Saint-Nazaire, and the Consul-General of the United States, accompanied by his vice-consuls, together with a large group of American army and naval officers. After dinner, over champagne, the American Consul-General delivered, in French, a carefully crafted speech, the full text of which was published in both newspapers the following day.

The Consul-General evoked the traditional friendship binding France and his nation, pre-dating La Fayette and based on the common ideal of liberty: an 'alliance of hearts' that would last forever because it was 'ordained not by man but by the Grand Master of the Universe'. Just as France helped America when it was fighting for its independence, so now the Americans had come to help France, and they did so 'without ulterior motive', out of love for the nation and its people. This was no territorial war, but the defence of modern civilisation against the barbarity of Prussian militarism: 'We have come to help France safeguard democracy in the world.'

The speech paid homage to the passion and bravery of the French army and to the endurance and suffering of the people. France would rise again, and 'shine with a lustre brighter than ever . . . as the emblem of the rights of man'. In the tail of the speech, however, there was a sting. In retrospect, the Consul's words seem to prefigure a new consciousness of America's potential as an international force, and the determination to create a new world order. In such a global context, Franco-American 'affinity', and indeed France itself, would have diminished importance:

We shall conquer and the colours of France and America like those of Great Britain, Italy, Belgium, Brazil, Japan and the other allied states will fly more serenely than ever in a world where individual freedom will exist along with the autonomy of nations in a League of Nations, in which treaties will be considered as sacred, and where arbitration will take the place of force, in a climate where honour and justice can reign. Long live France! Long live Brittany! Long live the city of Nantes![14]

It is not surprising that the Wilsonian postwar program should find its way into the Consul-General's speech, which was greeted with warm applause; and no doubt the good people of Nantes were flattered by the three-part final salutation, which so clearly moved its focus from the national to the local.

The shadow of difference between the American position and the French one darkens when we look closely at the response given by the Mayor before his compatriots in the Théâtre Graslin. Using the example of Lincoln, he introduced his first major theme, liberty:

Our wish for the whole universe is what the New World has achieved: to unite rather than to divide, to bring down the old forces of domination and tyranny with their dark Machiavellian schemes, and in their place to ensure the triumph of fresh energies of integrity, transparency and, indeed, political honesty.[15]

In the Mayor's mind, America appeared as a selfless provider of resources, undemanding and uncomplicated, to participate in sacrifice for the abstract ideals of justice and liberty.

The idea of partnership introduced the Mayor's second theme, that of equality. He acknowledged differences between the Old World and the New, but saw their destinies as convergent:

... When victory has rewarded our persistence and when its fruits have repaid all the blood that has alas been shed, allow us to hope that your youthful ardour will not turn its back on our old civilisation ... Europe and America cannot be rivals: they will work together, they will construct the League of Nations which, first and foremost, will be the League of Peoples who have desired the liberty of the world, the League of Allies.[16]

The explicitly European dimension of Bellamy's discourse is striking. To embrace the New World does not imply any weakening of Europe as a centre, but rather the prospect of an exchange of goods and culture that will produce 'greater well-being and a greater sense of fraternity'.

Liberty, equality, fraternity: unlike the American Consul-General's intimations of a new global order, the Mayor's speech was structured by the universalist values of the French Revolution. It was through these values that France, in welcoming the American presence, could offer hope for the future:

> Patience, gentlemen! The garden-beds will flower again and tomorrow, you and all our allies will carry from our home to yours the roses and laurels of the land of France.[17]

The confidence of this final statement brought wild applause from the audience. They appreciated that the Mayor's heartfelt assessment of France's terrible pain did not undermine his faith that his country still had something to offer, even to America the saviour. Indeed, while the American Consul-General declared eternal 'affinity' between his nation and France, one can interpret the Mayor's speech as redolent of the passion of a declaration of love: 'allow us to hope that your youthful ardour will not turn its back on our old civilisation'. The Mayor's vision of the future could hardly have been more symbolic of a seduction:

> As in the past, our city, the Port of the West, will throw open to you the estuary of the gayest of our French rivers, the one that leads you to the very heart of Europe.[18]

It was in this context—a spirit of victory shared, an unconditional partnership and an open-ended commitment—that the New York Infantry Band struck up its first tune. Little wonder that the concert, delayed though it was, got off to such a good start.

In the newspaper coverage, *Le Populaire* made only a few general remarks about the audience's appreciation of the band's energy, clarity and precision, the 'picturesque' and 'colourful' originality of the music, and the excellent quality of the musicians. The concert, while a point of focus, was only one aspect of the wider demonstration of Franco-American friendship: 'one of the most moving, and also the most comforting stories of the war, in the old city of Nantes'.[19] *Le Phare de la Loire* paid more attention to the music. The journalist saluted the 'sparkling array of brass and lively drums' and the 'first-rate vocal quartet' that delivered its songs 'with ease and spicy variety'.[20] The entertainment value of the band was further enhanced by the integration of dance:

> These singers, in addition to all that, turn into dancers on occasion, and in this way, their jig finale caused the audience great amusement and brought them frenzied applause.[21]

Europe's earlier experience as a creator and director of musical entertainments in New York was obviously put to good use in Nantes. This was no straight, static concert performance, but a fully choreographed show with an audiovisual synthesis between the punchy rhythms of the music and the physicality of the singing and dance. *Le Phare de la Loire* reserved a special mention for what the commentator perceived as the specifically American parts of the program, which he found fresh and unusual. But he was impressed, too, with the band's encore, a 'fiery rendition' of the popular French song *Madelon*, in which he saw not only Lieutenant Europe's sensitivity towards his hosts, but also his 'perfect understanding of French music'.

Despite all this, the ultimate meaning of the evening did not reside in the music or the performance. The concert ended with the playing of the two national anthems to an audience standing in silent respect, a conclusion that the journalist described as a 'religious symbol' of France and America joining in a sense of common purpose and direction. From this feeling of unity flowed the 'endless applause' that brought the evening to a close and marked it as an 'indelible date' in the memory of Nantes.

There was of course no recording made of the concert, but it is possible to get an idea of how it sounded from the recordings made by Pathé in 1919 after the band returned to the United States.[22] Some of these pieces (for instance, 'Memphis Blues' and 'Plantation Echoes') were on the program of the Nantes concert. For today's listener, the music may appear both familiar and quaint, but for 1919 French audiences, its syncopated drive, technical effects such as slurs, unconventional tonguing and rhythmic shifts, as well as the use of blue notes and mutes to colour tonal patterns, would have contributed significantly to the sense of newness.[23] Europe later recounted a discussion with the leader of the band of the Garde Républicaine after a concert for 50 000 people in the Tuileries Gardens in October 1918:

> After the concert was over, the leader of the band of the Garde Républicain [sic] came over and asked me for the score of one of the jazz compositions we had played. He said he wanted his band to play it. I gave it to him, and the next day he again came to see me. He explained that he couldn't seem to get the effects I got, and asked me to go to a rehearsal. I went with him. The great band played the composition superbly—but he was right: the jazz effects were missing. I took an instrument and showed him how it could be done, and he told me that his own musicians felt sure that my band had used special instruments. Indeed, some of them, afterward attending one of my rehearsals, did not believe what I had said until after they had examined the instruments used by my men.[24]

It has been queried whether Europe's music can be canonically defined as jazz,[25] and Badger concludes that it is a 'primitive sort of big band jazz'.[26] However, one should not overlook the significance, in Europe's routine, of the singing, and especially of the dancing that was so closely linked to the music. Jean-Christophe Averty's television history of jazz in France contains a clip of one of the dances: although brief, it gives an idea of the joyful energy with which the dancing soldiers were able to transcend the bulk of their uniforms and, by symbolic extension, the heaviness of the historical moment. For French audiences, this reintegration of physicality into music would be one of the hallmarks of the jazz experience.

There is thus an important historical coincidence of the emergence of early jazz and indications of an early French interest in jazz. However, it cannot be taken for granted, even from a musical perspective, that French audiences were already attracted by what would later be called the *specificities* of jazz. Badger entitles one of his chapters 'Filling France full of jazz',[27] but in truth, jazz, for much of its first decade in France, was only one of many elements present in an extraordinary period of artistic renewal that had begun during the Belle Époque, and continued more or less unabated during World War I.

As we shall see, the French avant-garde took to jazz because it was a new colour to add to what they believed to be an infinite rainbow of novelty. It is nonetheless evident that the James Reese Europe band and its performances were part of a crucial cultural discovery—one that promised an end to the deadlock of European history manifest in four years of relentless trench warfare. The band stood for America, the friend and liberator. The symbolically named American band leader seemed to open a window onto a new world full of hope, by conjuring up the image of a 'Europe' in which the inhabitants of the old continent could project *themselves* into something *other*, a promise of an untrammelled future. Badger notes 'a certain irony, and yet a certain appropriateness, in the fact that it was a black American lieutenant named Europe—a commander of machine guns, that most perfect symbol of depersonalised mechanical warfare—and his band that brought the welcome compensation of jazz to wartorn France'.[28] There were, however, deeper ironies at work, on both the French and the American sides.

From the French angle, the main irony lay in the complete failure to dissociate the music itself from an American presence identified as entirely altruistic and liberating. The story that the French constructed around the concert in Nantes is summed up in the headlines used to describe the event in both the local newspapers: '*Manifestation franco-américaine*'. It is a story of joint ventures, both past and future, and it is based on a belief in common values and in unshakeable friendship. One does not need to look very far forward to see that the enthusiasm of the mayor and people of Nantes was based on illusion. The winning of the war was not to be matched by good management of the peace, and Wilson's failure to persuade his own Congress of the virtues of a League of Nations meant that the process at Versailles would produce an increase in conflict rather than a diminution of it, setting in train the gradual isolation of France and the step-by-stumbling-step progress towards World War II.

In the city of Nantes, the awakening followed closely on the heels of Allied victory. During the war itself, the French had been caught up in various forms of Americanisation: they took to learning English, and rebaptised shops and hotels with English names; they imitated American fashion and followed the Americans' sports competitions with assiduous enthusiasm; they even developed a new interest in the work of American writers and artists. But local patience with the American presence was quickly eroded by the effects of the US preparations for withdrawal: deterioration of the roads because of heavy traffic, bullying requisition tactics, increased prostitution, and alcohol-induced violence on the part of American soldiers. By the summer of 1919, conflict between the US soldiers and the French locals was open and frequent: the Star-Spangled Banner, which for two years had been flown throughout Nantes as a symbol of salvation, was now subject to burning. Particularly shocking to the French was the brutal treatment by white troops of black American soldiers and dockers. The change of mood in the city was remarkable. While there had been a few grumbles since the time of the American arrival, they had been very much a minor under-current in the overall climate of optimism. By early 1919, overt hostility was the order of the day and the local authorities had difficulty in containing it.[29]

Europe and his band came out of that night at the Graslin Theatre elated by their reception, and convinced that their French audience was free of any colour prejudice. They were right enough about that, and could justifiably reach the conclusion that this was proof of their full status as Americans. At the same time they could be proud of their contribution, as black Americans, to this foreign perception of 'Americanness'. Their pride was reinforced when the band, along with the rest of the 369th Regiment, was integrated into the French army. On the battlefields of Champagne and beyond, the regiment comported itself with great valour, gaining the nickname 'the Harlem Hellfighters'. However, the sense of having been valued for their humanity, their skills as musicians, their bravery as soldiers, and their friend-ship as Americans would be a source of frustration and embitterment once they returned to the United States. The years following the war were to produce some of the worst race-based violence in the nation's history, with multiple riots, burnings and lynchings.[30]

After Nantes, the band travelled to Aix-les-Bains as part of the enter-tainment for the newly established leave area for the American Expeditionary Forces. It arrived with the first group of soldiers (283 of them —all white) and led the procession that marched through the town under the enthusiastic gaze of the assembled citizens and dignitaries. 'Applause rang out as the parade passed by,' reported the journalist of *Le Journal d'Aix-les-Bains*, 'accompanied by the band of the American negroes and the one from Aix-les-Bains.'[31] During this sojourn, which was extended for two weeks beyond the original plan, the local press was full of praise for Europe's music, noting 'a prodigiously skilful drum duo'[32] and generally brilliant per-formances by both band and singers.[33]

However, as distinct from the Nantes experience, Europe's performances were presented as part of a large-scale leave and recreation operation that involved a weekly turnover of thousands of soldiers, and as many—if not more—French artists and performers as Americans. The band was in Aix essentially to perform for compatriots, not for the French.[34] Indeed, town life was turned upside down: even if some local merchants benefited by raising their prices,[35] American habits of excessive washing, drinking, and otherwise amusing themselves provoked concern and, occasionally, alarm. For local spectators of so much American activity, it would have been difficult to separate James Europe's music from the general perplexity.

From Aix, the band proceeded to its tour of military duty. In late August, it went to Paris, and, among other performances, played in a major festival organised by the YMCA for the Allies in the Tuileries. This was essentially an American event, and was reported as such by the American press.[36] Europe's band opened the day's proceedings and also the concert section. But it was only one of five military bands—and not even the only band to play jazz[37]—and there were many other entertainments, including operatic singing and fencing exhibitions. The French press reports emphasised the mixed nature of the event: the variety of music emerges as an emblem of a new order of things in which national perspectives are blurred, and different cultures blended and layered. Jazz was part of a broader cultural fusion whose meaning was yet to be revealed.

> This afternoon's big outdoor festival in the Tuileries, organised in honour of the Allied soldiers by the American division of the Paris YMCA, attracted a considerable crowd . . . Many soldiers of the Allied army had accepted the kind invitation of the great American association: 'poilus', 'yanks', 'tommies', 'arditis', Belgians, Serbs, Greeks, Poles, Czechoslovaks, Montenegrins, and even Japanese, crowded into the broad paths of the gardens, and their varied uniforms of all shades from khaki to French blue melded pleasantly under the greenery of the tall trees.[38]

The difference in perspective between the American reports, full of burgeoning national pride, and the French ones, which reflect the need for cooperation, is, as we have already suggested, significant. It would not be long before the ephemeral nature of the friendship embodied in the Tuileries festival would become evident.

On their return to the United States, Europe's band led the 369th in a triumphant victory parade all the way up Fifth Avenue to Harlem. Europe resumed his career as a professional musician, using the 'Hellfighters' as his main vehicle. It was, however, short-lived. He arrived back in New York in February 1919, and by May he was dead, tragically murdered in a trifling dispute with Herbert Wright, one of his own drummers.[39]

The story of the 369th Infantry band's tour in France shows an engagement and interchange between the two cultures that extended well beyond the question of art. Those who reported on the 'Franco-American manifestation' recognised this, and without ignoring the originality of the music, used it to affirm the positive relationship between the two cultures. In more than one way, this event presents a model of how French culture would deal with the jazz phenomenon in the 1920s and 1930s.

During the last year of World War I, a small number of jazz musicians began to find work in the Paris music halls and cabarets, laying the groundwork for what would soon become a veritable revolution in France's musical entertainment. The most durable of these musicians was Louis Mitchell, who secured a residency at the Casino de Paris in October 1918,[40] and was to remain in Paris for many years. At the same time, something equally as significant for the French jazz age was happening on the other side of the Channel, when Will Marion Cook brought a large group of musicians together as the Southern Syncopated Orchestra. The name shows the seriousness of Cook's aim to elevate black American music to the highest levels of dignity, and it is an ironic coincidence that the Southern Syncopated Orchestra was in London at the same time as the all white Original Dixieland Jazz Band, whose rollicking antics Cook despised.[41] The SSO spent almost three years in Britain, performing at Buckingham Palace, the Philharmonic Hall, the Royal Albert Hall, and many other places. Under the direction of W. H. Wellmon, it performed in May 1921 at the Théâtre des Champs-Élysées in Paris. At its height, the orchestra included E. E. Thompson, whose success during the war as a military band master had earned him the nickname of the 'black Sousa'. It also included the trumpeter Arthur Briggs, later to become a fixture of the Paris jazz scene, and most importantly, from a historical perspective, Sidney Bechet, whom Cook allowed the privilege of improvising on his own composition, the 'Characteristic Blues'. Bechet would be the first jazz giant in France.[42]

One of the enthusiastic members of the SSO audience was Ernest Ansermet, the 36-year-old conductor of the Ballets russes who were in London performing the premiere of Manuel de Falla's *The Three Cornered Hat*. Ansermet was so moved by the SSO music that he wrote about it, and the article that he published in *La Revue romande* has been universally acclaimed as the first piece of serious jazz criticism. It does indeed mark the first time that a prominent musician of the high art tradition offered a considered reflection on the nature and importance of jazz. Ansermet was very much a man of what the poet Apollinaire called 'the new spirit'. It was he who conducted *Parade* in 1917, and his work with Diaghilev ensured that he was at the forefront of development in music, dance and theatre. During his 1916 visit to the United States, he collected ragtime sheet music which he shared with his friend Stravinsky, who in turn had no hesitation in building elements of the form into his own compositions, such as the 'Soldier's Tale', 'Piano-Rag-Music' and 'Ragtime for Eleven Instruments'.

Ansermet's 1919 article, 'Sur un orchestre nègre',[43] began by noting how pervasive ragtime had become. He distinguished between what he called 'authentic' ragtime and its facile imitations, defining authenticity by the degree to which the music stayed close to its ethnic origins. The music was the emanation of the genius of a particular race, whose African origins Ansermet saw as quintessential. This was the music of a people who, having been geographically removed from their roots, had nonetheless managed to graft onto the music they had learned in America enough of the fundamentals of their lost African world to create a place of their own in the new one. What delighted Ansermet especially was the musicians' complete absorption in the rhythm of their music, an effect that transformed their playing into a spectacle of movement and dance. And like the members of the Garde Republicaine listening to James Europe's band in the Tuileries Gardens, Ansermet had the impression that trombones, clarinets, saxophones, violins and drums were being transformed into different instruments by virtue of their being played by these black musicians.

Ansermet's use of a discourse so overtly grounded in the idea of race was not uncommon at the time. 'Race' was a concept accepted both in common parlance and in ethnography. This aspect of Ansermet's thinking inevitably provokes discomfort and suspicion today, the more so because of his apparent association of the oral tradition with less evolved forms of civilisation and culture. Is there not something paternalistic in his stance? There must be a question about whether his thrill at Cook's music does not arise, at least in part, from the ethnographic curiosity of a gifted and fully trained European musician finding himself able to observe, at close hand, a living example of a phase of musical development long forgotten in his own tradition. At the same time, Will Marion Cook explicitly aimed to promote 'the musical art of the Negro', and the ethnic specificity of his music was thus central to his project. And of course, the issue of whether jazz should be considered as *essentially* African-American, not only in its roots but in its very nature, remains vexed.[44]

There is no such ambiguity in Ansermet's treatment of Bechet. He singles Bechet out as 'an extraordinary virtuoso clarinetist' and 'an artist of genius' who, although unable to speak about his art other than to say that he is following his 'own way', may well be creating the way to the future. Later in life, Ansermet concluded that jazz did not have the scope, musically, to achieve the heights he had anticipated in 1919. He maintained—rather condescendingly—his affection for Bechet,[45] but even though he considered the rise of jazz to be significant in the history of music, he believed that the music itself, because of its folkloric nature, was doomed to self-perpetuation rather than to the kinds of enrichment and development open to 'great' music. Jazz, by its very nature, was destined to be a minor genre of music. In 1919, however, Ansermet did show himself to be prescient. He apprehended the role that jazz in general and Sidney Bechet in particular would play in the French cultural scene in the following decades, and he predicted the ways in which jazz would help open the future of French culture to extensive transformations. His personal enthusiasm was a forerunner of the warm reception that France would reserve for jazz. More subtly, his perception of the music as something that deserved not only to be listened to, but also to be written about, stands as a foundation of the music's legitimisation.

# CHAPTER 2

# SETTLING IN
## Between the Wars

**Above all, Combelle is a great swinger. His playing is extremely negro, and even in the U.S.A. there are very few white tenors who play as well as he in the purest negro style.**
**Hugues Panassié, *Jazz Hot*, March–April 1937**

As it emerged from World War I, France faced grave economic, social and political problems, and national life was fraught with contradiction and confusion. In the public sphere, there was widespread celebration of the victory over the 'hereditary enemy' and politicians trumpeted the return of the provinces of Alsace and Lorraine, relinquished in the Franco-Prussian War a half-century earlier. The authorities strove to cultivate an optimistic climate to create the impression that the war-battered nation would soon recover its prosperity, as well as its prestige and power in world affairs. Perhaps some public figures, like the good mayor of Nantes, actually believed for a time in their own morale-boosting propaganda. If so, they were surely deluding themselves. France was in fact entering a downward spiral into one of the darkest periods of its history.

The 1917 revolution in Russia, the rise of the United States to the status of a major power, the deliberate British foreign policy to foster continental instability, and the incipient ambitions of Japan had changed, almost overnight, the geopolitical order of the world. France was ill-equipped to deal with the new situation. Its economy was industrially archaic, still profoundly entrenched in its rural heritage; its workforce was cripplingly depleted by the huge war losses in dead and wounded; and its chronically low birth rate was destined to fall even further for the same reasons. At odds with its wartime allies about how best to ensure ongoing peace, France was politically exposed even before the postwar peace negotiations were complete, and at Versailles it walled itself behind a treaty that both isolated it further and virtually guaranteed an ultimate resumption of war with Germany. Despite frenetic and sometimes brilliant efforts at diplomacy through the 1920s, in the League of Nations, France would never be able to break out of an impossible dilemma which was partly self-inflicted but substantially imposed by factors beyond its control.

Internally, the nation was suffering from deep social and political divisions that fifty years of fragile democratic rule had not managed to mend. Indeed, subsequent events would demonstrate that the structures of the Third Republic, having grown out of adversarial attitudes and compromise, were inadequate to deal with the period of ideological and geopolitical turbulence that the country was entering. In 1920, when the French Communist Party was founded, it was the largest outside Russia. However, at the very same time, the royalist Action française—anti-Semitic and militaristic —was at the height of its strength. It is true that the experience of the war had contributed to greater understanding between the constituencies of the Left and France's vast traditional Catholic base, due to the universal conscription that threw priests, farmers, factory workers and shopkeepers together in the same trenches. However, the conflicts between anticlerical ideologies and traditional Catholic beliefs—which had reached their climax in the 1904–05 laws separating church and state—were far from resolved.

Despite these gloomy and unsettling portents, the vitality and vibrancy commonly associated with the postwar years were also a reality, though the traditional French label for the period, 'les années folles', carries in its evocation of carefree folly an edge of darkness. It was a time of great paradox, and this was evident in every area of the arts. Forces of renewal were at work, but so were terrifying memories of the war just past and anguished visions of the world to come. In the work of the great novelists of the period—Bernanos, Malraux, Céline, Mauriac—we find literary creation defined by a new and radical incongruity: innovative narrative techniques and the forging of powerful new poetic languages coincide with the bleak portrayal of individuals and a society in disarray. In the imaginary worlds conjured up by the nation's most potent storytellers, the postwar euphoria gave way to the uneasy feeling that France had already entered an interwar period. This was the context in which the French 'jazz age' came into existence.

The most prominent African-American pioneer of the new music was the enterprising drummer Louis Mitchell, who, with his Jazz Kings, became a drawcard for the American tourists who began to invade Paris at the end of the war.[1] Mitchell worked at the Casino de Paris, on the slopes of  Montmartre. Although it had already begun to lose some of its bohemian and artistic population to Montparnasse, Montmartre retained, for the transatlantic visitors, much of its reputation as the centre of Paris nightlife—a place where middle-class pleasure seekers could safely find ready thrills by rubbing shoulders with society's less reputable inhabitants.[2] For the African-American musicians themselves, Montmartre had an air of familiarity about it, a climate not unlike that of Harlem.[3]

Mitchell's band was well known. It made a series of recordings with Pathé (1921–23), and toured Europe regularly. In 1923 it began a long residency at a newly opened club, Le Perroquet. Located in the premises of the Casino de Paris, Le Perroquet was to become one of the most popular haunts of the mid 1920s, frequented by a regular French clientele including members of the surrealist group. Mitchell opened his own place, the Tempo Club, and reportedly also ran a restaurant, specialising in 'sausages and hotcakes and other dishes which the American palate craves abroad'.[4]

Another African-American musician, Eugene Bullard, a dancer turned drummer, elected to remain in France after the war because of the dangerous racial situation in the United States. He played at Zelli's, which, under the direction of the dynamic Joe Zelli, soon became another important jazz venue, where bevies of vivacious girls were reputed to enjoy dancing and drinking with the patrons.[5] It was Bullard who enticed to Paris the energetic 30-year-old Ada Louise Smith who, under her nickname 'Bricktop', became the leading female manager of the Paris jazz scene. Bricktop had been an entertainer in Harlem and had real flair, both as a singer and as an entrepreneur and organiser. Bullard brought her into the Grand Duc and she later took over Chez Florence (originally run by pianist Palmer Jones and his wife Florence in 1924), eventually opening her own place, Bricktop's, which thrived well into the 1930s.

There were other black musicians who took up residence in Paris at this time. Work was easy to find and well paid. Clubs sprang up in many parts of the city, drawing crowds of well-heeled Parisians who came to listen, and above all to dance. E. E. Thompson, Arthur Briggs and Bobby Jones had all worked in Cook's Southern Syncopated Orchestra, as had the drummer Buddy Gilmore. Others who drifted across the Atlantic were attracted by wages that were often much higher than what was on offer in New York. Cricket Smith, who played cornet at the Casino de Paris, boasted that he earned five to seven times what he had in America.[6]

The African-American musician community in Paris was much in the public eye. It was, however, a tiny community, numbering no more than a couple of dozen in the early 1920s, and only a few hundred even in the later part of the decade.[7] That such a small group of people should have had the impact that they did is a testimony both to their personal energy and to their music. Moreover, in France, Paris no longer had a complete monopoly on African-American jazz, with the entertainers following the rich holiday-making crowd to the Riviera resorts during the summer.

The Perroquet, the Grand Duc, Zelli's and the Tempo Club were all in the area around Montmartre. Closer to the centre of Paris, a different form of jazz experience was being developed. Shortly after the end of the war, in the Rue Duphot, adjacent to the Madeleine, Louis Moysès opened a bistro that quickly became the base of the city's young avant-garde artistic set. This was the 'Gaya' bar, whose success was so great that within a short time it was necessary to move to a larger space, a couple of blocks away in the rue Boissy d'Anglas. Rebaptised as 'Le Boeuf sur le toit', the new bar opened in January 1922. The pianist who provided the entertainment was Jean Wiéner, a 25-year-old conservatorium-trained musician with a gift for improvisation, who had fallen in love with ragtime before the war. He dazzled the opening night audience at the Gaya with the latest tunes by Gershwin,

Youmans and Henderson, extemporising from sheet music sent from America. He was accompanied by Vance Lowry, an African-American originally from the Louis Mitchell band, who played banjo and saxophone and also worked the basic drum kit that Wiéner had borrowed from Stravinsky.[8]

It would be easy to dismiss Wiéner's music as 'ersatz' (the term used by Hugues Panassié).[9] While it was clearly derivative, and already filtered through the compositions of white Americans, it was also the fruit of his own enthusiasm, and it allowed significant space for emotion-driven improvisation. If it was not jazz of the kind Louis Mitchell was playing, it nonetheless shared some of the freedom and feeling of Mitchell's music. Some critics welcomed the softening of the American music, and what they saw as its adaptation to French taste and aesthetic sense. The composer-musicologist Roland-Manuel, for instance, praised Wiéner and his partner Clément Doucet for naturalising jazz 'as French', by 'lightening and ennobling its spirit'.[10]

With their two-piano act, Wiéner and Doucet produced more than 2000 performances up to 1939, and there can be no doubt that they helped to open the French artistic sensibility to the sounds and rhythms of jazz.[11] In his memoirs, Wiéner notes one evening at the Gaya in 1920 when the audience was a veritable Who's Who of the Paris artistic world: Gide, Marc Allégret, Diaghilev, Picasso, Missia Sert, Mistinguett, Chevalier, Satie, René Clair, Picabia, Tzara, Cocteau, Radiguet, Anna de Noailles, Léon Paul Fargue, Auric . . . and the list went on. Fernand Léger put in a request for 'St Louis Blues', while Poulenc leaned on the piano listening. No doubt Wiéner's memory has somewhat romanticised this event; we have no independent evidence that all these people were indeed gathered on a single occasion. However, the feeling that he evokes is consonant with the sympathetic reception of jazz in French modernist circles, a topic to which we will return in the second half of this book.

Wiéner was also a keen and innovative organiser of concerts. These were characterised by what he described as his 'salad' approach: a mixture of music of sometimes startlingly different kinds in a single program. The first such concert on 6 December 1921 featured the Billy Arnold band (a white American six-piece combination), alongside fragments of Stravinsky's *Rite of Spring* arranged for player-piano, and Milhaud's *Sonata for Piano and Wind* with the composer at the keyboard. Roger Désormière's review of the concert in the *Courrier musical* gave almost as much space to Billy Arnold as to the other two works together, and expressed excitement at the possibilities that had been revealed:

> We must be grateful to Mr Jean Wiéner for being the first to think of introducing a jazz band into a concert hall for an audience of musicians. The moment has no doubt come to include the jazz band in the domain of chamber music. Will our young musicians, inspired by sessions like this one, soon be providing us with divertimenti or symphonies for jazz orchestra? I would like that to be the case, and I hope so.[12]

In various other concerts, Wiéner introduced ragtime works by Stravinsky as well as rags and blues of his own composition. One 1924 program included the playing of two phonograph recordings of African-American music, as well as jazz-related compositions written by Wiéner, Milhaud and Stravinsky, and Louisiana ballads.[13] The treatment of phonograph records as being somehow equal to live music shows astonishing openness on Wiéner's part, as well as prescience. Unsurprisingly, such efforts did not win universal approval, especially from more conservative critics. Louis Vuillemin, for instance, ridiculed them as 'mongrel' performances likely to produce gangrene at the heart of French culture:

> In truth, [the organisers] are unwelcome phonies who lack wit and are harmful musical dadaists. They all, except for some very rare exceptions, rush to discover everything that international bad taste has produced and import it into the heart of the capital, in the clear hope of putting it off its beat.[14]

But Wiéner's concerts were defended by Ravel and others.[15]

More central to the development of jazz as a distinctive cultural language in France were a number of other French musicians who, for the most part classically trained, worked their way into professional jazz careers during the 1920s. People like the trombonist Léo Vauchant, the trumpeter Philippe Brun, the pianist Stéphane Mougin, the saxophonists Christian Wagner, Alix Combelle and André Ekyan, and the drummer

Maurice Chaillou learned the hard way, through listening and imitation.[16] Vauchant, training as a drummer in the orchestra pit at the Théâtre Marigny, was barely into his teens when he first heard Mitchell's Jazz Kings, and was fascinated by the variations they produced each night from music the French musicians rendered with dutiful regularity.[17] Like Mougin, Brun and the others, he struggled to master the new musical syntax by mimicking what he heard in the clubs and on the jazz records that were gradually becoming more readily available—although the very limited release in France of American labels meant that they were jealously collected, and carefully shared only among fellow initiates.

At this time—the early to mid 1920s—the recorded music market in France was dominated by white American jazz musicians such as Bix Beiderbecke, Red Nichols and Jimmy Dorsey. As a result, the budding French jazzmen had extremely limited exposure to the range of jazz creation. In America, high-quality jazz was flourishing everywhere, and many of the greatest musicians were beginning to make their mark. Bessie Smith, Jelly Roll Morton, King Oliver, Fats Waller, Count Basie and Louis Armstrong had all begun recording, and were doing so more and more prolifically. Comparatively, what was available in France was a faint echo indeed. It is almost impossible to determine in any detail who heard what and when, but we do know, for instance, that the general release in France of Louis Armstrong's work did not occur until 1929,[18] several years after he had achieved star status in New York. The French musicians quickly seized upon whatever new music presented itself; but opportunities were not all that frequent.

Places where musicians could play publicly were also few, although a growing number of Paris bistros had begun to offer live music. It was popular at the time to alternate jazz bands with tango groups, to cater to the two dominant dance fashions. The tango had preceded jazz by a decade or so in France, and a number of would-be French jazzmen tried their hands at both styles.[19] For the public at that time jazz was, as we have seen, primarily dance music and not for passive listening. A listening culture was being fostered, however, through the creation of regular radio jazz programs around the mid 1920s.[20]

A significant change occurred in 1925 when the *Revue Nègre* arrived, bringing with it Sidney Bechet and Josephine Baker. The review itself was a landmark event in French entertainment history, and Baker, like Bechet, was to become an iconic figure of jazz in France. Bechet was by far the most accomplished jazz musician that Paris had ever seen. He was also a young man of somewhat unstable personality. After his musical triumph in England with the Southern Syncopated Orchestra, he had been arrested in 1922 for assaulting a London prostitute, and spent two weeks in Brixton prison before being deported to the United States.[21] Back at home, he had recorded with pianist Clarence Williams and also with Louis Armstrong, toured with Bessie Smith, and worked briefly with Duke Ellington. Ellington admired his musical aggressiveness, but had trouble managing his wild behaviour.[22] Bechet's role in *La Revue Nègre* was a cameo appearance, albeit widely remarked upon, and there was no real opportunity for French audiences to appreciate the musical skill that would later establish his stardom in France. However, his participation in the review allowed him to make the contacts he needed to stay on and work in Europe once the show was over. That, in turn, enhanced his reputation in America as a musician with a European following. This was a desirable attribute at a time when European culture was still very much a yardstick of legitimacy and respectability and it was one of the reasons why Noble Sissle chose Bechet for a further Paris trip in 1929.

*La Revue Nègre* itself was originally the brainchild of Caroline Dudley, a wealthy American expatriate and sometime impresario, who had little difficulty in arousing the interest of André Daven, the artistic director of the Théâtre des Champs Élysées. This theatre had fallen on hard times during the previous few years despite the presence of such major attractions as Pavlova, Loïe Fuller, Paderewski and Paul Robeson. The summer of 1925 marked a crisis point.

Dudley went to New York to engage a troupe of instrumentalists, dancers and singers for a hastily concocted spectacle choreographed by Louis Douglas to music by Spencer Williams. Daven turned to Jacques-Charles— universally acknowledged as the best music hall director in Paris—to tighten the rhythm of the spectacle, to accentuate the black eccentricities of the cast and their costumes, and to intensify the erotic content. It was this last factor that led to the choice of slim and sinuous Josephine Baker as the main star, rather than Maud de Forest, whose physique was judged too substantial to appeal to Paris audiences.[23]

The expectations that Daven had pinned on the New York troupe are evident in his recollections of the group's arrival in Paris:

That October morning in 1925 it was raining. The daily flood of dreary pale suburbanites was flowing from the Gare Saint-Lazare. All of a sudden the busy travellers were transfixed. On the platform, descending from the transatlantic train, a bustling little group—noisy, multicoloured, bearers of bizarre instruments, bursting with laughter, skirts coloured red, green and saffron, jeans the colour of raspberries, shirts with wide checked or polka-dotted scarves—was suddenly brightening the greyness. Unbelievable hats —cream, orange, poppy red—framed thirty ebony faces with big wild laughing eyes. Under an extravagant piece of headgear, and wearing black and white chequered gardener's overalls, a long-bodied supple young woman detached herself from the technicoloured group and advanced towards us.

And so this is Paris!, she cried.

That was Josephine Baker's first utterance before the conquest.[24]

But Daven's excitement was tempered by a paternalistic protectiveness towards the troupe, who he felt had to be shielded from the potential debaucheries of Montmartre's nightclubs. When they were not at the theatre they were virtually sequestered in their hotel in the rue Campagne-Première, travelling between the two in a specially hired bus.[25]

After a thorough advance publicity campaign, including a preview that set the press into frenzied excitement,[26] *La Revue Nègre* ran from 2 October to 19 November 1925. The Théâtre des Champs Élysées held 2200 patrons[27] and *La Revue Nègre*, during its run, must have drawn almost 100 000 spectators. The show had lavish sets, designed by the Mexican Miguel Covarrubias, around pink backdrops flamboyantly painted with hams and watermelons. It opened with a rowdy jazz band introduction, followed by the much quieter performance of a Bechet soprano saxophone solo. Bechet's poignant and melancholic music created a sudden focus, setting the mood for a new emotional experience.

The novelty of the show had been trumpeted well in advance, and appeal to Parisian infatuation with the exotic was undoubtedly one of the main causes of the spectacle's success. But it was the sheer sensuality of Baker's dancing that produced outcry. In her first appearance, she arrived on stage scantily clad, on all fours with her bottom high in the air, before launching herself into a frenzied demonstration of the Charleston, followed by an undisguisedly sexual tree-climbing act. The scene was transgressive enough to provoke some disapproval and departures, but most members of the audience rapturously embraced the show, many of them returning repeatedly. Adrienne Monnier, friend of Gide, Joyce and Sylvia Beach, experienced the 'liveliest pleasure'.[28] In the finale, Baker, completely naked, was spun around the head of her companion dancer, Joe Alex, before being lowered, statuesque, into an ultimate silent tableau that brought the house down.[29]

The flagrant eroticism of Josephine Baker's 'danse sauvage' not surprisingly divided the critics, with more liberal commentators enthusing about her audacious energy and vitality, and more conservative ones mocking what they heard as a confusion of sound, and what they saw as disjointed and ugly gestures. Whatever their leanings, however, most of the critics associated Baker with the world of wild animals.[30] In his praise of her, even the unconditionally supportive Daven acclaims the 'simian suppleness' of her body.[31] What lay behind this animal imagery?

Ludovic Tournès considers *La Revue Nègre* as a defining moment in the assimilation of jazz in France because it foregrounded so publicly and forcefully the link between the music and 'négritude'—that is, the consciousness of a culture specifically rooted in black Africa.[32] Indeed, the ethnic composition of the cast and the Dixie, Harlem and African themes of the tableaux were critical features in all contemporary published commentaries. Jody Blake's judgment that the show was 'a grotesque caricature of what was already a stereotype-laden theatrical genre'[33] also rings true: in many ways the review was a standard collage of acts that had been common in New York reviews for years. Paul Colin's famous poster for *La Revue Nègre* is deeply stereotypical: both grotesque and caricatural, it portrays Josephine Baker sexily propped between two clown-like black male faces, and all of the figures are exaggeratedly negroid with oversized eyes and mouths. However, race was not the only thing being debated in the diverging French reactions to the review.

With respect to the music–'négritude' nexus it must be doubted whether the music itself was central in any real way. It was essentially and almost exclusively a vehicle for the dancing. And as far as the dancing is concerned, the idea that it was stereotypical simply does not match up with the way the show was received. Josephine Baker, in both her blackness and her femininity—in what the audience perceived as a single entity of black femininity—pushed the boundaries of dance beyond anything that the French had previously known. Her dance was a revolutionary exhibition of unmediated physicality. And more than that, her performance presented her body as a new kind of instrument of female initiative and desire. It was Baker who led the band, and not the other way around. André Levinson actually saw the dance as 'giving birth' to the music,[34] an image that synthesises all the connotations of fertility and genesis associated with the Black Venus archetype. Klein is right to describe reactions to La Revue Nègre in terms of a fundamental conflict between what the spectators saw as 'nature' (that is, the untamed, visceral energies whose source is some mythical primal condition —the 'jungle' or 'Africa') and what they valued as 'culture' (such as the 'civilised' characteristics of modesty and control).[35]

Josephine Baker brought this conflict into tantalising focus. But there was more to it. La Revue Nègre fed into the existing dance craze of the 1920s, into the fascination with America and with primitivism,[36] but above all, the show's spontaneity and its driving rhythms were a call to participate. For audiences accustomed to a more passive attendance at shows, the dominance of the dance brought a new sense of freedom, as if their own bodies were being opened to the possibilities of improvisation being demonstrated before them. In this way, La Revue Nègre, despite its undisguised commercial motivations, was an authentic jazz experience for the Paris audiences, provided we understand 'jazz' in the French setting as covering a shifting set of meanings.

Following Paris, La Revue Nègre toured Belgium and Germany, breaking up in February 1926 when Josephine Baker returned to Paris and Sidney Bechet left for Moscow. After his sojourn in Russia, Bechet toured Europe for a time, including France. His work in 1929 with Noble Sissle at Les Ambassadeurs was not especially remarkable, except that it culminated in the event that caused the saxophonist to be unwelcome in France for the next twenty years. Bechet had continued to be prone to sharp flare-ups of temper when he had been drinking, often over trivial matters. On this occasion, an argument about chord changes with a banjo player provoked an exchange of pistol shots in the streets of Pigalle. Neither was hit, but some passers-by were injured, and Bechet was imprisoned for eleven months before being deported to America.[37] Although a relatively minor affair in itself, this episode draws attention to the violence, not always latent, that was associated with the world of jazz musicians, many of whom routinely carried pistols. It also shows the still startling gap between that world and the more demure patterns of Parisian society.

In the meantime, jazz in France was attaining a wider and more positive reputation through the development of the big-dance-band phenomenon, in which the American Paul Whiteman was the uncontested leader. In 1924, Whiteman had invented 'symphonic' jazz, one of the early steps in his lifelong ambition to establish the new music's legitimacy in the mind of the American public. Responsible for commissioning George Gershwin's celebrated *Rhapsody in Blue*, he had quickly been dubbed the 'King of Jazz' by the American media. Whiteman was highly aware that his version of the music was softer than that played by African-Americans—which he sometimes acknowledged as 'real' jazz.[38] His orchestra did, however, include recognised jazz players, some of them great ones, such as Bix Beiderbecke and Frank Trumbauer.

Whiteman carried out a successful five-month tour in Britain in 1923. A second European tour in 1926 took him back to Britain and also to the Continent, where the band performed in Germany and Holland before twin engagements in Paris in July. These were at the Théâtre des Champs Élysées (where *La Revue Nègre* had played the previous autumn) and the Café des Ambassadeurs, where Whiteman shared the billing with the black singer Florence Mills. Whiteman's orchestra, with its repertoire of light classics, tightly arranged popular music, and occasional improvised solos, caused nothing like the stir that had accompanied Josephine Baker. It was a big success nonetheless, and advanced Whiteman's goal of promoting the respectability of jazz and making the music stand for 'the spirit of a new country, an expression of the soul of America'.[39]

 But if jazz was seen by Europeans as just such an expression, it had in other ways already reached beyond its national origins. Jazz bands were springing up everywhere in Europe. One of them, an English jazz orchestra led by Jack Hylton and modelled on Whiteman's, began touring Europe in the late 1920s—its first appearance in Paris was in 1927—and continued to do so until World War II. Hylton's impact can be gauged by the fact that in 1929 alone, the band gave as many as 700 performances and sold over three million records. Hylton was hugely popular in France, and for a considerable cross-section of the public his name was synonymous with jazz. The

French government decorated him for his services to France and music, and in 1931 he gave a celebrated concert at the Paris Opera House.

Hylton's music was derivative but lively, and although it is unlikely that anyone today would collect his music as jazz, his historical contribution to the spread of jazz and to the transformation of French musical culture should not be underestimated. In addition to leading his own band, he sponsored the career of Coleman Hawkins and was responsible for bringing Duke Ellington to Europe. He also incorporated into his band three of the best French jazz musicians of the time, Léo Vauchant, André Ekyan and Philippe Brun.[40] Hylton was not just a symbol of the internationalisation of jazz; he was actively engaged in it.

Among others, Vauchant, Ekyan and Brun were active in forming the first French jazz bands, and hence in laying the foundations of an indigenous French jazz tradition. In the flux of these early years of French jazz, individual musicians were often shuffled from group to group, and few ensembles were settled enough to last long. The two most influential groups were 'Gregor and his Gregorians' and 'Ray Ventura and his Collegians', which gathered together the most inventive and competent French jazz musicians, including Vauchant, Ekyan, Brun, Alix Combelle, Stéphane Mougin, and the violinists Stéphane Grappelli[41] and Michel Warlop. These bands made a conscious effort to develop a distinctively French style in their music, and included French material as well as American standards in their performances.[42] Archival material gathered by Jean-Christophe Averty reveals the deliciously marked accents with which French bands delivered American songs, but whether the audiences of the time noticed this or not is another question![43]

The case of Léo Vauchant is particularly interesting. Having mastered several different instruments—classical percussion (for which he had a prize from the Paris Conservatorium), cello, trumpet, saxopohone, xylophone—he attained true virtuosity as a jazz trombonist. He was one of the few French musicians whom Chris Goddard acknowledges as world-class soloists of the period.[44] He made plenty of money through both playing and arranging, and he thrived on the near-delinquent zealotry cultivated by the French jazz clique in order to assert independence and originality. Jazz was more than music for Vauchant: it was a way of life, combining religion, sex, freedom and violence in ways that echoed the American jazz scene. In later life, he confessed to nearly killing a man at the Perroquet, where he had been flirting with the man's girlfriend. The jealous lover had grasped the bell of Vauchant's trumpet, driving the mouthpiece into his teeth, and Vauchant responded by trying to beat the man to death with it.[45]

Vauchant played with many bands, including those of Gregor, Ventura, Gluskin and Hylton. He was also an intimate of Maurice Ravel, whom he visited weekly throughout the mid 1920s to share insights into the harmonic and rhythmic structures of jazz, and the instrumental possibilities revealed by the new music. Vauchant moved to Los Angeles in 1931, where he ended up as the musical director at MGM Studios.[46] However, his pre-emigration trajectory illustrates, on a personal level, how French culture as a whole would respond to the jazz challenge. It epitomises the way in which the enthusiasm for jazz music was taken into the crucible of French cultural tradition and creativity before finding a new, broader cultural platform to transform the original inspiration into other expressions.[47] In 1930, however, jazz in France was still overwhelmingly dominated by foreign bands. Late that year, an official in the French musicians' union complained that of 68 jazz bands operating in Paris, only 24 were French; and there were only about 100 French musicians working in jazz, as compared to almost 240 foreigners.[48]

A whimsical example of the change that was taking place in the French music scene can be found in the comments of Sisley Huddleston. Huddleston was a correspondent for various British and American newspapers and in 1928 he published a memoir in which he gave vent to a mock-Villonesque lamentation that is both colourful and informative:

> Where are the hurdy-gurdy organs which used to be played in every court-yard? They have vanished with the duel and the fiacre. Where are the quadrilles and the cancan, danced with a dazzling display of froufrous at the Mabille and the Tabarin? Where are La Goulue and Nini Patte-en-l'Air, and the Môme Fromage, and Valentin-le-Désossé, and others of whom old Parisians still speak with affection? . . . The nude has replaced the agitation of petticoats, and negro jazz and tangos from South American houses of ill-fame have triumphed over the waltz and polka. A hundred of the lowest and most fashionable haunts of Montmartre and the Champs-Élysées are alive from noon to night with champagne and dancing parties.[49]

The 'snows of yesteryear' nostalgia voiced here by the foreign journalist was widely shared by a French population still struggling to come to terms with the loss of a world that had been swept away in the course of World War I. For a variety of social, cultural and even political reasons that we will explore later, jazz was still far from being accepted as a popular music form.[50] Nonetheless, by the early 1930s, France was well and truly established as a place receptive to visiting American jazz musicians, both white and black. Over the following years, Paris in particular enjoyed many visits by some of the great proponents of jazz. In 1929 Milton Mezz Mezrow played there, and in 1930 Sam Wooding and the Ted Lewis band, which included Jimmy Dorsey and Muggsy Spanier. Beyond their formal concert engagements, visiting musicians helped develop the jam-session culture of Paris night-clubs, such as the Music-Box in Pigalle (later La Rumba), Chez Florence, Bricktop's and L'Aéroport at Montparnasse.[51] Often enough, musicians from visiting bands remained in Paris. Such was the case, for instance, for the pianist–arranger Freddy Johnson and the saxophonist Willy Lewis, who found many opportunities to play in the clubs. Jam sessions often began well after midnight, and were hardly popular events. But they allowed the musicians to explore their music with complete freedom, and they heightened the passions of an emerging group of jazz fans—people such as Robert Goffin, Jacques Bureau, Jacques Canetti and Hugues Panassié, who would become the founders of jazz history and criticism, vigorously promoting jazz across the country to give it a wider audience.

Robert Goffin (1898–1984) was a Belgian lawyer and avant-garde poet, a frequent visitor to Paris where he moved in the same circles as Blaise Cendrars and Jean Cocteau. His article on Louis Mitchell's Jazz Kings[52] was only the second instance of jazz criticism to be published (after Ansermet's 1919 piece in *La Revue romande*), and he titled one of his first collections of poems *Jazz-Band* (1922). In 1932, he published *Aux frontières du jazz*, which is a serious attempt to present to the general public an account of the history and qualities of jazz and its musicians. Even today this work retains interest for historians as an account of the arrival and impact of jazz-based dance, song and music in France and Belgium. But even more importantly, it is a striking testimony of how jazz, a music 'twisted like barbed wire', tore its way into France's emotional heartland. Throughout his life, Goffin served the jazz cause with unchecked enthusiasm. In exile—like many

European artists—in New York during World War II, he was a regular columnist for *Esquire* and helped Leonard Feather organise jazz concerts. After his return to Europe, he continued his efforts through radio broadcasts and prolific writing.

Bureau (1912–    ) and Canetti (1909–1997) were both promoters of early jazz radio programs in 1931 and Canetti used his position as artistic director of Brunswick Records to launch a career as a jazz impresario. But one of the greatest legacies of this new breed of jazz fans was the energy and vision of Panassié (1912–1974). Panassié did much to earn his legendary status in the history of jazz, a status acknowledged in America as well as in France. Very considerable inherited wealth enabled him to devote himself entirely to the passion that he discovered in the mid 1920s, following a bout with polio that left one of his legs paralysed. Dogmatically opinionated, and wielding a sometimes violently polemical pen, Panassié would be no stranger to controversy, and his doctrinaire approach to jazz would eventually lead to his marginalisation.[53] His role in the reception of jazz in France was nonetheless crucial. Beginning his promotional activity in 1930 as a writer for the short-lived *La revue du jazz*, Panassié was engaged as a regular record critic for *Jazz-Tango*, but it was the creation of the Hot Club de France in 1932 that set him in a class above all other jazz promoters at the time.

The pillars of the Hot Club were Panassié, Charles Delaunay (1911–1988) and Pierre Nourry—not one of them a musician, but all of them purists devoted to the defence and promotion of 'real' jazz and its practitioners. Just what 'real' jazz consisted of was still in the process of being determined, but the members of the Hot Club believed their enemies to include the musical conservatives of high culture and those undiscriminating members of the public who thought that jazz was just what was played by Paul Whiteman and Jack Hylton. The decision to institutionalise what was essentially grassroots enthusiasm rapidly resulted in the creation of formal structures to help the club achieve its goals.

To begin, the club organised concerts, and although the first few were given by black Americans, they later featured French musicians along with resident or visiting Americans, some black, some white. There were also educative lectures illustrated with recorded jazz; there were radio broadcasts and recording sessions. Panassié and Delaunay even launched their own record label, Swing, to extend the availability of jazz in France. And in March 1935 they began publishing the periodical *Jazz Hot*, the first specialist jazz review in the world, with a circulation that grew over the next four years from an initial 200 to around 3000. The Hot Club was primarily a Paris affair, but a few provincial branches grew up before the war.[54]

There is no doubt that Panassié had somewhat dictatorial tendencies. He was highly intolerant of anyone who encroached upon what he saw as his domain—which included anything that had to do with the jazz world. He was irascible and inclined to break off relationships whenever he felt offended. He was furious when Canetti brought Louis Armstrong to Paris in late 1934, and thereafter never failed to shower Canetti with invective. Never one to accept defeat readily, however, his competitive spirit led him to respond by organising a Coleman Hawkins concert in the Salle Pleyel in February 1935.[55] In other words, no loss to jazz fans ensued from Panassié's rift with Canetti.

After Armstrong and Hawkins, the very top American bands soon followed, bringing to France the full force of the swing era. Duke Ellington performed to three full and fanatical houses in July 1933 at the Salle Pleyel, and returned to Paris for two further concerts, at the Palais de Chaillot, in 1939. The use of the Salle Pleyel and the Palais de Chaillot, as distinct from the music hall circuit or the nightclubs, was a symbolic consecration of jazz as music to be taken seriously. These concerts, like the ones given by Cab Calloway (April 1934), Louis Armstrong (November 1934) and Coleman Hawkins (February 1935), received extensive coverage from the music critics of the Paris press. This attention was by no means always favourable[56] and critics tended to divide along the sociopolitical and ideological fissures that characterised the France of the Stavisky affair and the February 1934 riots, one of the most unstable periods of the Third Republic.[57] The arrival in Paris of the best American jazz was, inevitably, conflated with the Great Depression, the rise of fascism, and the sharpening of ideological positions, including the growth of a culture of xenophobia and fear of decadence. While jazz enthusiasts were concerned principally with the beauty and energy of the music, for many critics, particularly those of the overtly extremist Right, jazz concerts were little more than an excuse for rehearsing their favourite racist themes. André Suarès, future collaborationist in occupied France, was particularly outspoken:

Jazz is, cynically, an orchestra of brutes with non-opposable thumbs and still prehensile feet in the voodoo forest. It is wholly excessive, and in that way, more than monotonous: the ape is set loose, without manners, without discipline, completely lost in the undergrowth of instinct, parading its flesh naked as it leaps about, and its heart which is an even more obscene piece of flesh. These slaves must be overcome.[58]

The growth in popularity of the music nonetheless continued, despite the efforts of its sourest detractors. Another important symbolic moment was the New York Cotton Club review at the Moulin Rouge in 1937. The Cotton Club was a legendary jazz venue in America, and the decision to bring it to Paris in the year of the World Fair was a deliberate attempt to maintain the prestige of the French capital as a major entertainment centre.

The show ran from 11 June until 23 July and had a success comparable to *La Revue Nègre* ten years earlier—though this time the audiences, more familiar with the spectacular sensuality of African-American performances, did not suffer the shock of their discovery of Josephine Baker. The review contained the stock 'cotton plantation' and 'jungle' scenes, featuring nudity and slickly oiled bodies. It also had a novelty dance sequence demonstrating the 'Suzy Q' and the 'Lindy Hop', the latter named after the aeronautical exploits of Charles Lindbergh. Hugues Panassié saw the show fifteen or twenty times, and loved the improvised music and dancing. At the end of the performance, around 1.30 a.m., the bands continued to play for those members of the audience who wanted to dance. Panassié presents a lively picture of post-review cavorting in the nearby Montmartre Boudon brasserie, where the performers would eat and drink until daybreak:

Girls, singers, dancers, musicians would take their places at the 'banquette' or drink at the bar or wander among the tables, calling out loudly from one end of the room to the other, tossing the salt or pepper shakers from one table to the next over the heads of the waiters. The waiters were running around like rats, frantic. Because most of these blacks didn't know a word of French, it was quite a job to find out what they wanted to drink or eat. Quite often, a few of my friends and I served as interpreters for half the room. The blacks made some incredible menu selections: they would eat omelette or sauerkraut with blueberry jam, whilst drinking pernod-grenadine which was their favourite beverage. At the start, the waiters couldn't get over it. One of them was assiduously pursuing one of the Lindy Hoppers, the charming Naomi Waller. She would cry out from time to time in a strident voice 'Go away! You're no good!' and the waiter would retreat terrified, while she burst into laughter.[59]

If this description underlines the cultural differences that separated the American visitors from their French hosts, it is also infused with the deep sense of pleasure, comfort and excitement engendered by the encounter. The Cotton Club experience in 1937, like the concerts of Ellington, Armstrong and Hawkins, suggests not only that American jazz musicians enjoyed their performances in France, but that the French themselves had come to think of their culture as a space in which jazz could be at home.

In an article published after the Ellington concerts, the pianist Stéphane Mougin, writing against what he saw as a trend among some critics to identify jazz uniquely with African-American music, stressed the heterogeneous nature of the French jazz audience. And he called upon the critics to take a greater interest in French musicians such as Brun, Ekyan and Combelle. Mougin believed that some French jazz musicians were already on a par with some of the best American ones:

> If jazz is interesting, and even beautiful, and if the music is in itself captivating, why should we care about the nationality or the colour of the performer? You must, dear friends, recognise talent and praise the hot French musician as much as the American black. Enough partiality and ignorance! In France too we can play jazz, and good jazz! [60]

It was through the Hot Club that France produced its first example of an original French jazz style, with Django Reinhardt and the Quintet of the Hot Club of France. Reinhardt was a French-speaking Gypsy, born in Belgium in 1910 to a basket-maker father and a dancer–acrobat mother. The vagaries of World War I drove the family to North Africa and then back to France. Django grew up in the 'zone' at the edges of Paris, an area which in 1920 was still a distinct, if bleak, territory between the city ramparts and the rapidly developing suburbs. Market gardens, junk merchants and garbage dumps coexisted with plank and tin shanties inhabited by the destitute. This was the place where the Gypsy community set up camp and made its daily life.

Django spent his early years as a minor delinquent, running with youth gangs and committing antisocial acts such as vandalism and theft.[61] He completely avoided formal schooling and remained virtually illiterate for the rest of his life. But it was music that saved him from social exclusion. He was completely self-taught, obsessively practising the guitar he received at the age of twelve until he was good enough to play with adult groups. Through the 1920s he gradually established his reputation as a café musician, often working with his younger brother Joseph.

In 1928 Django was badly burned in a fire that destroyed his caravan and left him unable to use two of the fingers on his left hand. There is some debate about whether it was this injury, or the efforts required to overcome it, that resulted in the unusual harmonies that would later distinguish the Reinhardt music. Stéphane Mougin, ever alert to original talent, recruited Django to his band in 1930, but it was while he was working in the south of France and continuing his recuperation from the injury that he was more systematically introduced to jazz records. The experience changed his approach to music and led to his seeking out further jazz contacts. In January 1934 he met Stéphane Grappelli, who later became the other featured musician of the quintet. Grappelli was two years older than Reinhardt. He came from a family of Italian immigrants and, like Django, was largely self-taught, although he did have some conservatorium training during his early adolescence.[62] At the time of the meeting, he was just beginning his own jazz career with the André Ekyan band.

Charles Delaunay was responsible for assembling the group that would make its fame as the Quintet of the Hot Club of France—initially for an unsuccessful recording audition. For a jazz band, it was a very unusual combination, made up of three guitarists, a bass player and the violin, with neither drums nor any front-line horn players.[63] However, the band's swinging energy and the extraordinary improvisational inventiveness and mutual musical understanding of Reinhardt and Grappelli created a completely new jazz sound. Soon after the first public concert in December 1934, the group made its first recordings, and for the next several years, changes of personnel notwithstanding, successful record sales and well-received concerts combined to create a wave of popularity at home and a growing reputation abroad. Their repertoire included American standards, but also works of their own composition. After their foray into the Salle Pleyel with Coleman Hawkins in 1935, a long residency in 1937 at Bricktop's The Big Apple during the Paris World Fair brought the quintet some of its best exposure, because of the constant flow of distinguished international visitors, who included Constant Lambert and Cole Porter.

Django was a true virtuoso, and despite personal unreliability exacerbated by a grandiose self-image that soon became notorious, he was much sought after by other high-quality musicians. He accompanied a number of French singers, including Jean Sablon; he recorded with the Americans Coleman Hawkins and Benny Carter, who marvelled at the guitarist's uncanny ability to create the perfect harmonic and melodic context for their playing; and he played regularly with both French and visiting American musicians in a way that gave him a special bridging role. When one listens to his work spanning the 1930s, the interplay between the different influences is evident in the evolution and enrichment of his musical language.

In the months preceding the first public concert of the quintet, the musicologist Blaise Pesquinne published two long reflections on jazz in France's major mainstream music periodical, *La Revue musicale*.[64] Pesquinne considered himself to be a jazz enthusiast, and argued that being a good jazz musician required as much talent as any other kind of music. If jazz had been such a refreshing surprise for Europeans, he believed it was because they had tended to neglect improvisation and melodic and rhythmic invention in favour of composition, complex harmony, and the science of orchestration. However, he could not see that jazz would provide any ongoing aesthetic interest for the European high-culture music tradition, because of its essentially exotic nature. Being based in the expressionist, non-written inspiration of African music, it was most usefully compared with other improvisational forms, such as the Commedia dell'Arte, or such music as Russian folk-songs and Gypsy or Magyar instrumental performances.

In one respect, Pesquinne's reflections seem to echo those of Roger Désormière,[65] in predicting that when jazz abandons its role as dance music, and subordinates improvisation to composition, it will turn into a form of chamber music.[66] In 1934, it would still be a long time before jazz took that path, but from today's perspective, the remark appears prophetic. On the other hand, the cultural divide that Pesquinne so attentively maps and strives to maintain was already breaking down. The melding of high and popular culture that he thought impossible had already occurred. In a way, his own love of jazz, despite his better judgment, was a sign of that transformation. And so was the Quintet of the Hot Club of France. Pesquinne's analytical methods would perhaps have allowed him to understand how Django Reinhardt came so readily to jazz, because of the kinship he saw between jazz and Gypsy music. But nothing in the musicologist's discourse allows for the Grappelli phenomenon, or for the musical fusion produced by the encounter of the classically trained violinist and the self-taught Gypsy.

The quintet proved that jazz was not, as Pesquinne believed, simple exoticism. It was a new and revolutionary idiom. In 1938, through the Centre d'Étude de Jazz, some of France's leading practitioners were actually publishing jazz methods: saxophone (Combelle), trumpet (Allier), guitar (Chaput).[67] Jazz had in fact become the single most important point of reference in popular musical development in France. By the late 1930s, the style of chanson typified by Mistinguett had been overtaken by the swing-influenced performances of Jean Sablon, Charles Trenet and Johnny Hess—and it was such singers, along with Django Reinhardt's music, that would drive French musical life during the Occupation years.

CHAPTER 3

# REVIVAL AND REVOLUTION
## World War II and After

**French boys and girls like better to dance in filthy cellars with
dirty bands, and the cellar has to be quite small to be a success.
Boris Vian, *Jazz in Paris*[1]**

When World War II broke out, the Quintet of the Hot Club de France
was in England. It had been booked for a long tour there, which was
supposed to be followed by trips to India and Australia. With the news of the
war, Django Reinhardt panicked and the group rushed back to Paris, except
for Stéphane Grappelli, who made the decision to remain in England where
he stayed until after the war.[2] During the months between the declaration of
war in September 1939 and the German attack in May 1940 (the so-called
'drôle de guerre' or 'phony war'), there was little change in the pattern of
Paris nightlife. Despite the climate of growing fear and unease, the city's
clubs and music halls continued their operations as before.

One change that did occur was that almost all of the resident American
musicians returned home, an exodus which immediately increased opportunity for their French counterparts. Two of the few African-Americans to
remain were Arthur Briggs and Charlie Lewis. Briggs was imprisoned in
Germany when the United States entered the war in December 1941. Lewis

53

managed to pass himself off as a native of the French Caribbean and continued to work in France throughout the Occupation.[3] It was at Jimmy's in Montparnasse, with Lewis on the piano, and with Alix Combelle, Philippe Brun and other French musicians, that Django Reinhardt, fresh from his aborted London tour, began the most intense and brilliant phase of his career.

That French jazz should have blossomed during the war is not really a paradox. First, the isolation produced by the partition of the nation and the occupation of more than half of it by Nazi Germany ensured a virtual exclusion of American influence. This was even more the case after the United States entered the war, when the German authorities imposed severe interdictions on all forms of American culture. Even before that, however, the continuing US diplomatic presence during the first eighteen months of the Occupation was no counterbalance to the mass departure of American citizens who had adopted Paris as their place of residence in the 1930s, or the dramatic fall in transatlantic tourism. American jazz remained available in the form of records, especially early in the war, and it continued to get air time on Radio Paris. However, live jazz—in high demand throughout the capital—became, by default, the monopoly of French musicians.[4]

In addition, for jazz musicians and fans alike, the music had escapist value.[5] Military occupation had brought with it pervasive material hardship and a climate of oppression. The media, both press and radio, were dominated by propaganda from two directions. On the one hand there were the heavily moralistic messages of the Vichy government with its reactionary invocations of national guilt and a return to traditional values; on the other hand, the virulently racist and imperialist rhetoric of Nazi Germany. As a music whose essence was freedom of personal expression, both for the players and those who (clandestinely) danced to it, jazz provided a space to breathe.[6]

Although the Vichy proponents of the so-called 'National Revolution' disapproved of jazz, the music was more than tolerated by the German authorities in the occupied zone. This apparent leniency was in fact wholly pragmatic. It stemmed partly from the general German policy of maintaining control by offering occupied populations a semblance of normalcy. It was also the case that the soldiers of the occupying army needed entertainment. In fact, except for the Vichy government, jazz seems to have become

popular with almost everybody, including some elements of the collaborationist press.

There is an important distinction to be made between the constant anti-
jazz carping of the Vichy moralists and the attitude of the Paris collaborationists, which was more complex. The latter attacked the 'swing' fans in the
name of order and morality, often associating the swing and jazz with
Gaullism and Jewishness (that is, as something degenerate and subversive).
But at the same time, they could be quite positive about the music itself.
Lucien Rebatet and Alain Laubreaux, two of the most notorious collaborationist journalists, both offer good examples of this ambivalence.[7]

**D**jango Reinhardt became a major star overnight. He was sought after as
a soloist and he played in a variety of bands—including a reconstituted
quintet, featuring Hubert Rostaing on clarinet to replace the absent
Grappelli. He performed in all the major entertainment centres: in the
music halls (the Olympia, the Normandie, the Moulin Rouge, the Alhambra,
the A B C), the Gaveau and Pleyel concert halls, and the most chic cabarets
(Ciro's, Chez Jane Stick, the Montecristo, the Impératrice). These were
places frequented by the Paris fast set—people like the shady socialite
Porfirio Rubirosa, and film stars Danielle Darrieux and Roland Toutain—as
well as by high-ranking officers of the German army. At a time when the
movement of civilians around France was severely restricted and complicated by the regulations governing the Occupation zones, Reinhardt toured
extensively throughout France, and also to Algeria and Belgium. Recording
sessions multiplied, and Django worked in many different musical combinations: with the quintet, with Alix Combelle, Noël Chiboust, Christian
Wagner, Pierre Allier and André Ekyan. During the four years of the Occupation, he recorded almost a hundred sides, nearly all of them on the French
'Swing' label, which moved quickly to fill the gap left in the market by the
departure of the American labels. Django composed a lot of original material
during this time, including some of his most complex work such as *Nuages*
and *Féerie*. Musically, it was an inspirational time for him.[8]

He was not a modest star. He was erratic, flighty and unbearably
arrogant, and his heavy gambling and frequent drinking bouts made him difficult and unreliable to work with. But the sound he created and the swing
that he generated were a passport that allowed him to circulate with total

freedom, admired, and indeed almost adulated, by French and Germans alike. With his propensity for getting into trouble, it is quite astonishing that Django had no serious run-ins with the Nazi authorities, whose persecution of Gypsies was notorious and systematic. The explanation probably lies in the fact that the guitarist had become such a legend as to be untouchable. Charles Delaunay tells an extraordinary story according to which Django, arrested as a spy in a cabaret at Thonon-les-Bains on the Swiss border, was released on the order of a German commandant who happened to be a fan.[9] Unlike many of the prominent French wartime entertainers, he even managed to avoid the normally mandatory cultural tour to the German heartland.[10]

Other jazz musicians who thrived during the war included Alix Combelle, who realised his longstanding dream of running his own band, Le Jazz de Paris. With this eleven-piece ensemble, which included some of Django's musicians, Combelle used tight arrangements to achieve a polished, full sound modelled on pre-war American big bands.[11] André Ekyan and Gus Viseur ran busy small groups while Fred Addison and Raymond Legrand (the father of Michel) also directed big swing bands. The singers Johnny Hess and Charles Trenet, both extremely popular entertainers, cultivated jazz and swing styles that contributed strongly to the Paris wartime jazz boom. Hess's 'Je suis swing' became the catchcry of the younger generation, and Trenet's recording of 'La cigale et la fourmi' with the Quintet of the Hot Club of France was an instant and enduring hit.

Before the war, Hugues Panassié had been the major organiser of jazz life in France and had very much dominated the activities of the Hot Club. When he chose to spend the duration of the war at his country retreat at Montauban, Charles Delaunay, who had until that time been a loyal lieutenant for Panassié, began to play a more prominent role in the organisation and promotion of jazz. Son of the famous painter couple Sonia and Robert Delaunay, Charles was himself a gifted visual artist, as evidenced by his drawings of jazz stars, which appeared regularly in *Jazz Hot*. Perhaps from a desire to be different from his parents, he turned away from art, and in his early twenties developed a passion for jazz. It was jazz—the music and the whole associated cultural phenomenon—that would become the canvas for all his future endeavours, absorbing the dazzling energies of his entrepreneurial intelligence and his undeniable creativity. General secretary of the Hot Club of France under Panassié, he directed *Jazz Hot*, managed the Reinhardt-Grappelli Quintet, composed the first exhaustive jazz discography (1936) and created the recording company 'Swing' (1937).

Delaunay had served in the artillery at the start of the war, and after his demobilisation at the time of the armistice, he had briefly contemplated emigrating to the United States, fearful of the fate that jazz would suffer at the hands of the Nazis. He was therefore surprised, when he returned to Paris, to find jazz flourishing everywhere in the city. Musicians had work, record sales were brisk, and the music itself had taken on the liberating symbolic value of 'forbidden fruit'.[12] It was a climate in which Delaunay detected strong, if hidden, hope. He was inspired by the urge to revive the Hot Club of France, and particularly its objective of reaching out to young people to cultivate their musical taste. For this apostle, jazz was not so much a form of rebellion as a call to a deeper sense of personal freedom.

From the club's headquarters in the rue Chaptal (near Pigalle), he set out to re-establish the kinds of activities that were taking place before the war: lectures, concerts, recordings, and, given the paper restrictions that prevented publication of *Jazz Hot*, the distribution of a regular newsletter. His efforts were rewarded. There was a doubling of the number of large-scale jazz concerts compared with the pre-war period, and a rapid growth in the number of Hot Club branches, from five in 1939 to twenty-nine in 1944. Sales of the quintet's records also increased significantly.[13]

Delaunay gave his lecture series not only in Paris, but also in a number of provincial cities. In an attempt to avoid unwelcome attention from the Germans, he tried to pursue an apolitical line, and encouraged the spread of a strategy developed by musicians, in which forbidden American tunes were given French names. Thus, for example, 'Two Left Feet' became 'Deux pieds gauches', 'Exactly like you' became 'Pour vous' and 'Honeysuckle Rose' became 'Chèvrefeuille'.[14] He also served the French cause more directly. While moving about, chiefly in the occupied zone but with occasional clandestine excursions across the demarcation line, Delaunay sometimes transported information and documents for the Resistance. Having a Jewish mother, he was at considerable risk, despite an 'Aryan' certificate obtained through a Hot Club member who worked in the Jewish Affairs Commissariat.[15] At one point, he was arrested and briefly imprisoned. The Hot Club also raised money to support French prisoners of war and other charities. Delaunay's activities during this period provide a valuable example of how unwise it is to try to categorise life under the Occupation in terms of a simple Resistance–collaborationist dichotomy.

Most of the keenest supporters of the jazz wave were young people, and they came from all social backgrounds: students and workers, as well as the strangely garbed rebels known as 'zazous'.[16] Despite the controls imposed by the Occupation, diversity among French youth remained strong during this period and represented a powerful obstacle to any broad-based entrenchment of totalitarian ideologies. Even the official Catholic Church hierarchy, generally very supportive of Pétain and the Vichy government, was unyielding in its refusal to permit collaborationist politicians to introduce the kinds of unified youth movements that had taken root in Italy and Germany.[17]

The zazous were extreme examples of youthful anarchy, defying all the rules of polite behaviour and good taste as well as rejecting the general mood of resignation. Flaunting Django Reinhardt dark glasses and moustaches, the young men wore long hair, oversized jackets, gloves and flamboyant scarves; the girls painted their lips and nails bright red and got themselves up in big pullovers and short skirts. They walked with an affected syncopated strut, and when they danced they waved their forefingers in the air above their heads, a gesture that (no doubt to their satisfaction) particularly irritated their critics. Some of them peppered their conversation with English words. Without necessarily being politically committed, they were capable of taking serious political risks, as on the famous occasion when, after the introduction of the law obliging Jews to wear the yellow star, they paraded down the boulevard Saint-Germain in Paris with Stars of David inscribed with the words 'swing' or 'zazou'.[18] This, and similar incidents in other French cities, was seen as a serious irritant by the Nazi administrators, leading to the arrest and internment of a number of protesters.

For the young, jazz was a territory in which they could express themselves with a freedom denied to most aspects of their lives. While the nature of its impact is complex and often indirect, the music was an undeniable part of the birth of a new phenomenon in France. It was one that would become fully manifest only after the war, but whose emergence clearly dates from the Occupation: for all their foppish eccentricity, the zazous were the pioneers of a culture that, in a self-conscious and outspoken manner, sought its identity and its autonomy specifically in youth.

As early as 1942 the music historian André Coeuroy, in his *Histoire générale du jazz*, ascribed the vital link between jazz and youth culture to the fact that jazz had brought with it a physicality, a re-*incarnation*, that had been lost to European musical art:

> Jazz is no longer exoticism; it is no longer entertainment; it is no longer  luxury or leisure, it is a new form of the art of living . . . Swing restores a sense of physicality to music and to the listener . . . This is the new and profound reason why jazz has real meaning for the young, and why, by its very presence, it is instructive in a way which, at this time, could not be more salutary for them. It is curious, and healthy, that these young people should be sustained by swing, in which malcontents see only chaotic frenzy, but where we are able to discover, simply and refreshingly, the force of life which continues patiently and never despairs.[19]

Coeuroy's own ideology is, to be sure, suspect. It feeds into the Vichy discourse that saw French culture as decadent and in need of reinvigoration, and at the same time it is tinged with a Eurocentric superiority that seeks to appropriate jazz by cutting it off from its roots:

> Jazz has only been black by chance. Its principal elements have come from whites, and European whites. In its history and in its substance, jazz is ours; its future is in our hands.[20]

In denying the undeniable historical origins of jazz in the experience of African-Americans, Coeuroy is plainly wrong. However, despite this confusion, one of his fundamental insights was accurate. Jazz was serving to reintroduce an emphasis on sensual pleasure into patterns of artistic activity and reflection that had become abstract and intellectualised, and for the young this was a natural and powerful magnet that would become even more attractive during the Liberation period.

The liberation of France was an extended process, beginning with the June 1944 Allied invasion of Normandy. Military operations spread throughout the country and lasted until the end of that year, when the tenacious German forces were finally driven from French territory. But the turmoil of bombings and massacres that accompanied the German withdrawal from France disrupted every aspect of national life. Material damage from the hostilities was itself catastrophic. More importantly, the aftermath of the final German defeat revealed, quite abruptly, how fundamentally the governing principles of pre-war life had been altered. The economy was in tatters. The framework of political life—based on a shaky tripartite agreement among socialists, communists and Christian democrats—was completely unstable. The nation was faced with multiple, simultaneous crises: acute shortages of consumer goods and energy supplies; the return of almost two million prisoners of war; the even more troubling return of political and racial deportees, whose stories of horror and genocide would become a permanent blemish on the national consciousness. Attempts to purge from public life those held responsible for the shame of the armistice and the years of collaboration were messy and drawn-out, and were ineffective in restoring order. In the midst of all this, France had to seek a place for itself in the postwar world, at the same time as its colonial empire was beginning to break up.

Although few realised it at the time, it was a situation in which the rebuilding of the nation could not occur without a radical revision of thought and behaviour patterns. From many points of view, the postwar reconstruction of France is still an unfinished story. But one has only to revisit Renoir's 1939 film masterpiece, *The Rules of the Game* (*La règle du jeu*), to comprehend the revolutionary nature of the changes that have occurred in all aspects of French life. Renoir analyses a social and cultural order that would have been still fresh in the memories of many who had lived through the Occupation—a world to which, despite its foibles and hypocrisies, they would have expected to return after the end of hostilities. Few would have known how completely it belonged to a past that could never be revived. The pre-war social hierarchies, with their clear codes of conduct, were now gone forever. Neither the rules nor the game would ever be the same.

It is perhaps symbolic of the pace and scope of those transformations that the career of Django Reinhardt quite speedily declined. Given his unparalleled popularity during the war, it might have been expected that the Liberation would bring him even greater opportunities, especially after Grappelli's return from London in 1945. His reputation was such that the first contingent of American soldiers arriving in Paris flocked to hear him. He had major performances at the Tabarin and the Olympia, and others with Fred Astaire and musicians from Glenn Miller's band. Invited to work in America with Duke Ellington, whom he had met before the war, he played with his usual virtuosity, but drew the wrath of critics by the unprofessional nature of his conduct: on several occasions he turned up late for performances, or not at all. Django was a genius, and an inspired improviser, but while these qualities were sufficient to have ensured his success in occupied France, they were not sufficient to satisfy American expectations of professional musicians. In New York there was nothing like the French and European tradition that tolerated the shortcomings of great artists: he was simply castigated for behaving badly.

There were still a few good times. Dizzy Gillespie came to see him and play with him during his February 1948 trip to Paris. But Django had never reacted well to pressure, and faced with the increased competition of a new influx of American musicians after the Liberation, he was bewildered and disgruntled by dwindling audiences. He began to lose interest in music. Poorly organised playing engagements at American army bases in Germany were disastrously received, and other tours to England, Belgium and Italy left him so discouraged that he decided to abandon his guitar and take up painting. When invited to play in a 1950 Paris concert with Benny Goodman, he simply did not turn up. An attempted comeback in 1951, two years before his death, was overshadowed by the sense of a growing distance between his style of music—which just a few years earlier had seemed so far ahead of its times—and the revolution that had occurred with be-bop.[21]

The French jazz musicians who made their mark during the immediate postwar years had begun their careers during the Occupation, often participating in the amateur jazz competitions organised by the Hot Club. Like Django, they had had no opportunity to hear the new sounds that were leading jazz development on the other side of the Atlantic. In New York, Charlie Parker, Thelonious Monk, Kenny Clarke and Dizzy Gillespie had unleashed a storm of experimentation, transforming the melodic and harmonic foundations of the music as well as its rhythms. This was the music of a new, infinitely more powerful American society and it was a form of jazz through which a dynamic group of African-Americans were restaking their claims in a musical territory they felt had been too comfortably appropriated by the white musical establishment. In Paris, the style French musicians continued to cultivate was very much New Orleans–based, which helps to explain the enormous success that greeted the return of Sidney Bechet in 1949. Whereas in America the fractures between traditional and avant-garde tendencies had by 1945 given jazz language an enormous range and capacity to expand, France's enforced isolation had kept it in a state of relative innocence. The enthusiasms of first discovery and emulation of the early masters were far from exhausted.

In this backwater, the Claude Abadie band grew out of a student group that began in Lyon in 1941. It was reconstituted in various combinations by the clarinettist leader after his return to Paris the following year. The band was an amateur one, at most semi-professional: while they were generally paid to perform, all of the musicians had primary commitments to other fields—Abadie himself was a banking executive, for instance. At the same time, their amateur status allowed them to play what they wanted, rather than succumb to the commercial dance-music demands often imposed upon professionals. Shunning the traditional white band jackets so that they could mingle and dance with the patrons when they were not on stage, they found plenty of work, especially in entertaining the American troops who flooded into liberated Paris. The Americans paid them in kind, with doughnuts, omelettes, chocolate and coffee—all luxuries in a city where basic food items were still tightly rationed. Claude Léon, the band's drummer, recalled the group's surprise in discovering how little the American soldiers knew about jazz. The Frenchmen were puzzled and amused to find themselves introducing the music of such composers as Duke Ellington to his compatriots.[22]

The cornet player in the Abadie band was Boris Vian, a trained engineer who was both a major character in the jazz story in France and a pivotal force in some of the wider cultural shifts in the postwar era. His horn-playing was not the most remarkable of his artistic talents, but it was not insignificant. Above all, it gave him a practical apprenticeship and understanding that would allow him to transfer jazz principles readily and effectively to other dimensions of his art. As a trumpeter, Vian modelled himself on Bix Beiderbecke, emulating the same kinds of extended lyrical lines across the range of traditional jazz standards. Because of a congenital heart condition that would eventually kill him, Vian was unable to keep up his trumpet-playing beyond 1950, but through his singing, his jazz criticism across a wide range of media, and his role as an indefatigable organiser of musical events, he became a dominant personality in Paris, earning the nickname of 'King of Saint-Germain-des-Prés'.

Vian was not the first to create a jazz cellar, one of the tiny, cramped, smoke-filled holes with their narrow slippery steps, which became the symbol of postwar French nightlife. That honour fell to Claude Luter, another student band leader, who had discovered jazz during his time in the 'Chantiers de jeunesse', the youth public-service camps instituted by the Vichy government in lieu of military service. At night, after days chopping wood, Luter would imitate famous clarinet solos that he had learned by heart.[23] Vian considered him the most interesting French jazz musician since Django Reinhardt.[24] In 1946, Luter set up a standing engagement with his group beneath a hotel called the Lorientais, at the Latin Quarter end of the boulevard Saint-Germain. He adopted the name of the hotel for the band, which became a favourite of the dance-happy students at the nearby Sorbonne.

But the cellars that Vian helped launch, the Tabou (in the rue Dauphine) and the Club Saint-Germain (in the rue Saint-Benoît), were equally influential, because of the quality of visiting American musicians who played there as well as the press coverage that the clubs attracted. In the public imagination, the jazz cellar culture soon became identified with different aspects of Liberation life: the noisy antics of unfettered youth, the infatuation with America, the explorations of avant-garde intellectuals such as Sartre, de Beauvoir, Eluard and Queneau. Sartre's sometime secretary, Jean Cau, would later claim that the Saint-Germain phenomenon never existed,[25] but the evidence is against him. The effervescence was real, and jazz was one of its principal means of expression. For Anne-Marie Cazalis, the scene at the Lorientais was one of almost religious fervour:

> Crowded into this warm, dark hole, a mystical young crowd listened to jazz, with mouths set and eyes vacant. The future cellar rats were practising. The faithful tapped their feet and moved their heads in time with the music for hours . . .[26]

It is worth emphasising that, for the audiences, jazz was still primarily associated with dancing. A newspaper report on the Luter band gave a tongue-in-cheek account of the energy required:

> No dancer has yet proved able to keep up with the rhythm of Luter's clarinet. A black, who tried to 'hang in', found himself forbidden to dance by his doctor. He was completely exhausted.[27]

The journalist obviously admired Luter's ability to serve up rhythms that were challenging even to those considered natural masters of the music. Such praise for a French musician was highly significant in the context of the Paris jazz scene, where the influence of the great American players was beginning to reassert itself in no uncertain way.

French jazzmen discovered be-bop through the records of Dizzy Gillespie in 1946,[28] and the experience produced a polarisation similar to that which had occurred in America a few years earlier. Some embraced the new sounds, exhilarated by the dazzling technical virtuosity deployed by the likes of Gillespie and Parker, and which could be regarded as a natural and inevitable evolution in jazz. Others rejected be-bop out of hand as mere acrobatics: a perversion, or even tuneless noise. There is no sign that the French understood anything of the specifically African-American rebellion involved in the origins of be-bop, that is, its affirmation of a black creativity and individuality against music that had been softened by the American mainstream. Rather, what attracted or repelled the French musicians and commentators was the openness of be-bop as a musical form, its avant-garde experimental nature, its self-conscious artistic boldness. As Delaunay put it:

> It was even hard to distinguish what was written from what was improvised. But as we kept listening to these records, it became obvious that we were listening not to the fruits of chance but to elaborate exploration.[29]

The taste of jazz players and listeners in France was slow to evolve. In the 1947 *Jazz Hot* referendum, Louis Armstrong was four times more popular than Cootie Williams and six times more popular than Dizzy Gillespie. Johnny Hodges was ten times more popular than Charlie Parker.[30]

The Gallic version of the battle over jazz is best rendered in the bitter and sometimes comic rift between the nation's two most prominent pro-moters of the music, Hugues Panassié and Charles Delaunay. Panassié, because of his absence from Paris during the war, had lost the momentum and prestige he had acquired during the 1930s, when he was the undisputed leader of the jazz movement in France. Delaunay, for his part, had taken over at the centre of activity, greatly increasing his sphere of influence by maintaining and extending the activities of the Hot Club of France. Both men were charismatic, and both of them were selfless in their devotion to jazz, but differences in personality, taste and approach produced increasing friction between them, and quickly led to a complete breakdown of their collaboration.

Some aspects of this split, which greatly affected the Hot Club de France both in its organisation and in its publication activities, can only be fully explained by reference to the wider French cultural context, which will be treated in the second part of this study. In purely musical terms, Panassié had locked himself into a New Orleans–Chicago purism that declared any other form of jazz to be heretical. Before the war, Panassié's authority had been recognised as so complete that he was given the title of 'the Pope of jazz'. The same term was now used to deride his absolutism. Delaunay, much more balanced, believed that jazz was a music flexible enough to accommodate growth and evolution without losing contact with its origins.

This balance was evident in his 1948 preface to Michel Dorigné's *La guerre du jazz* (The Jazz War).[31] Dorigné's polemic was an all-out attack on those who failed to understand the progressive nature of jazz. Delaunay was careful to point out that while he did not share all of Dorigné's opinions, he saw the enthusiasm of such writing as an overriding value. He would certainly have agreed with Dorigné's view of jazz as 'an art of peace and communion'[32] and he would also have concurred with the presentation of Panassié as a man who, despite his contributions to jazz, was flawed by his own dogmatism.[33] It is less likely that he would have accepted Dorigné's demolition of Claude Luter, dismissed as a mere imitator, as 'the great heretic of jazz music', and as 'a geriatric before his time'.[34] Delaunay's tastes were broader, but what he appreciated in Dorigné was the underlying conviction that jazz was not simply a musical form, canonical or otherwise. Rather, to the embattled young of postwar France, it offered 'a way out that takes us back to the most natural and hidden human well-springs'.[35]

In the longer term, inevitably, the future was with the Delaunay camp, firmly ensconced in the nation's capital and including most practising musicians as well as the influential Boris Vian. During the immediate postwar years, however, the tensions between Panassié and Delaunay led to spirited rivalry. Despite the fiery controversy surrounding their competition, it was actually beneficial to the development of jazz, and not only in France. It was Panassié who took the lead, as artistic director of the Nice Jazz Festival in February 1948. This was the world's first international jazz festival, and it provoked a dramatic boost for France's reputation as a place where the music was taken seriously. Panassié's American guests included Louis Armstrong—universally acknowledged as the single most important figure in jazz—and bands led by Rex Stewart and Mezz Mezzrow. The French bands were the Quintet of the Hot Club de France and, more surprisingly and contentiously, Claude Luter's Lorientais, who were at best semi-professional but who had received Panassié's blessing as the best French exponents of New Orleans style.

The festival was an unmitigated success, filling the halls of Nice's opera house and casino for six days with audiences from France and abroad. It was covered enthusiastically by the whole range of national media: press, radio, and even cinema newsreels. In the history of jazz, the Nice festival is an important landmark.[36] It was the prototype for a whole tradition of festivals in France, and it also pointed the way to the Newport Festival of 1954—the first American jazz festival—and other large-scale jazz events in the United States, Europe and the rest of the world. Furthermore, it institutionalised pathways by which American musicians could visit France regularly and easily, beginning the process that brought live performances by the best jazz musicians to French audiences over the next couple of decades.

Charles Delaunay used the Nice festival as a springboard to further his own ambitions as a jazz promoter. A few days before Nice, Delaunay had managed to improvise a concert in Paris by the 17-piece Dizzy Gillespie band, which was touring Europe. He thus succeeded in being the first to present authentic be-bop live in France, and he did it with considerable flair. It was not, strictly speaking, Gillespie's first performance in Paris, since he had been the second trumpet in the Teddy Hill band that played in the 1937 Cotton Club review, at which time he had been likened by Panassié to Roy Eldrige, and praised for his strong swing and temperament.[37] But the following decade had transformed Gillespie from a journeyman into a revolutionary soloist, and the February 1948 Salle Pleyel concert was received with what Delaunay called 'general stupefaction', the audience staggered by the band's 'violence and stridence'.[38] The concert was broadcast nationally. Boris Vian noted the preponderance of young people in the audience, and suggested that it was their familiarity with the music that created such an enthusiastic reception: '[W]ith Dizzy Gillespie, be-bop, the latest development of jazz music, has conquered Paris.'[39] It is worth noting that while some of the press saw Gillespie as the modernist representative in the jazz war, a number of Louis Armstrong's musicians did not hesitate to attend their compatriot's concert.[40]

In May 1948 Delaunay organised a 'jazz week' at the Théâtre Marigny, as a response to the narrowness of taste that Panassié had demonstrated in his choice of music for Nice. Delaunay took a much more universalist approach, both geographically, in that he invited the Australian Dixieland band led by Graeme Bell as well as French and American groups, and aesthetically, in that all tendencies in jazz were represented, from New Orleans to be-bop. There was even a kind of band 'cutting' competition, with Boris Vian acting as referee.[41] Delaunay increased the pressure on Panassié by launching a series of weekly jazz concerts in the heart of the city's theatre district and by staging, in May 1949, the first formal International Paris Jazz Festival. This was a major event, and it carried Delaunay's signature as the promoter of an inclusive concept of jazz. Sidney Bechet was featured as the principal figure of the New Orleans tradition, and Charlie Parker and Miles Davis as the chief representatives of the frontier-probing contemporary sounds. In the audience at the opening concert, the young Louis Malle was awestruck, noting in his personal diary his special enthusiasm for the polished, velvety sound of the Davis trumpet that would become so important to his own work as a film-maker a few years later.[42]

In December 1950, Delaunay, in collaboration with Jacques Souplet, stretched his organisational talents even further. They coordinated a monumental International Jazz Fair, which had the dimensions of a giant artistic, commercial, industrial and educational event. Under the official patronage of the Ministry of Education, it included concerts by top musicians such as Roy Eldridge and James Moody, and also 'how-to-listen' classes, and exhibits by record companies, music and book publishers, and instrument makers. It hosted the annual competition for amateur jazz bands, and an exhibition of paintings inspired by the jazz age. With 20 000 to 30 000 local and foreign visitors, the fair was an impressive coup, extensively covered by the media.[43] It marked a kind of apotheosis for Paris, in that it created a brilliant international showcase for jazz, and constituted irrefutable proof that the city had reclaimed its role as a centre of cultural innovation. While many of the residual problems left by the French wartime experience would take at least half a century to resolve, Delaunay's grand gesture had a confidence that makes 1950 a symbolic turning point in the French cultural liberation process.

The fifteen years following the end of the war were arguably the richest and most exciting in French jazz history. In addition to the feverish activity on the part of French musicians and enthusiasts such as Panassié and Delaunay, there was a significant influx of American musicians. Paris was quickly re-established as a major world centre for performance of jazz of all styles. Dizzy Gillespie had been preceded by Don Redman and Rex Stewart, and he was followed by Louis Armstrong, Bill Coleman, Charlie Parker, Miles Davis, Mezz Mezzrow, Duke Ellington, Buck Clayton, Benny Goodman, Big Bill Broonzy, Mahalia Jackson, Lionel Hampton, the Modern Jazz Quartet, Billie Holiday, and so on. Between 1948 and 1960 Duke Ellington gave more than two dozen concerts in France, a number of them broadcast on radio or television.

France's postwar reconstruction needs had given rise to generous immigration laws which, although primarily aimed at industry, made it easy for foreign musicians to find work. Thus, for instance, it was possible for Eartha Kitt, one of the few African-American women to relocate to Paris, to work with Frede at the very chic Carroll's, and also with Bill Coleman and Don Byas at the Perroquet.[44] Notwithstanding the efforts of some of the French band leaders to maintain the monopoly they had enjoyed during the Occupation, the situation produced unprecedented freedom of movement for individual musicians and a much higher degree of musical collaboration between French and Americans. The latter brought with them a level of professionalism that helped transform the French jazz scene, which, like Django Reinhardt, had never matched inspiration with discipline.

It was at the end of 1950 that Sidney Bechet made the definitive decision to settle in France. There was no sense of exile in this decision. For both Bechet and his French hosts, it was a homecoming: the French treated him as one of their own, and it was a role that he relished until his death at the end of the decade. The thunderous welcome he had received on the opening night of the first Paris Jazz Festival, when he played with Claude Luter's band, was a sign of adoption. His music was jazz as the French most loved it, a style that drew deeply on its New Orleans roots and that revealed an authenticity and continuing vitality that even the most progressive jazz fans could appreciate, commanding the respect of the boppers themselves. For the local audience, the fact that he was a French-speaking Creole added to his personal charisma.

Bechet became a French national treasure. He enjoyed his stardom and cultivated it with good-natured diligence. With the Claude Luter and André Réwéliotty bands, he sustained a heavy schedule of performances in Paris while also touring extensively in the provinces, including summer engagements on the Côte d'Azur. Alongside the New Orleans standards, he frequently introduced new pieces: tunes of his own composition, such as 'Les Oignons' and 'Petite Fleur', which became signature works and sold over a million records; and also songs by some of the major French *chansonniers* of the day, such as Georges Brassens.

According to his secretary, Marlène Gray, 'he would have been capable of giving an honourable concert to marble statues',[45] but he did not need to. He drew huge crowds—18 000 to an open-air concert at the Arènes de Lutèce in 1955—and on occasion he even relived a bit of the scandalous behaviour of his earlier life. After his October 1955 concert at the Olympia he almost triggered a riot. The disturbance, caused by a much larger than expected acceptance of invitations, was reported with dry humour by Jacques Nosari in *Le Figaro*:

> At the doorways, on the boulevard and in the rue Caumartin, the music-lovers did not hesitate to use their elbows somewhat brutally to force their way in. A violent brawl ensued. Called in as reinforcements, the police had to intervene to disperse the youthful crowd that had just smashed the big mirror of a nearby shopfront. At the Olympia, window panes were also broken, and marble tiles pried off the façade. While some 2500 lucky (?) ones managed to flood into the theatre, thousands of others were turned away. Result: two people mildly injured, and two others arrested for rioting. So there are four students who will remember this evening, during which another, more fortunate, 'fanatic' got Sidney Bechet to autograph . . . a piece of a theatre seat.[46]

*Le Monde*, more overtly disapproving, reported four injuries, including two hospitalised, and reproached the management of the Olympia for refusing to press charges against the 'hooligans' who had broken the furniture and souvenired the band photo posters.[47]

Ludovic Tournès's assessment of Bechet as France's first real jazz 'star'[48] overlooks the fact that Django Reinhardt had enjoyed that honour ten years before. It is, however, true that by the time Django died in 1953, Bechet had eclipsed the guitarist's fame, and occupied a far greater space in the French public imagination. Bechet, from the hooligan (and in fact criminal) deportee that he had been in 1929, was now the very incarnation of artistic legitimacy. His social circle included the likes of Simone Signoret and Yves Montand, and in the great Paris music halls he performed alongside the very top stars: Brassens, Catherine Sauvage, Mouloudji, Jacques Brel, Charles Aznavour. In 1954, he had a ballet—*La nuit est une sorcière*—staged in the capital, and during the mid 1950s, as performer or composer or both, he played in eight films.[49] By 1956 he had his own fan club. And just as his marriage in 1951 had been a national event, so was his death in 1959. While it did not earn him the state funeral that awaited his former partner Josephine Baker in 1975, it provoked a widespread sense of mourning for the man who had done more than any other single person to open French ears to jazz.

Among other American musicians electing to live in Paris—and the list included Jimmy Gourley, Don Byas, Mezz Mezzrow and Albert Nicholas—one of the earliest and certainly the most influential was the drummer Kenny Clarke. With Thelonious Monk, Clarke had been a member of the house band at Minton's Playhouse, on 118th Street in New York, during the formative years of be-bop. He stayed on in Paris after the Dizzy Gillespie tour in 1948, and immediately began working with a range of French musicians, touring and recording for the Swing label. His first sojourn lasted three years, and he returned again in 1956, this time permanently. Through his formal teaching and his activities at the centre of French jazz recording, he became a veritable jazz master. Towards the end of the decade, he became the anchor at the most distinguished jazz club in Paris, the Blue Note. It was at the Blue Note, with Clarke on drums, that the pianist Bud Powell would take up his legendary five-year Paris residence in 1959.

The possibility of playing regularly with the Americans—in jam sessions, pick-up groups, or more long-term bands—produced a rapid diversification of French jazz styles. The more traditional music not only survived but thrived through the contact with Bechet and Mezzrow: the most successful bands were those of Claude Luter, André Réwéliotty (until his death in a car crash in 1962) and Maxime Saury. Saury's group ensured that fans of New Orleans jazz had a permanent home at the Caveau de la Huchette, in one of the Latin Quarter's archetypal ancient streets. At the other end of the scale, the clarinettist with the Abadie band, Hubert Fol, converted to be-bop. As early as 1947 he formed a group provocatively called the Be-Bop Minstrels, which explored the challenges of playing and recording recent American compositions such as 'A Night in Tunisia'. Kenny Clarke's occasional participation greatly aided the development of the group's style. The talented pianist of the Be-Bop Minstrels, André Persiani, toured with Mezzrow, and enjoyed a successful professional career in the United States in the 1960s.[50]

As in most places where jazz was taking root, France also had a strong current of music that was mainstream progressive, drawing on both traditional and avant-garde sounds and rhythms. Pianists Jack Diéval, Claude Bolling and René Urtreger; saxophonists Barney Wilen, Guy Lafitte, Michel de Villers and Jean-Claude Fohrenbach; the trumpet player Roger Guérin; the bassist Pierre Michelot: all were good musicians, some outstanding, and they helped establish the foundations of a lasting indigenous French jazz 'family'. Its members were fully capable of creative engagement in the international 'conversations' that jazz made possible and desirable.

It is debatable whether the Paris of the postwar decades was once again, as Juliette Gréco believed, 'the capital of the world',[51] but France was a dominant jazz centre. American musicians, and especially African-Americans, loved to play there, and many chose to stay for prolonged periods. They liked the warmth of the audiences, the intellectual seriousness with which the music was treated, and, overwhelmingly—although there were a few exceptions—they experienced unfamiliar and welcome comfort in being seen as human beings without reference to their race. As Stovall remarks: '. . . [M]ost blacks have felt Paris offered a degree of freedom not available at home. The African-American community in Paris symbolises the potential of African-American life in general once it is fully liberated from racism.'[52]

The creative symbiosis experienced by American jazzmen in their relationship with France is given emblematic value in John Lewis's compositions 'Django' and 'Delaunay's Dilemma'. Lewis, the pianist and leader of the Modern Jazz Quartet, was strongly motivated by the need to restore a sense of dignity to jazz. The music's reputation had suffered from the wild atmosphere generated by and around Charlie Parker, whose breathtaking inventiveness became confused for a time with his uncontrolled alcohol and narcotics abuse. For Lewis, France was more than a haven; it was a place of artistic originality and stimulus. His 'Django', a homage to the first truly original French jazz musician, echoes the melodic feeling of a traditional

French ballad and evokes a limpid, wistful beauty. 'Delaunay's Dilemma' is a more complex tune, reflecting the tension between the basic harmonic changes of traditional jazz and the more jagged, unresolved lines of be-bop.

Charles Delaunay, when writing his autobiography, chose to take up Lewis's title because it so insightfully caught the difficulties facing the Frenchman in his promotion of jazz during this period of extreme polarisation in musical taste. Lewis's foreword to the book praised Delaunay's perspicacity and courage:

> We jazz musicians will remain eternally grateful to Charles for becoming a courageous and tireless defender of our art . . . At a time when most jazz writers seemed to appreciate only the early conventions, Charles Delaunay recognized the value of the new school, [ . . . defending] not a particular style, but nothing less than all of jazz.[53]

The MJQ made its first trip to France in 1956. With its quiet cool control and its borrowings from baroque and classical counterpoint, it took some time to win full approval from French jazz fans, but Lewis, who had shared the excitement of the 1948 Dizzie Gillespie tour, never wavered in his enthusiasm for France.[54]

The strong musical connection between French and American jazz musicians during this time resulted in part from the historical links created in the 1920s and 1930s, when the French jazz audience had begun to grow in size, knowledge and sophistication. Over the same period, concert and recording circuits had been developed and the first generation of local musicians had established themselves. The war brought a new generation into the French jazz scene, whose musicians shared a youthful diffidence towards the past. They were people ready for the new and radical sounds of be-bop and progressive jazz. While the coexistence of these different generations frequently provoked conflict, it also served to broaden and strengthen the bases of French jazz culture.

From the point of view of the Americans, France had never lost its status as a cultural icon, and with work readily available in the postwar era, it became more attractive than ever. The French–American jazz interchange of the 1940s and 1950s thus stemmed from both a reciprocal fulfilment of needs and a trading of freedoms: each group found in the other opportunity for self-expression and development. For the African-Americans, in particular, the French welcome was an affirmation rarely experienced in their still segregated homeland. Stovall documents how, after the war, a number of writers joined the African-American drift to France that had been initiated by the musicians, and quotes the acerbic comment of Chester Himes, who had generated a substantial French audience for his detective stories: '. . . now I was a French writer and the United States of America could kiss my ass'.[55] Kenny Clarke and Sidney Bechet could easily have made similar comments.

This kind of Franco-American jazz love affair points to the communicative potential of the music. Like many love affairs, it had its share of illusion, self-deception and disappointment; but it also had an inner spirit that transcended the banalities of the everyday. The recordings of Sidney Bechet from these years, and those of Bud Powell, are examples of a musical body of work of substantial volume and great beauty, representing an artistic achievement that would not have been possible without the powerful and mutually liberating exchange between the two cultures.[56]

Many of the qualities of that exchange can be seen in the personal relationship that developed between Miles Davis and Juliette Gréco. Davis first met Gréco during the first Paris Jazz Festival in 1949.[57] Although he did not realise it, he was more advanced in his career than Gréco. He thought of her as being already a prominent star. In truth, although she had gained some notoriety in the press as the hot-headed woman of the Tabou existentialist clique—*Samedi Soir*, for instance, reported her as having used a coin-laden handbag to belt the son of the famous pianist Alfred Cortot, and to knock an eminent politician unconscious[58]—her reputation as an actor and singer was hardly born. Davis had already launched the 'birth of the cool', bringing about a major direction shift in jazz, and the band that performed at the festival had been a huge hit. He was full of confidence, and although he was already married, he fell in love:

> The only other times that I felt that good was when I first heard Bird and Diz in B's band and that time in Dizzy's big band up in the Bronx. But that was just about music. This was different. This was about living . . . It was the freedom of being in France and being treated like a human being, like someone important. Even the band and the music we played sounded better over there . . . Juliette was probably the first woman that I loved as

an equal human being. She was a beautiful person. We had to communicate with each other through expressions and body language. She didn't speak English and I didn't speak French. We talked through our eyes, fingers, stuff like that ... Paris was where I understood that all white people weren't the same, and that some weren't prejudiced and others were ... She was independent, her own thinker, and I liked that.[59]

Arm in arm with Gréco, Davis wandered the quays of the Seine, absorbing the exoticism of the smells, as if he 'had been hypnotised, was in some kind of trance'. At one point, Sartre even suggested that he, the good-looking African-American, should marry the white-faced beauty with the long black hair. But even though he was tempted to follow Kenny Clarke's example and remain in Paris, he only stayed a week or two.

Back in America, he became depressed and fell into a heroin habit. It was some years before they met again, and when they did, in New York, Gréco had indeed become a major star. She invited Miles to her room in the Waldorf Astoria, perhaps unaware of the scandal that would be aroused among the hotel staff by a black man calling on a white woman. He went, but he treated Gréco abominably, demanding and getting a sizeable sum of money. If the romance was not dead, the innocence had certainly disappeared from it.

In 1956, another European tour (with Lester Young and the musicians of the MJQ) allowed Davis to revive the relationship. The following year he was back in Paris as guest soloist at the Club Saint-Germain with Kenny Clarke, Pierre Michelot, Barney Wilen and René Urtreger. It was through Gréco that Davis met Louis Malle, and came to write the music score for one of the first films of the French New Wave, *Ascenseur pour l'échafaud*.[60]

I saw a lot of Juliette and I think it was on this trip that we decided we were always going to be just lovers and great friends. Her career was in France, and she loved being there, while my shit was happening in the States. And while I didn't love being in America all the time, I never thought about moving over to Paris. I really loved Paris, but I loved it to visit, because I didn't think the music could or would happen for me over there ... I think it has to do with being surrounded by a culture that you know, that you can feel, that you come out of. If I lived in Paris, I couldn't just go and hear some great blues, or people like Monk and Trane and Duke and Satchmo every night, like I could in New York. And although there were good, classically trained musicians in Paris, they still didn't hear the music like an American musician did. I couldn't live in Paris for all those reasons, and Juliette understood.[61]

Davis's observations here show a profound understanding both of himself and of his relationship with Gréco and France. In this romantic couple —in their intimacy and their ultimate distance—we have a critical example of a passionate cultural encounter. Miles Davis, in choosing to accept America, with all its internal contradictions, as the culture he had 'come out of', was cementing his destiny as one of the great musical innovators of American jazz, a voice of the nation's most original musical form.

Gréco rose to stardom in France at a time when jazz activity was at its highest point, and when more French musicians were mastering jazz than ever before. Yet, in the French cultural context, jazz would never have the centrality that it had in the United States. Gréco's music gave voice to the work of major figures: Prévert and Kosma, Sartre, Mauriac, Ferré, Gainsbourg, Vian, Desnos, Aznavour, Marguerite Duras and Georges Delerue, Seghers, Queneau, Sagan, Moustaki and Brel. Her orchestrators included Bolling and Michel Legrand. But although Gréco's music was jazz-influenced, it was not so much jazz as it was a continuation and development of an older French musical tradition, that of the *chanson*. And while the *chanson* derived new life from its encounter with jazz, and indeed drew on jazz to extend its range of possibilities, its practitioners remained faithful to its cultural integrity.

What we see in the Miles Davis–Juliette Gréco story is the image of a love that, far from failing, produced a different kind of fulfilment for each of its participants. A cultural *exchange* is not a melding of cultures, but rather a mutual enrichment. Davis and Gréco's relationship encapsulates much of the deeper cultural relationship that the jazz phenomenon would stimulate between France and America. The reason why these two people could play this symbolic role was because both were so profoundly imbued with their own cultural traditions.

# CHAPTER 4

# FRENCH JAZZ COMES OF AGE
## The Contemporary Scene

I believe in . . . something . . . I like the philosophy of the present
moment, appreciating what I am living now, not making plans
for the future—we can never know what life has in store for us.
**Michel Petrucciani,** *Jazz Magazine*[1]

From the 1960s on, the history of jazz in France has continued to unfold
according to the broad contours of developments in America. America
remains the undisputed source of major innovation and directional change,
and the story of American jazz still sets the pattern for what happens elsewhere, including in France. Compared with the earlier periods, however,
because of the increased rapidity of communication technology and the
greater mobility of the musicians themselves, French jazz has evolved with
less delay relative to America than ever before. Moreover, as the music has
become more institutionally entrenched in France, French musicians have
become more confident about their own artistic autonomy.

In the United States, one of the effects of the be-bop revolution was the
detachment of jazz from the current of popular dance music. Over the postwar decades, although the Armstrongs, Ellingtons, Basies and Goodmans
were still performing for substantial audiences, those who danced to their

music grew older, and younger generations sought their dance rhythms in other forms of music. Jazz was eclipsed by rock, country, and folk music: from representing 70 per cent of recorded music in the 1930s and 1940s, by the 1970s it could claim no more than three per cent.[2] It is hard to imagine a sharper decline. Charlie Parker, Dizzie Gillespie, Kenny Clarke, Thelonious Monk and their like had made jazz a more creative and exploratory language; but in doing so, they had reduced its immediate entertainment value by turning it into constructions of sound and rhythm that denied listeners the comfort of familiar emotional response, and challenged them to more thoughtful reflection. Any dancing that this music stimulated was most likely to be in the mind. In this way, jazz converged to a considerable extent with the 'high culture' music tradition, and in line with the predictions made by Pesquinne and others thirty years earlier, it became a kind of classical music in its own right—an independent form—with a gallery of virtuoso instrumentalist improvisers, and a growing repertoire of original compositions enriching the older 'standards'.

At the same time, the boundaries between black and white jazz became more porous. The American pioneer had been Benny Goodman, who in the mid 1930s had created a mixed-race quartet by inviting Teddy Wilson and Lionel Hampton to join him and Gene Krupa in public concerts.[3] Such a band would have been no novelty in France, where blacks and whites had frequently played together from the beginning. In America, it was a radical —even revolutionary—statement, and the desegregation that it achieved can be seen as a significant precursor to the movements of social and political emancipation that shook the United States over the following decades.

Three major developments in the American jazz scene had almost immediate impact in post-1960 France. The first two—namely the increased emphasis on the musician as an individual creator (with the associated emergence of extended solo playing), and the 'free jazz' movement—can be seen as growing out of be-bop. The third came from the encounter of jazz with new forms of popular music and became known as 'fusion'.

The greater prominence, in the wake of Charlie Parker, of the soloist–creator was illustrated by a whole range of towering figures, such as John Coltrane, Charles Mingus and Bill Evans. These were not only musicians who produced personal 'sounds' that imposed themselves as instantly identifiable and compelling: they were creators of musical universes of such complexity and beauty that they command the utmost respect and attention. There is no more convincing example of the wealth of available musicianship in 1960s America than the Miles Davis quintet, which, with Herbie Hancock, Ron Carter, Wayne Shorter and the teenage Tony Williams, was both an outstanding band and the seeding ground for another generation of masters.

So-called 'free' jazz was launched by the saxophonist Ornette Coleman through an eponymous 1960 recording. It sought to remove as many constraints as possible from the process of spontaneous expression—those associated with the instrument itself as well as more formal questions of rhythm, harmonic structure and melody. Although its actual practitioners—particularly Coleman and the other best-known free jazz player, the pianist Cecil Taylor—were uncompromisingly extremist, and had difficulty attracting large audiences, free jazz principles were integrated into more mainstream styles by other musicians such as Coltrane or Eric Dolphy (who had performed with Ornette Coleman on the original record). Furthermore, jazz, along with almost everything else, was swept up in the waves of politicisation that unsettled all aspects of American life in those years. Free jazz cut across music and ideology, melding with the angry struggle against white supremacy and neo-colonialist capitalism, embodied, for instance, in work such as Mingus's 'Fables of Faubus'.[4] It intermeshed with the sexual revolution, echoing the increasingly aggressive demands for respect and power, and for freedom from the tyrannies of the established order. As the nation became more deeply embroiled in the impossibilities of the Vietnam War, it was part of the polarisation and protest.

As for 'fusion', it too had extramusical motivations. In attempting to come to terms with the developments of rock and electronic music, it was seen as a means by which jazz could re-establish its audience. Fusion sought to cater to the tastes of the public at large, and particularly those of the young, for whom music was absolutely central to their quest for alternative ways of life. In many respects, there was nothing fundamentally new in this move. From its very gestation, jazz had taken in a wide range of influences, and except among a few dogmatic purists, it had continued to do so. It had embraced the popular music of Tin Pan Alley and Broadway, and it had engaged with European and Latin American traditions. So when Miles

Davis once again—starting with his 1969 album, *Bitches Brew*—took up the pioneering role he had played in the 'birth of the cool' and began to make a form of jazz that used electric guitars and synthesisers and electronic distortion techniques, there was no reason to treat it as anything other than a new step in the evolution of jazz. It was an important one, because it pointed the way to new possibilities of musical hybridity that would eventually lead to the polymorphism that jazz has assumed today.

By 1960, visits of leading American jazz musicians to France were more numerous and more routinely part of the annual cultural calendar. Paris concerts and provincial tours by the bands of Norman Granz's Jazz at the Philharmonic, Armstrong, Ellington, Count Basie, and the Jazz Messengers were regular events. In any given year, there were multiple opportunities to hear live performances by the best artists: Gerry Mulligan, Oscar Peterson, Mahalia Jackson, Thelonious Monk, John Coltrane, Cannonball Adderley, Sonny Rollins, Charles Mingus, Don Cherry, Ornette Coleman, and so on.

During this period, the French continued to be very active in the development of the culture of jazz festivals. Following Panassié's initiative in Nice and Delaunay's in Paris in the late 1940s, a number of towns began to organise festivals on a more or less regular basis: Antibes, Rouen, Caen, Dijon, Avignon. By the end of the century, Marciac, a small village in France's deep south-west, had established itself as a major summer drawcard for jazz musicians and fans: begun with a modest budget in August 1977, the 'Jazz in Marciac' festival expanded its audience in ten years to over 20 000, and to more than 50 000 in twenty. Over the same period, the length of the festival was extended from three days to ten. It gradually attracted enough sponsorship from big business to be able to bring in the big stars of jazz: Branford Marsalis, Liz McComb, Shirley Horn, Herbie Hancock, Wayne Shorter.[5]

Even grander festivals are held in Vienne, where the restored Roman amphitheatre can hold up to 9000 spectators for a single concert, and where total numbers reached 85 000 in 1998,[6] and Nice, where numbers can be as high as 130 000. All in all, more than 200 jazz festivals are held each year in France.[7] Although many of them are mainly of local interest, and many more combine jazz with other contemporary musical styles, the overall pattern in France is that contact with the music, and in particular with touring

American musicians, is now taken for granted as an established part of ongoing cultural life.

A handful of world-class musicians ensured the transition of French jazz from a position of dependency and imitation to one of relative autonomy vis-à-vis the indisputable American dominance of the music. The bass player Pierre Michelot (born in 1928) began his career at the age of twenty in the Jazz Parade concerts organised by Charles Delaunay, and quickly established himself as a sought-after band member. Not only was his rhythmic sense utterly reliable, but his melodic lines were clear and quietly inventive—he won a *Jazz Hot* composition prize in the early 1950s. He was also musically adaptable, as much at ease playing with Django Reinhardt and Mezz Mezzrow as with Lester Young and Miles Davis. The high points of his work were in his years with the Bud Powell trio (1959–62, with Kenny Clarke), and in his contributions to the soundtracks of Louis Malle's *L'Ascenseur pour l'échafaud* (1957, with Miles Davis) and Bertrand Tavernier's *Round Midnight* (1986, with Dexter Gordon and Herbie Hancock), but he was valued over several decades by many of the stars. Don Byas ranked him with Oscar Pettiford as his favourite bass player, and both Dizzie Gillespie and Lena Horne offered him the chance to work with them in America.[8] In the 1990s he was playing with the American pianist Hank Jones, both in New York and in Paris.[9] Michelot set and maintained the standard of French bass playing, and opened the way for the following generation of players, among whom Henri Texier, Patrice Caratini and Didier Levallet have earned esteem. The last, although largely self-taught, went on to become the musical director of the National Jazz Orchestra.[10]

André Hodeir (born in 1921) began playing violin in the Ekyan band during the war while he was studying harmony, counterpoint and music history at the Paris Conservatorium, in all of which he won first prizes. He worked for a year with Messiaen, and was a fellow student of Pierre Boulez. With such a background, it is not surprising that when he joined the jazz world that revolved around Panassié, Delaunay and the Hot Club and became editor-in-chief of *Jazz Hot* (1947–51), Hodeir championed a form of jazz commentary based on serious musicological analysis. He did not pioneer this approach: from the time of Ansermet, many French music critics— Shaeffner, Coeuroy and Pesquinne, among others—had treated jazz as an object of conscientious musical attention. But Hodeir brought a new level of technical expertise to the process.[11] Although he continued playing in the early postwar years—notably with Kenny Clarke in an effort to master the advances of be-bop—his analytical bent soon led him in the direction of composition.

Hodeir's work provided important precedents for the ready crossovers that many of today's jazz musicians make between jazz and classical music, even though a lot of his own compositional experiments ultimately failed.[12] He was fundamentally motivated by the belief that the explorations of jazz and those of contemporary avant-garde music could be brought together. More particularly, he believed that jazz provided a sufficiently rich musical space to resolve some of the bigger compositional issues confronting music: atonalism, the application of serialist principles, and the detachment of musical material from the melodic and harmonic conventions of the past.

His credentials were impeccable. In jazz, he had extensive experience: as a player, as one who had reflected and written on the work of all the great American musicians, and as a teacher (he gave classes in harmony and orchestration through the Paris Hot Club). He had composed jazz pieces of his own, and had done orchestrations for Reinhardt and Grappelli. On the other hand, he was also a committed participant in the French contemporary music avant-garde. He was involved with Pierre Schaeffer's experiments in concrete music, and was part of the group working with Boulez in the founding era of the 'Domaine musical'. His search for a new musical synthesis was ambitious. He hoped to enrich jazz—which he saw as being emotionally strong in its swing and its blues roots, but formally impoverished—and at the same time to overcome what he saw as the austerity and hermeticism of the contemporary music field.

Hodeir was aware that his project was paradoxical, and indeed his first serious compositions (from 1954) bear the name *Paradoxe I* and *II*. But these, like much of his work, succeed neither as jazz nor as serious contemporary music. Although their reflective intellectualism commands respect, they lack the rigour of a Boulez, and they generate none of the excitement of the jazz masters in whom Hodeir sought his inspiration (especially Ellington and Monk). Hodeir's jazz is tuneful, but the excessively controlled and technical approach seems to block out excitement or passion. The quest for greater formal complexity is something he shared with any number of post-be-bop musicians, but in his case, it resulted in music that is entirely written—

in other words, in the sacrifice of real improvisation. What he called 'simulated' improvisation (written lines that give an impression of improvised creation) could never be a substitute for the freedom of expression that unites jazz players and their audiences. The ensemble that he constituted especially to perform his music—the Jazz Groupe de Paris—lasted from 1954 to 1960, but its existence was only ever fitful, and its members were obliged to get most of their work elsewhere.

Hodeir's opus is modest in volume and, in the long run, it has had little exposure. He did receive contracts for a large number of film scores, but performances of his work have generally been limited to a form of personal homage. At his best, Hodeir is a musician's musician, and it is a little sad that the activity in which he invested his highest ambition brought him the smallest degree of achievement. Although his compositions reflect some elaborate and advanced musical thinking, they do not communicate his indisputably real and great musical passion. Hodeir's work as an analyst and critic of jazz is an important contribution to the history of the music, but it is hard to see his own compositions as any more than an epiphenomenon.

Martial Solal, a few years younger than Hodeir, began as a relative outsider to the French mainland jazz scene. Born in Algeria in 1927, he discovered jazz as a teenager through listening to recordings of some of the giants of jazz piano: Fats Waller, Art Tatum and Teddy Wilson. With a reasonable amount of classical piano training, he turned professional at eighteen. After five years in Algiers, he decided to try his hand in Paris. Despite initial difficulties, his apprenticeship in the 'big league' proved to be relatively short. He worked briefly with Noël Chiboust and Aimé Barelli, and in 1953 joined Django Reinhardt and Pierre Michelot for what was to be the guitarist's last recording.

This was a symbolic event, since Solal is often seen as Reinhardt's immediate successor in the family of French jazz masters. It is certainly the case that by the following year, when Solal took up the post of resident pianist at the Club Saint-Germain, he had acquired—like Django before him—the special aura that seems to accompany virtuoso innovators. From his earliest recordings, Solal approached jazz as a forward-looking, evolutionary mode of expression. His treatment of the standards is only incidentally a link with tradition. Rather, the way in which he breaks up melodic lines and rhythms is a form of personal appropriation—sometimes playful, but always determined. He was soon a regular accompanist for visiting American stars—

Dizzy Gillespie, Stan Getz, Clifford Brown—but it was with his own groups that he demonstrated the greatest originality. He worked first with a quartet (1956–60) with Roger Guérin (trumpet), Paul Rovère (bass) and Daniel Humair (drums), and subsequently with a trio (1960–64) with Humair and Guy Pedersen (bass).

Solal's compositions are quirky, even eccentric, and his whimsy is reflected in the surrealist word-plays that he uses for his titles: 'Thème à tics', for instance, which carries both the idea of 'thematics' and that of a 'theme with tics'; or 'Volez, balles', which is both a homophonic rendition of 'volleyball' and a command for balls to take to the air. But his humour does not undercut the seriousness of his musical purpose, which involves elaborate and sophisticated exploration of and challenge to some of jazz's most familiar characteristics. Solal's work is marked by tempo variation, the rejection of the standard 32-bar structure, and the dissolving of the theme and variation development pattern into a kind of ongoing musical conversation between instrumentalists.

Had he chosen to do so, Solal could undoubtedly have made a successful career in the United States. After his appearance at the Newport Festival in 1963, which made his international reputation, there was no lack of offers. However, his decision to remain in France allowed him to extend his experimental work in a number of directions. He played in duos—for example, with Lee Konitz and with Stéphane Grappelli. He also worked with bigger bands, as he had already done in 1959—famously, for the scores of Jean-Pierre Melville's *Deux hommes dans Manhattan* and Jean-Luc Godard's *À bout de souffle*—and as he did again in the 1980s.

Later in life, Solal reflected on the difficulties of finding an educated audience for jazz:

> To be a jazz musician is madness when you think about how much deafness there is around, about the almost complete indifference of the mainstream media, and about how, just to exist, you have to play for ears that don't know the difference between a tin whistle and a grand piano.[13]

It was even harder if you were French:

> But worse than being a jazz musician is being a French jazz musician. Open most of the books which claim to be 'jazz history': you'll find that the few French (or Europeans) judged worthy of having their name printed in

these masterpieces are grouped under a special heading reserved for non-American musicians. In other words, they are not seen as part of the 'true history of jazz'.[14]

Although Solal's career was somewhat eclipsed by the radicalism of free jazz during the late 1960s and early 1970s, his marginalisation was short-lived. In 1998, *Jazz Magazine* collected comments on Solal from twenty-seven internationally prominent pianists—both jazz and classical—and the admiration was unanimous. Oscar Peterson praised his creativity and originality as significant for the history of jazz, a sentiment echoed by McCoy Tyner, while Joe Zawinul lauded Solal's honesty, finesse and sensibility as those of a great pianist. Jackie Terrasson, amazed by his technical mastery, also credited him with establishing the reputation of French jazz in America.[15]

Michel Portal (born in 1935) grew up near Bayonne, in the French Basque region. His family was musical enough to ensure that, early in life, he was given a clarinet, and it was through this instrument that he discovered jazz during his adolescence, listening to Jimmie Noon, Jimmy Giuffre, Barney Bigard. Sent to study at the Paris Conservatorium in the late 1950s, he emerged with the first prize for clarinet. At the same time, he was becoming familiar with some of the more advanced jazz styles, including that of Eric Dolphy. From then on, he developed his musical activity along three parallel tracks.

First, he forged a career as a classical concert musician. He earned respect as an important interpreter of such masters as Brahms and Schumann and won various international prizes as a clarinettist. His second strand was more experimental. He developed and pursued interests in contemporary dodecaphonic and serial music, with performances of Stockhausen, Berio and Boulez. Pressing the concept of musical freedom as a direct expression of emotion, and underlining, in this context, the centrality of collective improvisation, he co-founded in 1971 a group called New Phonic Art as a vehicle for his explorations. Jazz was the third major direction he followed, and given his background and musical orientations, he quite naturally concentrated on free jazz. He formed a different group—the Michel Portal Unit —for this purpose, but also played (mostly on saxophone) in small groups with all of France's leading experimental jazz musicians.

For Portal, the musician and the instrument have to perform as one, both of them subject to complete mastery so that there is no impediment to the immediate and accurate transmission of thought and emotion:

*James Reese Europe's Military Band at the Chambéry train station in February 1918, shortly after its successful concert in Nantes.*

*Poster advertising* La Revue Nègre *in Paris 1925 features the American star of the show, Josephine Baker.*

(Image Bibliothèque nationale de France, Paris)

*The leaders of the Quintet of the Hot Club of France, Django Reinhardt (right) and Stéphane Grappelli (left), perform together on 6 December 1935.*

*Whyte's Hopping Maniacs dance the 'Lindy Hop' at the 1937 New York Cotton Club review at the Moulin Rouge in Paris.*

*American performers delight French audiences with the Jungle dance at the Cotton Club review.*

*The Tramp Band in its jazzy performance at the Cotton Club review.*

*Charles Delaunay (right) presents Sidney Bechet (centre) with a gold disc celebrating the sale of his millionth record with Vogue at the concert held at the Olympia on 19 October 1955. Behind, banjo player Claude Philippe (left) and trombonist Benny Vasseur (right).*

*Count Basie (left) jokes with Hugues Panassié (right) at the Salle Pleyel in Paris in October 1963.*

*Young jazz-loving Parisians dance in the street outside the famous club, Caveau de la Huchette in Paris, 1957.*

When I improvise on a standard or on the blues, I have in me only the project of a certain harmonic development. I can get a lot of pleasure giving it expression, but I do not go beyond that, and in a sense I am a bit detached from the experience. When I play free jazz—and it is perhaps commonplace—I don't cheat, I am myself, I am at home. I conjure up a series of 'inner states', I undergo 'moods', a violence of unknown origins. That is why free jazz is a music 'of the essence' ... Free jazz is not a fashion, but a possibility. A possibility that allows certain musicians to dare. To dare something different. Free jazz is also a challenge, based on a will for permanent change ...[16]

This kind of jazz is conceptualised as being entirely without compositional features, as a completely open creative space with which the music is perfectly coextensive: there is no pre-existing harmonic, rhythmic or melodic framework. In the absence of external constraints, joint improvisation obviously requires exacting attentiveness from the individual musicians involved, for each one's expression is constantly in tension with the voices of all the other members of the group. But Portal's jazz is focused on the musicians' creative freedom, rather than on the audience or the music. This is what distinguishes it from both the mainstream jazz tradition and the experiments of a Boulez.

Being centred on the freedom of expression of the players, Portal's work shares with other forms of contemporary music the lack of concessions made to listeners' habits or expectations. Portal acknowledges this problem with bemused equanimity:

Often, in my music, when the concert ends without an event that clearly marks a finish, people feel very awkward. They exchange upset looks, caught in a straightjacket that makes them always want to have familiar guidelines for their listening.[17]

In America the emergence of free jazz coincided with the social and political radicalisation of the 1960s: the anti-war movement, campus activism, the quest for sexual freedom and alternative lifestyles, the use of psychedelic drugs, the affirmation of the right to power of black, Hispanic and Native Americans. What happened in France was both similar and different. The country had been profoundly divided at the beginning of the 1960s by the last phases of the Algerian war. This was, in every way, the most difficult of France's colonial withdrawals, because of Algeria's longstanding status as one of France's *départements*: a fully fledged part of the nation's political structure. The war itself was fought with unparalleled violence and cruelty that made long-term repercussions inevitable. The sense of betrayal and abandonment on the part of French settlers was pervasive, and the level of terrorist activity in mainland France verged on civil war. While the great majority of people within France approved de Gaulle's broad strategy for decolonisation, his authoritarian system of governance alienated many sectors of the population—the armed forces, the traditional political parties (who were bypassed in the decision-making of a president governing largely by decree), the trade unions, and the intelligentsia. Fractures developed within French society that were not mended by the end of the Algerian war or by de Gaulle's resignation in 1969.

The crisis culminated in the events of May 1968, when students and trade unions briefly joined in an explosive, if indecisive, confrontation with the political establishment. While falling well short of the revolutionary changes demanded by students nourished on Mao's 'Little Red Book' and the Chinese Cultural Revolution, the outcomes of May 1968 were significant enough for the date to become a landmark in French cultural history. Even if France's post-1968 social and political structures have evolved very differently from what the activists of that time sought, and much more slowly, the impact of May 1968 on the nation's intellectual and cultural climate must not be underestimated. It heralded a number of crucial transformations of consciousness and values: an explosion of awareness of the global nature of human existence, and in particular of the gross inequalities separating the developed and the developing world; a fundamental questioning not only of existing authorities but of the very principles of authority; and a rejection of the notions of hierarchy that validate the unequal treatment of particular groups or individuals.

The French free jazz movement was both a product of the turbulent debates that led up to May 1968 and a participant in them. Musically, the inspirational role of the American Don Cherry was widely recognised by French jazzmen. After the first formal presentation of free jazz (with Sonny Rollins) in Paris in 1963, Cherry played regularly in the French capital, working with many of the more experimentally inclined local musicians.

During this period, the visits of Cecil Taylor and Archie Shepp also helped to launch the French movement. But with one of the key tenets of this music being the subversion of all authority, it was inevitable that the French musicians sought to assert their independence vis-à-vis their American models, and to create their own versions of the new music.

In 1965, the pianist François Tusques formed a sextet that included Michel Portal, to produce France's first free jazz recording. Although the record title—*Free Jazz*—was a direct copy of Ornette Coleman's from five years before, the music itself sought its moorings in the colour and feeling of local experience. As Portal put it:

> We in Europe should not be repeating free jazz clichés, we should be inventing sounds and rhythms that will establish the reality of what some of us are reaching for.[18]

A number of these musicians—Portal, Tusques, the bassist Jean-François Jenny-Clark, and the drummer Jacques Thollot—played for political protest meetings. In the spirit of May 1968, a Committee of Musical Action was created, whose goals included undercutting the influence of the multinational record companies by gaining control of production and distribution channels for their music.[19]

Just as French free jazz followed the broad pattern of what was happening in America, but with its own particularities, so it was in the field that came to be known as 'fusion'. France's fusion pioneer was Barney Wilen (born in 1937). Wilen—whose father was American, but who was born in France and mostly raised there—had grown up musically as part of the bebop generation. He played with Miles Davis on the soundtrack of Malle's *Ascenseur pour l'échafaud* in 1957 and composed the music for Édouard Molinaro's *Un témoin dans la ville* in 1959, the year in which he also represented France at the Newport Festival. After dabbling in the free jazz movement, Wilen followed Miles Davis's lead in trying to create a fusion of jazz and rock, with his 'Free Rock Group' in 1967. Ultimately, however, while some forms of French fusion would continue in this direction (mixing jazz with rock or, later, with techno), most of it developed along more distinctively French paths.

One of these continued the musical style established by the 'chansonniers', Trenet and Hess, in the 1930s, combining the lively rhythms of jazz and swing with music and lyrics that remain deeply French. Of course, many French singers have performed jazz and swing in ways clearly influenced by their American counterparts: this is the case with some of the work of Yves Montand and Charles Aznavour, for example. But even in these cases, it could be argued that their extraordinary international success has depended on their French character as much as on their use of jazz. From the late 1960s, various artists have made more concerted attempts to integrate jazz and chanson by melding their personal poetic inspiration and the spontaneity of jazz. Two of the most popular and enduring are Claude Nougaro and Michel Jonasz: neither would be described as a jazz singer, but their music is completely steeped in the feeling of jazz.

A second typically French type of fusion has occurred through the interaction between jazz and another pre-jazz Gallic music tradition, that of the 'bal musette'—the small-scale popular dances that, to the music of an accordion band, provided entertainment in the neighbourhood café or square. There is obvious nostalgia involved in this particular mix, whose instrumental sounds and tempos evoke the past in rose-coloured romance and simplicity, but from the 1990s the music became extremely popular among all generations. Its chief exponent is the accordionist Richard Galliano (born in Nice in 1950). Galliano, whose father was a professional accordionist and teacher, trained as a classical musician at the Nice Conservatorium, but was drawn to jazz and dreamed of making the accordion a jazz instrument. After years of imitating American accordionists, he had a liberating apprenticeship with Claude Nougaro, and, in addition, he was given precious advice by the great Argentinian Astor Piazzolla, who taught him to connect his music with his French roots.[20]

The 'New Musette', as it has become known, uses waltzes as its principal material—some of them standards of the genre, some recently composed—but it subjects them to a treatment involving both swing and improvisation, giving them a contemporary rhythmic and melodic edge. The 'New Musette' is music to dance to. For contemporary audiences the fusion of jazz with the musette tradition carries with it the pleasure of tradition rediscovered and chosen rather than the tedium of tradition imposed or woodenly imitated. During the 1990s Galliano also achieved his goal of having the accordion accepted as a serious jazz instrument, through his recordings with Michel Portal and several others of the French free jazz school.

Another insight into the ways that French jazz responded to the multiple influences at work in popular music from the 1960s on is afforded by the case of Eddy Louiss. Louiss was born in 1942 in Paris, but his musician father was from Martinique and led bands specialising in Latin rhythms. After formal classical training, Louiss discovered jazz, and by the age of nineteen was working as a professional on a number of instruments. In the early 1960s he briefly became part of the singing group, the Double-Six, an ingenious combination led by the singer Mimi Perrin.[21] Having discovered the Hammond organ, he found a long-term position backing Claude Nougaro, while continuing to develop his jazz interests by playing with people such as the violinist Jean-Luc Ponty, Kenny Clarke, Jimmy Gourley and Stan Getz. Louiss also worked with piano, trumpet and electronic sounds, and in the late 1970s he began to explore more systematically the links between music and ethnicity, with trips to Africa and New Orleans, finding his way into his own style of musical hybridity with a band called Multicolor Feeling.

That Louiss has remained committed to jazz is no doubt because he belonged to a generation for whom jazz was still seen as an overarching language of popular music expression. Had he been born fifteen or twenty years later, his story may well have been a different one. Today, the most distinctive forms of fusion music emerging from France are those that draw on the musical traditions of former colonies in Africa, North Africa and the Caribbean. In this music, links with jazz—where they exist—are often tenuous, filtered through other influences such as rock and rap.

An eclecticism like that of Louiss characterises the music of the two violinists who grew up in the Grappelli lineage, Jean-Luc Ponty (born in 1942) and Didier Lockwood (born in 1956). Both were brilliant students, both abandoned promising classical careers to take up jazz, and both threw themselves into the maelstroms of jazz–rock fusion, electrifying their instruments and using dramatic distortion effects. Ponty has worked principally in the United States, playing with Frank Zappa, John McLaughlin and Chick Corea, and must be considered an expatriate. Lockwood, on the other hand, although he spent some time in New York in the mid 1980s, has remained in France, mixing his fusion activity with periods of acoustic playing.

Jazz was recognised as an important ingredient of the French music scene by the 1960s. Two decades later, it was given even greater official status by its inclusion in the offerings of the Paris Conservatorium, where classes begun in 1985 under Michel Portal attained full departmental strength by 1992. This initiative resulted from a broad government strategy for music education in France, which began in the mid 1970s but was given dramatic impetus with the 1981 appointment of Jack Lang as Minister for Culture under the Mitterrand presidency. Inspired by a belief in cultural pluralism, Lang greatly increased funding for popular culture generally, and for popular music in particular. In the space of ten years, the number of jazz classes available in national, regional and municipal music schools rose from a handful to several hundred.[22] Another product of this policy was the creation, in 1986, of a National Jazz Orchestra. Housed at the Cité de la Musique at La Villette and funded by a mix of state and private subsidies, as well as by the receipts of its busy concert season, the ONJ (Orchestre National de Jazz) seats a score of musicians. Over the fifteen years of its existence, it has provided its successive directors with a flexible and dynamic platform for big band experimental music.[23]

In the spring of 1986 the Bibliothèque nationale organised a week of jazz, with concerts, lectures and discussions, in honour of Charles Delaunay, who had recently turned seventy-five. Delaunay had decided to offer his massive collection of records, books, magazines, photographs and personal papers to the people of France. Although his own children would perhaps have preferred this collection to remain in the form of a private foundation,[24] the man who had devoted his life to promoting the performance and under-standing of jazz among his compatriots concluded that his final contribution should be a symbolic legacy to the nation. The Bibliothèque nationale was, perhaps a little pretentiously, described in 1954 by the great film-maker Alain Resnais as the world's memory ('toute la mémoire du monde'). It is without question a quasi-sacred site of *national* memory, and the inclusion of Delaunay's material in its official collections amounts to a historic recognition of jazz as an enduring phenomenon that had earned its right to a per-manent place among France's cultural treasures.

These signs of official, institutional integration of jazz are proof that the music that began its French adventure as an exotic imported subculture has now been thoroughly domesticated and absorbed into the cultural main-stream. It can be argued that the powerful centripetal nature of the French cultural process has assimilated jazz in ways that are analogous to those in which it assimilated the energies of German romanticism a century earlier. And, as with German romanticism, jazz has acted on the host culture as a major transformative force. It has enriched and reshaped the nation's musical landscape with new rhythms and with a spirit of openness deriving from its emphasis on improvisation, and it has helped to widen the accepted patterns of what constitutes 'good' music, and what kinds of music can be learned and taught in the nation's educational institutions. Furthermore, it has been a catalyst for change and creation in non-musical areas—in philosophy, writing and cinema, for instance—which are examined in the next section of this book, and which have contributed to the ways in which French culture has dramatically renewed itself and its interactions with the world at large over the past century.

France differs from other places in which jazz has made its home. France constitutes a cultural space of sufficient international standing to have made a substantial contribution to the legitimisation of jazz everywhere. Considerable numbers of African-American musicians have found their connections with France to be not only congenial in terms of the enthusiasm of the audiences, but also an important source of recognition of their music as an art form. The French cultural habits of categorising and historicising have also created a favourable climate for the different forms of the music as it evolved. It was France that produced the first jazz discographies, and the first specialist jazz reviews and histories. While these pioneering initiatives have since been overtaken, their foundational role cannot be neglected.

Few French jazz figures have captured the public imagination as much as Michel Petrucciani (1962–1999), who found in jazz the very kind of freedom that life seemed to have denied him. Born with a debilitating bone disease that prevented growth and made his bones extremely brittle, Petrucciani was a musical prodigy. His dwarfism was severe, but he had broad hands, and, encouraged by his family, he subjected himself obsessively to the practice regimen of eight or nine hours per day in classical piano technique that is required for virtuoso performance. His father and both his brothers were jazz musicians, and after his inspirational discovery of Errol Garner, he chose to make his career in jazz as well. By his early teens he was already playing professionally.

His handicap initially made public appearances complicated and difficult. His mobility was limited and he had an alarming tendency to break fingers, therefore, few concert managers were willing to take him on. The sheer quality of his work soon changed that. This tiny man, who had to be carried onto the stage, quickly came to be seen as a living and charismatic personification of one of jazz's most persistent images: transcendence over pain and life's bad deals. At twenty, he moved to the United States where he remained for ten years. He played more than a hundred concerts a year, sometimes in solo performances and often with some of America's top jazzmen, including Jim Hall, Charlie Haden, Wayne Shorter and Dave Holland. During this time, he issued seven records with Blue Note, comprising renditions of standards and a large number of his own compositions. His success continued after his return to France in 1993. He recorded albums with Eddy Louiss and with Stéphane Grappelli, and toured widely in France and Europe. His complete technical mastery made him a pianist of great flexibility, whose style—influenced variously by Art Tatum, Bud Powell, Oscar Peterson and Bill Evans—is markedly percussive while allowing at the same time the development of strong lyrical and melodic lines.

Petrucciani's sudden death in New York in 1999 from galloping pneumonia was greeted in France as a national tragedy. The Minister of Culture lamented the loss of a 'national genius' and President Jacques Chirac, not previously known as a jazz fan or specialist, praised the pianist's renewal of the language of jazz.[25] Never slow to see symbolic dimensions in such occasions, the French press pointed out not only that the diminutive pianist had proven the strength of French jazz by his brilliant conquest of America, but that his last public concert took place in the presence of Pope John Paul II, at the Vatican. Petrucciani, in these panegyrics, momentarily became both hero and saint—something of a cross between Astérix the Gaulle and Joan of Arc. Such exaggerated glorification aside, Michel Petrucciani touched the hearts of his compatriots in a way that few other jazz musicians had done before him, though he perhaps never quite reached the stardom enjoyed by Django Reinhardt or Sidney Bechet, nor the revered status of Stéphane Grappelli. What Petrucciani gave to the image of jazz in France was something akin to what Edith Piaf gave to song: a moving expression of frailty and pain overcome. It is surely no accident that in that great memorial catalogue of French culture, the Père Lachaise Cemetery in Paris, the jazz pianist Petrucciani should lie not far from Piaf, and only a few metres from Chopin.

**PART 2** | **JAZZ IN FRENCH ART AND THOUGHT**

# CHAPTER 5

# FOLK HOT OR MODERN COOL?
## Jazz and Modernism

America had unthroned forever the old European dances which,
by turning in endless circles, had ground to a standstill.
Adventure and space were reclaiming their rights.
Robert Goffin, *Aux frontières du jazz*[1]

The interaction of jazz with French culture in the modern period is a complicated story. It changes over time, with significantly different elements before and after World War I, and changes again after World War II, when the jazz form was itself radically modernised. It is a story that intersects with some of the great and fertile confusions of French thought and art—such as primitivism, surrealism and the birth of ethnography—and it threads its way through the social and political tensions of a rapidly mutating culture in which longstanding values and traditions were subject to fierce and even violent debate.

 Change is perhaps the dominant element in French modernism. The theoretical discussions that have sought to clarify modernism as a historical phenomenon have had varying degrees of success, and an examination of the reception of jazz in France does little to resolve the issues of the debate. If anything, our focus on jazz serves rather to emphasise the turbulence and contradictory forces at work during this period.

Jazz was a relative latecomer to the French modernist experience. From the poetic intuitions of Baudelaire in the late 1850s, musicians, writers, sculptors, engineers, architects, mathematicians, scientists and philosophers were all reshaping their fields with extraordinary intensity and brilliance. Invention was apparent in every sphere of life, medical and industrial as much as intellectual and artistic.[2] With the turn of the century, the nation entered what was to be baptised as 'La Belle Époque'.[3]

The word *modernisme* has always had as its dominant meaning a propensity to appreciate or to seek out the new, rather than to accept the continuities of tradition. The scholars and historians who have focused on the movements and productions of French culture in the late nineteenth and early twentieth centuries have often overlooked this broad semantic context.[4] Most of these writers also tend to forget that the first ideologically charged use of 'modernisme' occurred in the schismatic polemic of l'abbé Alfred Loisy (1857–1940) opposing the newly declared papal infallibility.[5] Loisy's *L'Évangile et l'Église* (1902) argued that new discoveries could be incorporated into religion without conflicting with church doctrine, allowing the church to move with the times. It was probably Pope Pius X who provided the first definition of modernism as a doctrine (and denounced it) in his 1907 decree *Lamentabili* and in the subsequent encyclical *Pascendi Dominici Gregis*. To ignore this dimension in a culture whose Catholic identity was still essential is to risk misunderstanding the nature of the changes that were taking place.

For French culture as a whole, then, modernism was not a movement, and certainly not a single or coherent philosophy: it was more a spirit or force, not to be contained within the existing parameters. It was an impulsion to create ways of seeing and being that were free of tradition, where the future could be fashioned without reference to the patterns of the past or to geographical frontiers. In art, the flourishing of impressionism and orientalism exemplifies this blurring of perspective and of cultural borders. It is no accident that many of the revolutionary artists of the first two decades of twentieth-century France were foreign-born or of foreign extraction: Picasso, Miró, Kandinsky, Stravinsky, Apollinaire, Diaghilev, Tzara, Arp. Not only was the cultural effervescence of the nation, and of Paris in particular, a powerful attractor for artists from everywhere, but an integral characteristic of French cultural modernism was its voracious curiosity: its self-assured openness to engagement with alien ideas and influences.

What France did not invent, it borrowed, adapted, or appropriated, driven by a powerful collective faith in its own identity and the inherent value of progress, including the technological advances that revolutionised the concepts of time and space.[6] Many products of these beliefs were of great practical value—such as the discoveries of Pasteur, the cinematographic inventions of the Lumière brothers, and the engineering feats of de Lesseps —but the underlying dynamic of the time was directed as much to the *processes* of experimentation and creation as to any material outcomes. The Eiffel Tower still stands as a quirky, identity-defining emblem of a mentality that, in its airy, open-lattice wrought-iron structure, valued the dream as strongly as the laws of physical stress.

It was an age of upheaval and instability, generally optimistic before the outbreak of World War I and increasingly gloomy thereafter. The modernisation of France's culture did not occur smoothly, quickly or uninterruptedly. Against the forces of change—represented in science by the likes of Louis Pasteur (1822–1895) and Étienne Jules Marey (1853–1904), or in philosophy and linguistics by Henri Bergson (1859–1941) and Ferdinand de Saussure (1857–1913)—stood a formidable array of forces of conservatism and reaction. These were both secular and religious, and they militated variously in the name of social order, morality, patriotic sentiment, religious authority and even God. The descendants of those who, under the Second Empire, had already brought literary geniuses Baudelaire and Flaubert to trial for the transgressive 'obscenities' of *Les fleurs du mal* and *Madame Bovary*, were at the end of the century railing against Rodin or Debussy, or calling for the blood of Captain Dreyfus, or demanding a return of the monarchy.[7]

In addition to the closely fought debates between the supporters of change and its opponents, there were also contradictions within modernism itself. In the rapid urbanisation of Paris and other major cities, for example, the ferment of wealth and optimism had its corresponding shadows: rural villages drained of their life by the rush of young men and women to the cities, overcrowded suburbs where the new working class was proliferating, frequently inhuman conditions of poverty and exploitation of those whose toil kept the mines and factories going. Such dark areas were not used as mere elements of contrast that put material progress into relief: they were integral to the experience of modernism. The paradoxes of the age are evident in the lives and work of many key modernist figures. Rimbaud, the most iconoclastic poet of his age, ended his life as a cynical gun-running colonialist; Monet applied his innovative techniques to objects such as cathedrals and haystacks as readily as to the bridges of industrialised London; Gide, whose revolutionary 1902 novel *L'Immoraliste* was the archetypal user's manual for modernists, became for some years a supporter of the reactionary and racist Action française.

One of the constants of French artistic modernism was its resistance to any notion of progress articulated in purely materialist terms, or, as in popular interpretations of Darwinism, as something predestined and inevitable. For its artists, modernism was about individual choice, personal responsibility, and freedom of expression. Baudelaire, once again, was an important precursor. In his comments on the 1855 'Exposition universelle',[8] he attacked the notion of material progress, and even included an early intimation of what would become a permanent French suspicion about the role of America in the promotion of this 'perfidious beacon':

> Ask any good Frenchman who reads *his* newspaper in his local bar what he understands by progress. He will reply that it is steam, electricity, and gas lighting—miracles unknown to the Romans—and that these discoveries are ample testimony of our superiority over the ancients . . . The poor man is so Americanised by his zoocratic and industrial philosophers that he has lost sight of the differences which distinguish phenomena of the physical world from those of the moral world, and those of the natural from the supernatural.[9]

In a similar vein, Proust's monumental novel *À la recherche du temps perdu* (1913–27), universally recognised as one of the great expressions of literary modernism, is on one level a great circle of regret that the author traces around the society whose inevitable extinction he so painstakingly documents.

In the light of this contradictory climate, in which the open embrace of novelty was in uneasy ongoing tension with reticence and apprehension, it is hardly a surprise that jazz, when it arrived in France, provoked a wide range of reactions. We saw in the first part of this book that the antecedents of jazz—ragtime, and dances such as the cakewalk—made their appearance around the turn of the century, with jazz itself entering France with African-American troops during World War I and exerting greater influence in the 1920s and 1930s. These two phases offer different, complementary angles of approach to the relationship between jazz and French modernism.

In the pre-war period, two distinct strands of modernism converged to create a positive climate in France for the new American music and dance: the first was a fascination with what was called the 'primitive', the second a predilection for the expressions of popular culture found in the circus and music hall. Each of these was part of the modernists' outward-looking reaction against the centralised traditions of French civilisation, with its chauvinistic hierarchy of aesthetic values.

Primitivism was an attempt to break with tradition by reaching back to what some artists imagined as the origins of human creativity. This happened in two discrete ways, one focused on the life of the individual, the other on encounters with cultures from other parts of the world. The work of Henri (le Douanier) Rousseau and of Erik Satie provides good examples of the first aspect. Rousseau's paintings evoke an imaginary and personal world of ele-mental visions and emotions, the tracings of a psyche that discounts hun-dreds of years of art history and technique in favour of a new naiveté. This work is childlike in its immediacy of feeling, and in its dreamlike qualities. It is primitive in the sense that it reaches back to a form of perception predat-ing and abolishing the compositional sophistication accumulated over time and by tradition. Much of Satie's music is of a similar kind. Spare and simple melodies declare their resistance to the massive orchestrations of the Wag-nerian school, and the recourse to ancient modal harmonies points to a musical future quite different from the atonal explorations of Schoenberg. Rousseau and Satie were both embraced by the innovative artists of their day because their art, as well as being highly individual, was felt to be infused with the spirit of the times, which included strong nostalgia for childhood.

The second form of primitivism was in some ways a continuation of dis-coveries made during the voyages of exploration of preceding centuries, voyages which had generated richly illustrated accounts that nourished the growing curiosity of the French literate classes about distant lands and cus-toms. Artistically, this form of primitivism was also linked to the exoticism and the 'orientalist' tradition of the eighteenth century, which Delacroix had injected with new energy and direction through his North African paintings of the 1830s. During the Belle Époque, it was Gauguin who most clearly represented the aspirations of an art that sought its authenticity in human cultures untouched and unspoiled by Western civilisation. Gauguin spent time in both Martinique and Tahiti, experiences central to the imagery that he contributed to French art. He was not seeking any form of ethnographic representation, but rather the evocation of a *mood* that would express his dream of a new kind of relationship between humanity and nature. He had no qualms about drawing on other exotic art forms as varied as Egyptian, Aztec and Indian, and the eclecticism of his inspiration was an essential part of his legacy.

The painters of the next generation, such as Picasso and Matisse, brought to primitivism a specific interest in African art and cultural objects. From the late 1870s, one of the manifestations of French colonial pride had been the regular exhibition of groups of African people at the Jardin d'Acclimatation in Paris, as well as at the Expositions universelles. These exhibitions, which continued into the 1930s,[10] included reconstructions of African village life, complete with costumes, crafts, music and dance, and fetishistic rituals. They were hugely popular, stimulating interest in musicological circles and among painters and writers. The stylisation of African art objects and the tom-tom rhythms of African drums were attractive additions to the armoury that the modernist artists brought to bear in their attack on the rules and traditions of French society.[11]

France's colonial enterprise never escaped a tangle of embedded racial and cultural stereotypes that were, inevitably, a part of the background of the primitivist movement. One source of this was the concept of colonialism's 'civilising mission', which depended on largely unquestioned attitudes of the cultural superiority of Europe in general and of France in particular. Both the Comte de Gobineau's writings on the inequality of human races and Édouard Drumont's viciously anti-Semitic *La France juive*[12] had already sown the seeds of the ideological racism that would spring up more generally in the 1920s and 1930s. The stereotypes were pervasive and enduring, and were shared by those who were attracted to the cultures of the 'uncivilised' world as well as by the xenophobic conservatives.

These attitudes are depicted, with characteristic derision, in Céline's *Mort à crédit* (1936). The narrator, Ferdinand, is taken by his father to the 1900 Exposition universelle, to visit the 'natives':

We only saw one, behind a fence, he was boiling himself an egg. He wasn't looking at us, he had his back turned. It was quiet there, so my father started gabbing again with lots of animation, trying to enlighten us about the curious customs of tropical countries. He wasn't able to finish, the nigger was fed up, too. He spat in our direction and disappeared into his cabin.[13]

The colonialist myth of a 'civilising mission' is dealt a sardonic blow by Céline in this portrayal. It needs to be pointed out, however, that the translation of 'nègre' by 'nigger' carries a degree of vilification not present in the original. Indeed, the evolution of the acutely stereotypical word 'nègre' can be highlighted as an important indicator of the confused and changing attitudes across the period. While it was certainly used perjoratively by racists, it was also widely and neutrally accepted by blacks in France until the mid 1920s, and even when it began to fall from favour and to be replaced among colonial authorities and assimilationist blacks by terms such as 'noir' (black) or 'gens de couleur' (coloured people), it was still claimed as a positive term of self-definition by many of the more revolutionary African activist groups.[14]

There was never anything truly innocent about the ambient racial stereotypes of the turn of the century, but the benevolent paternalism of French colonial policy was such that non-European races could for many decades be perceived as curious, rather than menacing. Until World War I, there were very few people from the colonies in France itself. After the war a trickle of emigrants and a handful of students arrived, but the most common encounter of ordinary French people with blacks was through the regular parades of the 'tirailleurs sénégalais'. These were the regiments of African soldiers who had fought with great courage during the war—including in the emblematic Battle of the Marne—and of whom twenty to thirty thousand remained stationed in France. As well as being seen as the 'happy children' of the colonialist regime, Africans thus acquired the status of heroes, associated with the glories of French victory.[15] Racism was sternly forbidden by government policy, which declared the absolute right of 'people of colour to receive equal treatment to whites'. Prime Minister Poincaré famously affirmed this policy during the 'Tovalou incident' of 1923, when a native of Dahomey who had come to France before the war was violently ejected from a fashionable Montmartre bar by a group of white American tourists. The bar's licence was cancelled.[16]

A benevolent partiality for things 'nègre' became a real fashion, heightened in the years following the war. In the wealthy bourgeois society such as that portrayed in Aragon's *Aurélien*, a standard entry-hall fixture was a life-size, white-clad 'nègre', symbol of a completely tamed exoticism.[17] It was also chic for Parisian socialites to frequent any of the 'bals nègres' where they mingled and danced with blacks from Africa and the Caribbean.[18] The gallery owner, Paul Guillaume, who had been exhibiting African sculpture since 1919, believed that 'art nègre' was capable of regenerating Western art. As the art editor of *La Dépêche africaine*, he went so far as to claim that this art was 'the vivifying sperm of the West'![19]

Another aspect of modernism facilitating the implantation of jazz in France was the growth in popularity of the circus and the music hall. These mass entertainment forms were very public manifestations of the way in which the boundaries between high and popular culture began to disappear. The music hall had its origins in more intimate forms of café entertainment largely limited to song and instrumental performances. Through the 1870s and 1880s, however, café-concert artists progressively introduced into their repertoire a great variety of entertainment, including theatre, dance, acrobatics, animal acts and so on. Expanding audiences required expanded spaces, leading to the creation of the great music halls that would make Paris the nightlife capital of the Belle Époque world: the Folies-Bergères, the Casino de Paris, the Moulin Rouge.[20] These, together with the Lido, the Alhambra, the Olympia, the Théâtre des Champs-Élysées, Les Ambassadeurs and Bobino, would become internationally renowned as venues for the new entertainment forms, including cinema and the tango. They would also remain one of the principal homes of jazz, throughout its history in France. The music hall was not unique to France; London and New York were also rich in such entertainment places. But at the turn of the century, no show could qualify as 'international' if it did not pass through Paris.[21]

As popular entertainment forums, music halls allowed audiences to experience a vast range of repressed energies and taboos. In the shows, the public could, without losing its sense of security, witness freakishness and baseness as well as feats of daring that put lives at risk. It could ogle at nudity, chuckle at the sonorous exploits of a 'pétomane',[22] and experience a multitude of strong emotions—horror, fear, astonishment, delight, desire—all in the safety of a theatre seat.

Like the music halls, the circuses of Paris (the Cirque d'Hiver, the Nouveau Cirque, the Cirque Médrano and the Cirque Métropole) featured an open, eclectic approach to entertainment. It was at the Nouveau Cirque in the 1902–03 season that French audiences first saw the cakewalk, in a rag-time pantomime entitled *Les Joyeux Nègres*. The cakewalk became an instant fad taken up by the music halls and by the fashionable society set in their own salons. This dance, although it does so embryonically, shows how neatly jazz links in with the strands of modernism we have discussed. Along with the excitement of the new, the cakewalk embodied convention-defying movement, the mechanised modernism of America and the foot-driving rhythms of Africa, and allowed Parisian sophisticates to relive, at least momentarily, the unfettered exuberance of children at play.

The spontaneity experienced by music hall and circus audiences was to a certain extent illusory: the productions were highly organised and highly commercial operations.[23] Nonetheless, the *climate* of spontaneity was an important expression of the ethos of the time, and corresponded to indi-vidualistic experimentations in art, as well as to more reflective manifes-tations such as those found in Henri Bergson's *L'Évolution créatrice* (1907), with its praise of instinct and 'élan vital'. It was through their emphasis on novelty that the music halls and circuses became a natural and congenial welcoming place for jazz.

The artistic break with the past was accelerated and radicalised by World War I, whose impact reached into every corner of national life. In every field of expression, new creations broke the rules and conventions that had structured the previous order of things, dissolving established criteria of dis-crimination, challenging the most basic assumptions of perception and relationship. Despite the fears of cosmopolitan influence expressed in novels like those of Bourget and Barrès, despite the trumpeting nationalism that permeated the lead-up to the war, and its conduct, it was the willingness to change, and indeed the will to change, that dominated the cultural scene. Even conservatives such as the ultra-Catholic novelist Georges Bernanos understood that the language of the past had no purchase on present reality and that new means of expression had to be forged:

Whoever was holding a pen at that time found themselves obliged to reconquer their own language, to throw it back into the forge.[24]

Such new languages were everywhere, many of them originating before the war but gaining impetus and urgency in its wake. In painting, Picasso, Mirò, Kandinsky, Braque, Matisse and Delaunay continued the process of renewal begun earlier; in music, Maurice Ravel and the members of Les Six developed new musical paths in the terrain opened by Debussy, Stravinsky and Satie. It was Diaghilev's Ballets russes that had the greatest impact on the vocabulary of theatre, with their sheer physicality, their spectacular convergence of movement, colour and sound. In poetry, the 'new spirit' summoned by Apollinaire in his call to artistic revolution[25] was above all the determination to create a different imaginative reality, to reshape the minds of people in ways that would free them from the destructive logic of the past. This logic was most evident in the horrors of the war itself, which perpetuated age-old hatreds and the patterns of conflict that sustained them. A form of 'esprit nouveau' appeared in the dadaist revolt initiated by Tristan Tzara and Hans Arp in Zurich in 1916 and brought to Paris after the war as visual art, theatre and performance art. Apollinaire did not live to see this manifestation of the artistic avant-garde, nor the word he had coined, 'surrealism', turn into the movement organised by André Breton. But his own work had been prophetic, in its formal experimentation and, most potently, in its emphasis on the capacity of the human imagination and the spontaneous expression of emotion.

This was the climate in which the young Jean Cocteau (born 1889) grew up, and it is through Cocteau, more than any other single figure, that the intersection of jazz and other aspects of French modernism can best be articulated. Cocteau was one of the participants in the creation of the 1917 event *Parade*, with Satie, Picasso, Apollinaire, Diaghilev and Ansermet, and at the end of that year he was in the audience of the Casino de Paris show *Laissez-les tomber!*, starring the song and dance team Harry Pilcer and Gaby Deslys. This was a revelation for him:

The first time I heard a jazzband (it was behind the curtain at the Casino de Paris before the Gaby Deslys and Harry Pilcer dance) I pricked up my ears like a circus horse. I recognised the music I had been craving and waiting for. In the space of a second I realised that it would not be a passing fashion, but a form of orchestra that would last and evolve.

My certainty came from the fact that jazz was better than a rhythm, it was a pulsation. I was holding the pulse of the Muse. I could feel her red blood beating. It came from the heart. It was frightening. It was reassuring.[26]

Cocteau's claim to have sensed the lasting value of jazz on the basis of this initial experience was probably informed by hindsight, but he was to be a faithful supporter of jazz all his life, first as a pillar of Le Boeuf sur le Toit, and later, as the Honorary President of the Academy of Jazz (L'Académie du jazz) from its foundation in 1954 until his death in 1963. In *Le Coq et l'Arlequin*, first published in 1918, his excitement overflowed:

This is how the dance was. The American band was accompanying on banjos and big nickel pipes. To the right of the little group in dinner suits was a noise-making barman under a golden pergola laden with bells, rails, planks and motorcycle horns. He made cocktails out of them, sometimes adding a zest of cymbal, standing up, lolloping and grinning beatifically.

To this hurricane of rhythm, Mr Pilcer and Miss Deslys danced a kind of tamed catastrophe that left them totally intoxicated and myopic under a flood of six searchlight projectors.

The audience gave them a standing ovation, dragged from its lethargy by this extraordinary number which is, when compared to Offenbach's extravaganzas, what a tank is to an 1870 carriage.[27]

Cocteau's use of imagery here is significant. For the young poet, the jazz experience had several interlocking essential qualities. The first association was with America, a name already carrying connotations of the new. Then there is the representation of the drummer as a barman making cocktails. In  the early perceptions of jazz in France, the word 'jazz' first designated the drum kit, then by extension the band, and only later the music itself. Cocteau's focus on the new pulse was linked with the cocktail, itself a novel experience. However, the fashion of colourful mixed drinks imported from America was already taking on metaphorical dimensions, the blending of unexpected ingredients becoming a symbol of new ways of thought and creation and, indeed, of a whole new era. The term 'cocktail epoch' is ascribed by Sisley Huddleston to the painter Van Dongen,[28] but it was in the air. Cocteau's own layering and mixing of images mirrors the aesthetics of variegation and juxtaposition already being practised in Stravinsky's music, Diaghilev's dance theatre, Apollinaire's poems and the collages of the avant-garde painters. It is his own version of a cocktail. But, in acknowledging the obvious and specific impact of jazz on Cocteau's artistic thinking, we must not forget that jazz was feeding into an older aesthetic current, going back a half-century to Baudelaire's exploration, in *Les Fleurs du mal*, of synaesthesia —the hidden 'correspondences' between different orders of sensation and perception.

In his description of the Pilcer–Deslys performance, Cocteau also emphasises the elemental violence of the rhythm, and its ability to provoke a dance that actually overwhelms the dancers, leaving them in apparent disarray. This was a larger-than-life music, a power that buffeted the artists beyond their limits of control, and Cocteau's jubilation came from hearing something with a scope that offered a way of grasping the reality incarnated in the war. The comparison between the tank and the carriage is that of an immense contemporary mechanised force against a lost elegance. Artistically, what Cocteau was celebrating in jazz was its potential to inspire a new creativity, one equal to the needs of its time and able to replace the likes of the now obsolete Offenbach as an expression of popular sensibility.

He did not, however, see jazz as an answer in itself. Cocteau's view at the time, and in *Le Coq et l'Arlequin*, was that jazz was not art. Rather, through the strong emotions that it generated, it was the kind of stimulus that artists might find in the music hall or the circus:

> These spectacles are not art. They are sources of excitement, like machines, animals, landscapes, or danger.[29]

It is perhaps surprising to find such an apparently conservative position expressed by an artist whose work was part of the avant-garde that sought to challenge the canons of high culture and to embrace popular forms: the very title of *Parade* owes a great deal to the circus and the fairground. But contradictions of this kind were not rare in the modernist maelstrom.

Cocteau's view of jazz as one of a number of possible sources of inspiration rather than as an art form in its own right was largely shared by the French 'high culture' composers who took a serious interest in the new music. (And not all did, by any means. Roussel walked out of the concert organised by Jean Wiéner in 1921 when the Billy Arnold band played,[30] and Francis Poulenc never hid his distaste for jazz.)[31] We will remember that Erik Satie had used ragtime as an ingredient of his musical setting for *Parade* in 1917, and he returned to the jazz inspiration in 1924 in his background music for the surrealist film *Entr'acte*, used as an interlude in the Satie–Picabia ballet *Relâche*. But in both instances, jazz is little more than an echo in a musical conception that owes more to the relentless rhythms of the factory.

Darius Milhaud and Maurice Ravel, at least temporarily, were drawn to more penetrating exploration. Milhaud travelled to the United States in the early 1920s and sought out opportunities to listen to jazz in its home territory—Harlem. His reflections led to a much more sophisticated level of understanding than what one finds in Satie, not just of the external forms of jazz, but of its inner spirit as a music expressing ethnic and communal suffering and the quest for liberation. It was to this dimension of jazz that he turned in composing *La Création du monde* in 1923, and conjoined with strong elements of the Jewish musical tradition. This is music conceived for ballet rather than popular dance, but the exquisite modulations of the work constitute a homage to the emotional power that Milhaud, at that time, recognised in jazz.

It must be noted, however, that in 'Impressions of America', published on his return, the composer showed far more interest in the 'high' music tradition than in jazz. His article concentrates at length on the American public's openness to the work of Satie and Les Six, and on the lectures he gave to leading universities and cultural associations, comparing the young French and Viennese schools. His allusion to jazz is too specific for it to be considered an afterthought, but his sense of the music's future derives very much from a background in classical music history, informed by the idea that jazz must naturally progress from its folk origins to something more 'serious':

> I took advantage of my stay to work on negro folklore . . . The young American school understands the importance of jazz, its innovative rhythms and sounds, and I hope it will be an American composer, one of the very young ones, who will lift jazz out of the dance music category and put it into that of chamber music.[32]

Ravel, for his part, was almost fifty when he discovered jazz, and his recognition of the music's interest was tempered by the maturity of an experience well acquainted with exotic sounds. Attracted originally by the vitality of the Billy Arnold band, he studied jazz and the blues closely over a four-year period, from 1924 to 1928, including frequent detailed discussions with jazz trombonist Léo Vauchant, and began integrating elements into his own compositions. In *L'Enfant et les sortilèges* (1925), it is the childlike and exotic elements of jazz that Ravel uses to create a parodic foxtrot that accompanies the lament of a Chinese teacup and a Wedgwood teapot. In this work, Ravel exploits musical forms of many origins, and jazz is only one allusion among others. However, his Sonata for Violin and Piano (1927) and the two heavily syncopated, blues-influenced piano concertos (both completed in 1931), show clearly the serious attention that Ravel paid to jazz, as well as the ways in which he used the knowledge and techniques of contemporary composition to extend its limited possibilities. It is unsurprising that his music would become an important reference for the jazz musicians of the be-bop generation as they sought to break jazz free of the constraints it had developed. Questioned during a 1928 United States visit about his use of jazz and the blues, Ravel gave an answer similar to Cocteau's statement of a decade before:

> ... these popular forms are but the materials of construction, and the work of art appears only on mature conception where no detail has been left to chance ... despite the unique nationality of their initial material ... the individualit(y) of (the) composer (is) stronger than the materials appropriated.[33]

While some gifted composers in the classical tradition were able to take jazz in their stride without being swept away by it, they were not representative of the way in which jazz affected the wider community. The very word 'jazz' became a virtual synonym for everything that was contemporary  and modern. To a certain extent, this was a matter of sheer fashion, with 'jazz' acting as a metonymic buzz-word both for those who wanted to prove how up-to-date they were, and for those who strove to resist what they saw as a corruption of France's cultural values. Throughout the 1920s and 1930s, dozens of popular texts appeared which included the word 'jazz' in their titles, often evoking little more than a festive, bubbly spirit. But at the same time, the operative power of the word was widely recognised.

For instance, when Marcel Pagnol came to have his 1925 play *Phaéton* produced, the director Rodolphe Darzens overcame the author's hesitations and persuaded him that the title should be changed to *Jazz*. The recent success of the *Revue Nègre* was a factor in Darzens' reasoning, as was, more importantly, his belief that the title would appeal to the public imagination. Any links between jazz and the play's subject matter were, to say the least, oblique: it is the story of a university professor who spends his life reconstituting what turns out to be a fake manuscript of Plato; with the loss of his reputation and of his hopes of marriage, he falls into debauchery and commits suicide. The only mention of jazz in the play is in the last act, where the hero Blaise meets the ghost of his youth in a Montmartre nightclub, and this act was cut after the first few performances because the work was judged to be too long. One could postulate that the deep theme of the play is the loss or death of artistic tradition, and that the new title carried, for the audience, the connotations of the rupture that provokes the hero's death. What is more certain is that Darzens' calculation seems to have paid off. The play was a considerable success: it ran for over a hundred performances, stopping only because of a previous commitment by the lead actor, Harry Baur. But when it was put on again in 1929, with another actor and under the original title of *Phaéton*, it flopped. From then on, it was as *Jazz* that it entered the French theatrical repertoire.[34]

Another example of jazz serving as an umbrella modernist concept (with no necessary connection to music) can be seen in the monthly magazine launched in 1928 by Elisabeth Sauvy (better known under her pseudonym 'Titaÿna') in association with Carlo Rim: *Jazz: l'Actualité intellectuelle*. Although it only ran for fifteen issues, *Jazz* offered a broad-based, contemporary, hybrid approach to culture and, with its double title, reinforced an idea of jazz embracing everything that the intellectual avant-garde was about. It carried essays, poems and stories, as well as reviews of what was happening in the theatre, the cinema and the music hall, in painting and literature, and even in sport. It made no value-based distinction between high and popular culture. Amply illustrated with drawings and photographs, it included work by René Clair, Pierre MacOrlan, Jean Prévost, Pierre Bost, and of course Titaÿna herself, a fearless adventurer whose ideas of modernity resolutely embraced female emancipation. And that included emancipation of the body, with the last of the fifteen published numbers of *Jazz* being devoted to the practice and pleasures of nudism. *Jazz* did have a music section, with reviews by Louis Laloy of recently released recordings. And here again, the principle of openness is pushed to the limit, with sympathetic attention accorded in equal doses to such diverse work as the 'finely written' orchestrations of Paul Whiteman, the exoticism of Ted Lewis, and the mysteries of *Petrushka*.[35]

It was, without doubt, in surrealist circles that jazz was given the greatest degree of artistic credit. Several of the surrealists—Man Ray, Philippe Soupault, Francis Picabia, Tristan Tzara, Michel Leiris, Louis Aragon, Robert Desnos—were among the early French jazz fans who regularly haunted the Montmartre bars such as the Tempo Club, le Grand Duc and Bricktop's.[36] Desnos and Soupault were also patrons of Le Bal Nègre, where the music and dancing were a seductive part of the jazz era.[37] Whether the music was understood to be something autonomous or simply a source of inspiration, the surrealist aesthetic enterprise recognised and shared its transgressive spirit, its energy and spontaneity. Building on the rebellious mood that the dadaists had brought to Paris in 1919, the surrealist group sought the most radical possible breaks with the past in all expressions of art and thought. The notion of 'automatic writing' ('écriture automatique'), developed by Breton and Soupault in their 1920 text *Les champs magnétiques*, had clear affinities with jazz, since its principal quality was collective improvised composition that proceeded by spontaneous association of words and phrases.

Interestingly, the surrealists also associated jazz with the deliberately destructive side of their own enterprise, the most infamous example of which was Breton's description of the ideal surrealist act as that of a man walking into the street with a revolver and discharging it at random into the crowd. Soupault's 1927 novel, *Le nègre*, portrays jazz as the funeral music of a dying Europe:

> I am watching a death and it pleases me that it is surrounded by songs that are melancholy or too gay. The few notes rising from Welmon's [*sic*] piano were, for me, the beginning of a funeral march or of a murderous anthem.[38]

Soupault had discovered jazz as a young man at the Tempo Club in Montmartre, where W. H. Wellmon, who had brought the Southern

Syncopated Orchestra to Paris in 1921, played the piano. He uses this experience as the starting point for *Le nègre*, which narrates stories of the life of a black protagonist, Edgar Manning. Manning is presented variously, across a period of years, as a white slave trader, a gambler, a drug dealer and a murderer. This figure is, from one angle, an incarnation of surrealism's revolutionary ideals, and the narrator expresses admiration for Manning's unbreakable independence, as well as for his freedom from any sense of morality or rationality, and his willingness to bend rules to his own needs of the moment. The Manning figure obviously continues and renews the primitivist strain of modernism discussed above, and Soupault, for all the sympathy with which he presents the character, does not escape the stereotypes prevalent twenty years earlier.

Michel Leiris and André Schaeffner, who had both developed ethnographical interests, attempted to approach jazz more scientifically. They recognised its ethnically hybrid origins—indeed, Schaeffner invented the neologism 'afro-américain' to describe it[39]—and saw in its combination of primitive (African) and modern (American) elements an energy strong enough to challenge the rules and habits of the European high-art traditions. The ethnographic approach, in acknowledging the autonomous value of cultures other than European, opened the way to a more global notion of cultural pluralism. Even within France itself, traditional monolithic universalism was breaking down—despite the persistence in colonialist circles of the rhetoric of France's 'civilising mission'.

In April 1929 Leiris and Schaeffner, along with Georges Bataille, were involved with the launching of an ambitious illustrated ethnographic periodical, *Documents*, which sought to combine new methodological approaches to the cultures of the ancient world with commentaries on the most explorative of contemporary artists such as Picasso, Paul Klee and Stravinsky.[40] Later that year, *Documents* paid special attention to the second Paris visit of Lew Leslie's *Blackbirds* troupe.[41] Leiris, disillusioned with what he saw as the crusty and oppressive atrophy of European civilisation, praised the show for its defiance of the canons of taste, intelligence and morality.[42] He described its energies in terms of a pre-art natural creativity, a glimmer of frenzy that might draw the audience out of its bored self-sufficiency into rebellion.

Leiris's early thinking on the uniqueness of jazz and black American dance was governed by his belief that African-American art resulted from the encounter of two contradictory polarities. On the one hand, the African element was seen as exemplifying an atavistic and ancestral primitivism, which Leiris identified as fundamentally maternal. (This idea, articulated before Leiris ever went to Africa, relied on the common Eurocentric stereotypes.)[43] On the other hand, the American element presented a civilisation at the forefront of capitalist development. This combination of the primitive and the extremely modern gave birth to jazz, which Leiris describes as a 'hermaphroditic' art, dominated nonetheless by its maternal primitivism. Because of its inner conflicts, he predicted that African-American art would not be durable.[44]

Later, when he looked back on this period, Leiris saw jazz as a personal inspiration for his own interest in ethnography, but at the same time, as something belonging essentially to the past:

> In the period of rampant freedom that followed the conflict, jazz was a rallying sign, an orgiastic banner in the colours of the moment. It acted magically and its mode of influence can be compared to a state of possession . . . Caught up in the violent gusts of warm air from the tropics, there were in jazz enough echoes of dying civilisation, of humanity blindly submitting itself to machines, to express the full possibilities of the state of mind that at least some of us shared: the more or less conscious demoralisation born of the war . . . our self-abandonment to the animal joy of yielding to the influence of modern rhythm, our underlying aspiration for a new life, where greater space would be given to all kinds of untamed ingenuousness, for which we had a devouring—although as yet quite formless—desire. It was the first manifestation of the *nègres*, the myth of the coloured Edens which was to lead me as far as Africa, and, beyond Africa, to ethnography.[45]

Significantly, and quite explicitly, the older Leiris distanced himself from the process by which jazz had become a more modern music in the intervening years. While acknowledging that the jazz that had so stirred him up in his youth was technically mediocre and coarse, and that in its almost complete reliance on repetitive rhythm it was not especially inventive, he nevertheless preferred his memory of the earlier music to the reality of what he was currently hearing:

. . . at that time, jazz came across as a frenzy that we miss in most of what we hear today, which is so 'artistic' and so stilted, even though it has unquestionably become much more refined.[46]

The shift towards nostalgia is understandable: a lot had happened in the intervening years. The economic crisis that spread through France in the early 1930s had produced a sharp and inevitable upsurge of xenophobia, exacerbated by the rise of fascism in Italy and Germany and Hitler's seizure of power in 1933. Throughout the 1930s, French racism and black racism began to feed and infect one another with an increasing distrust, in which the utopian pluralisms imagined by the ethnographers had no place.

Leiris's fellow surrealist, Aragon—later turned communist—offers a similarly retrospective view of jazz in *Aurélien*, published at the end of World War II. The novel acknowledges the music as de rigueur in fashionable circles in the 1920s: the young poet figure who plays the piano in society salons is expected to respond equally enthusiastically to requests for Chopin and for jazz; and jazz, along with the tango, is the music of the expensive nightclubs frequented by the characters. But for the Aragon of the World War II communist resistance, looking back on the world of his youth, jazz is essentially the music of a society that was falling apart, a world of frivolous masked balls and the childish pranks of the dadaist–surrealist avant-garde.[47]

A different light was cast on the links between jazz and the modern by yet another surrealist, Georges Ribemont-Dessaignes, who took a particular interest in the mechanical reproduction of music through recording and the phonograph. In *Le Phare de Neuilly*, a short-lived but feisty review run by Lise Deharme (Breton's 'lady with the glove' from *Nadja*), Ribemont-Dessaignes pleaded for the phonograph not to be treated as a simple means of reproducing music, but as a 'magic box' capable of creating a common experience analogous to poetry. He considered that jazz records were especially valuable because of the collective activity underlying their creation. Recommending, among others, Fletcher Henderson, Duke Ellington and the Savannah Syncopators, Ribemont-Dessaignes extolled their emotive power:

In [this music], the feelings that we are most proud of, common feelings, or secret and exceptional ones, are turned over in the sun or in the shadows, with elephantine grace, with politeness or jovial indecency and a certain supernatural obscenity that compensates for the dull tranquility of our poetic expression.[48]

In another issue of the review, the vitality of jazz, both the white Chicago and black styles, is defended through the recordings of Eddie Condon, Don Redman, Earl Hines, Andy Kirk, the Boswell sisters and the Mills brothers. At the same time, Ribemont-Dessaignes defied the expected outrage of conventional musicians, and, in praising a Berlin Philharmonic recording of the No. 2 Brandenburg concerto, claimed a direct link between Bach and jazz:

> ... Bach's music is *hot Jazz* that has been written down once and for all. Bach's genius is such that this capturing of life through writing includes no germ of death. The freedom of the instruments, their expression, the intense vitality of the parts—a kind of magic dance around a central subject —have no equivalent in any music in history except in jazz.[49]

It is not surprising that Ribemont-Dessaignes should have discovered this kinship between jazz and Bach through the composition that gives such free rein to a dazzling solo trumpet. The common characteristics—freedom, the sense of immediacy, the pluralist principles underlying the polyphony, the rhythms that stimulate a desire to dance—are also those of surrealism. Jazz was being enlisted as an ally in the struggle against a civilisation whose creativity had been stifled by convention, whose sensibilities had been diluted by excessive sublimation, and whose power structures had kindled the murderous horror and destruction of total war. By putting jazz on the same level as Bach, Ribemont-Dessaignes was reaching, metaphorically, back to an important moment of Western culture, when tonal and formal patterns were set that would dominate for 200 years. By interpreting jazz as a similar moment in history, and as a similar renewal of language, he was expressing a faith in the human capacity to renew life by probing beyond what he caustically described as the 'corpses found in public ears'.[50]

For Ribemont-Dessaignes, jazz was American only accidentally: its essence and message are perceived as universal, a gift and an opportunity for all humanity. A similar position was adopted by Gaston Criel in the slim book, *Swing*, that he wrote during his deportation in World War II. Criel, a surrealist poet, was an early member of the Hot Club de France.

The artistic and emotional sincerity of his book was saluted by Sartre, Le Corbusier and Picabia, among others, and in the postface by Charles Delaunay:

> Gaston Criel wrote this hymn of Hope and Faith during his captivity, in the same conditions as the oppressed Blacks of the plantations of Louisiana, a slave of the Nazis as the Black is still the slave of the White American master.[51]

That no American jazz historian could accept such an analysis is evident: in its well-meaning universalist sympathy for victimhood, it obscures the specific characteristics of the African-American experience from which jazz emerged. Whatever conceptual *similarities* there may be between forced labour in Nazi Germany and racial oppression in the United States, to present them as being the *same* conditions is not only to blur their particular qualities, but to reject any detailed approach to them. But national specificity was one of the areas, precisely, that European modernism was most suspicious of, an attitude even more acutely present in the surrealist avant-garde, especially because of the blatant associations between nationalism and the recent war. For this reason, Criel espouses a pluralist account of the origins of jazz (not unlike the one expounded by Coeuroy):

> Our 'hot' is a world in a perpetual state of birth. It is a gravity, a gravitation fighting the virulence of the planet; it is a return to virginity by those who created it and who create it each day; the rediscovered purity of the four civilisations—native American, African, Latin (Franco-Spanish), and Anglo-Saxon—fused in America in the 'hot' she has bequeathed us.[52]

In this vision, the American origin of jazz is merely geographical, and its African origin only partial. And in any case, it is perceived as a heritage, a gift, gratuitous in its provenance and global in scope. The use of 'hot' as a noun is symptomatic of Criel's extension of the concept beyond the category of jazz to evoke the notion of passionate creative regeneration at the level not of France but of humanity. From today's perspective, Criel's faith in the power of jazz seems extraordinary, but it can be explained by the intensity of his postwar hopes for the future.

Implicit in Criel's writing was the sense that jazz was an evolving form. This contrasted with Leiris, for whom the musical excitement of jazz was limited to its earlier expressions—and the similar attitude of those jazz fans who, in accord with Hugues Panassié, defined the authenticity of jazz by its resemblance to the New Orleans style. Criel linked jazz to the broader, forward-looking thrust of modern art. While his work predates the arrival of be-bop, it makes room for it by conceptualising the music in terms of perpetual renewal and development.

Those most in favour of jazz during its first decade or so in France were also most in favour of modernist trends, and they tended to see jazz as a catalyst for needed change. During the interwar years, it did not matter much whether the music itself was 'modern' in the sense of seeking to expand, develop or enrich its own vocabulary and terms of reference. Just as the French modernist experience, in its pluralism, was far from coherent or consistent, so the reception of jazz as part of modernism depended on the attitudes and predispositions of the recipients. For many, it was little more than a flavour of the times, one sign among others of welcome novelty; for others, it heralded deeper transformations. Some, especially among the avant-garde, saw it as an instrument to be used in the revolutionising of Western civilisation.

With the arrival of be-bop, jazz music could stake its own claim as an avant-garde art. In doing so, it left behind many who had been its ardent supporters in the 1920s and 1930s. Some of the earlier generation, like Cocteau and Delaunay, had no difficulty with the radical break created by Gillespie and Parker, but the ethos of extreme dynamism embodied in the new jazz was too much for many earlier fans, who preferred forms of the music that (paradoxically) had now come to be called 'traditional'. Before World War II in France, jazz was the major music of a society whose artistic creation mapped a deep process of modernisation. After the war, by becoming so self-consciously experimental, it engaged the enthusiasm of a new, younger generation of artists, but lost its hold on the mainstream.

Not unexpectedly, during the jazz era the strongest opposition to jazz is found among cultural conservatives, in the same circles where one finds the greatest opposition to the changes brought about by modern life.[53] Cultural conservatism came in many guises and many degrees, and it was perfectly possible to be conservative in some areas of life while being dramatically innovative and even iconoclastic in others. Sisley Huddleston turns Camille Mauclair, the art critic of René Coty's *L'Ami du peuple*, into something of a stereotypical arch-conservative:

> As a patriotic Frenchman, he attributes the change to the influence of Germans, Russians, and Jews—particularly of Jews, whom he estimates at eighty percent of the Montparno population ... Every composer who obtains applause for his ear-piercing cacophonies, every writer who attracts attention by his incomprehensibility, every savant who insists on the libido, every painter whose ambition is to earn a livelihood by giving a section of the public the pictural [*sic*] follies it demands, is, like the vendor of cocaine, enrolled, consciously or unconsciously, in a Slavo-Teutonic army whose purpose is to destroy France! It is by art that the *élite*, who have hitherto upheld the banner of culture, can be made the allies of Semitism, German-ism, and Communism![54]

Allowing for the caricature, this is not a bad portrayal of the kind of paranoia to be found on the nationalist Right, where the likes of Mauclair, Lucien Rebatet, Léon Daudet and Charles Maurras indulged in all the scur-rilous slander that lax press laws permitted, disseminating their fears about French identity, and its dilution or destruction through external influence, as polemic. The Mauclair case exemplifies the contradiction and confusion that reigned throughout French modernism. As one of those innumerable *hommes de lettres* that late nineteenth-century France produced so prolifi-cally, the young Mauclair wrote symbolist poems and novels, and travel lit-erature imbued with the spirit of orientalism. He was also part of the circle of Mallarmé, the most innovative yet hermetic poet of his generation. Mauclair came to shun André Gide, who was part of the same group, when the latter wrote in favour of homosexuality and communism, but his nostal-gic attachment to Mallarmé was lifelong.[55]

Jazz was not the only foreign threat that such people feared, but it was a particularly good target because of its associations with America (whose role as villain in the international arena was subtantially embellished by the Versailles peace negotiations and their fate), as well as with the primitivist stereotypes of black Africa.[56] Coeuroy cites René Brancour, curator of the Paris Conservatorium museum: 'If Saint Vitus dance and the antics of chimpanzees are an aspect of the art of choreography, then the jazzband is an aspect of the art of music.'[57] Other critiques of jazz involved agricultural images (jazz as phylloxera threatening the French vine), or biological ones (jazz as an infectious germ).[58] There were also pseudo-anthropological attempts to show that French ancestors had jazz-like rhythms already. Some psychoanalytic explanations posited the jazz craze as a form of regression, and 'dance-o-mania' as a form of mass hysteria. Others, including Catholics, attacked jazz dancing as a kind of 'moral bolshevism' that was subverting French culture, and above all, destroying the decorum of young women. Some doctors believed that jazz caused constant sexual arousal, and claimed that it was provoking nervous disorders and insomnia in men, and lesbianism in women.[59]

Even among those who defended jazz, there were many who continued the racist stereotypes. There were bitter debates about whether jazz really had its origins in Africa, or whether it was a black American adaptation of European music. Equally, arguments flared over whether white musicians were capable of playing jazz. Significantly, these disputes were aired in serious mainstream music periodicals such as *La Revue musicale* and *Le Courrier musical*. In other words, they were carried on in the kind of forum in which the guardians of French cultural canonicity determined questions of exclusion or right of entry. The depth of racial prejudice present in these texts is staggering, the more so because its perpetrators were completely unaware of it. For example, the musicologist Arthur Hoérée, who believed that jazz was 'less an essentially black music than a black interpretation of an art of white European origin', was a master of stereotype, concluding a long article in the *Revue musicale* in the following way:

> America, a brand new chess-board where whites and blacks had to play out the game, was a fertile soil, the more so in that the conquering pioneers were of the Jewish race whose assimilative power we know. For Berlin is the son of a Russian rabbi and several names which come to mind recall their Jewish origin: Gus Kahn, Erdman, Snyder, Abel Baer, Youmans, Kern, Silver, Cohn. Finally, the two Frenchmen who have best absorbed the spirit of jazz are Darius Milhaud and Wiéner.[60]

Similarly, André Schaeffner, a prominent music critic and future head of ethnomusicology at the Musée de l'Homme, while holding that jazz was essentially black, was capable of the following statement:

If the black borrows, it's because laziness, perhaps native in him, finds a certain satisfaction in it. But it's above all because that gives him so much more to return: an instrument in a perpetual state of reception, his physical endurance as a dancer and instrumentalist is there to prove it. The extent of the saltatory and rhythmical gifts of the black (African or Afro-American, it doesn't matter) constitutes a fact that is primordial and probably without equivalent elsewhere.[61]

In summary, we can see that while the impact of jazz within the framework of the French modernist movement was considerable, it was also complex and uneven. As a social phenomenon, it was a reasonably reliable but far from infallible indicator of where people stood in relation to the sweeping changes that were occurring. Those who enthused about jazz were, generally speaking, the ones who welcomed trains, automobiles, short skirts and other signs of social progress. But it should be remembered that the coincident timing of the arrival of jazz and the end of World War I also gave jazz a special status as the music of the postwar euphoria—the release from four years of sacrifice, deprivation and massacre. Hoérée, in explaining how jazz owed its sudden expansion to the 1918 armistice, portrays this cultural explosion colourfully:

> For the time came, as after every war, when an irresistible desire arose to dance on the dead in order to forget their distress, to flaunt the mask of a joy that was at first artificial, and then real . . . Dance-halls sprang up from the earth, and private hops proliferated like so many hopes for liquidating the stock that four years of matrimonial suspension had accumulated.[62]

Associated in the first instance with the liberating role played by America, the music carried connotations of the energy of the New World, but there is little evidence that such connotations were anything but superficial. Much more than the music of the liberators, jazz was the music of liberation.

It is true that the impact of jazz was intense enough to entrench it as something stronger than a fad, but the element of fashion was nonetheless important. Among the conservatives, this elicited the hope that jazz would fade away, and indeed there were periodic pronouncements that this had already occurred—which led Ribemont-Dessaignes to retort that it was not jazz that was dead, but rather most listeners, with Viennese waltzes playing the role of maggots.[63] On the progressive side of the cultural divide, however, the innovative freshness of jazz, its qualities of spontaneity and emotivity, its physicality and freedom from scruple were readily linked to a desire for a new way of life.

Artistically, the early years of jazz in France fitted well with the general climate of experimentation that characterised modernism, but there were only a small number of French musicians who attempted to master the new forms and the new style of playing. Only a few composers of moment sought to integrate jazz effects into their work, especially into serious works. Milhaud and Ravel were exceptional in this respect, and although their jazz-related works are significant ones, jazz remained only one point of reference among others, and a minor one at that. Similarly, in most other art forms—poetry, painting, fiction, theatre—jazz was perceived, if at all, as a potentially beneficial catalyst, or a kind of sympathetic parallel, rather than as a source of transformative inspiration.

French modernism was most directly affected by jazz where avant-garde artists were trying to build bridges between 'high' cultural forms and the popular cultural forms of the circus, the cabaret and the music hall. This was the aspect of modernism that most effectively encouraged the presence and persistence of jazz, and it is through this pathway that jazz would ultimately be fed back into other forms of creation. Jazz would eventually become a robust force in the development of French modernism, and hence in the evolution of French culture. It is, however, fitting to close this introductory reflection on jazz and modernism with a brief analysis of Henri Matisse's *Jazz*, a significant work from the visual arts, which is perhaps the most widely recognised face of French modernism.

*Jazz* was composed by Matisse during World War II and first published in 1947. It is a series of brilliantly coloured collages, accompanied by a handwritten text on art and life. In the final text, Matisse describes his work thus:

> Jazz. These images, with their lively and violent tones, derive from crystallisations of memories of circuses, folktales, and voyages. I've written these pages to mollify the simultaneous effects of my chromatic and rhythmic improvisations; pages forming a kind of 'sonorous ground' that supports them, enfolds them, and protects them, in their particularities . . .[64]

It is not completely clear whether Matisse or his publisher, Tériade, chose the title *Jazz*. It is likely that it was the latter. Matisse completed the collages for *Jazz* in the first half of 1944 and at that stage the painter had still intended to use the title 'Cirque'. The written text of *Jazz* was added later as a kind of counterpoint that, rather than being an illustration or a support for the images, develops its own themes. The handwritten pages, black on white, have an obvious spontaneity, with their generous large curves, different sizes of lettering, and unplanned layout of the writing on the page.

This syncopated composition is clearly what Matisse felt was the visual counterpart of jazz music. After its publication, the artist was reported to have commented, '*Jazz* is rhythm and meaning' . . . Matisse has taught the eye to hear.[65]

Matisse's hesitancy about the title draws attention to the link, in the artist's mind, between jazz and the world of the circus—a relationship discussed earlier in this chapter. In *Jazz*, many of the twenty collages are explicit allusions to circus figures: the clown, the ringmaster, the woman on horseback, the knife-thrower, the sword-swallower, and so on. Like the circus, jazz had for Matisse the vitality of popular art and culture, something that would appeal directly to the emotions and that would have the honesty and innocence of childlike creativity.

As can be seen in a piece like *The Bouquet*,[66] Matisse's work, subordinating intellect to instinct, tradition to immediate personal inspiration, and conventional sensual categories to a more holistic synaesthesia, blurs accepted artistic order in the interest of creative freshness. It is a profoundly modernist gesture. In calling it *Jazz*, Matisse—like Pagnol before him who had used the same title for a work in a very different genre—was paying his respects to the most distinctive music of his age, and to the values that jazz music shared with the rest of the modernist enterprise. At the same time, he was also expressing those values by performing them, in the most natural and uncomplicated way, and in a medium of his own choice. That an artist of Matisse's stature should use 'jazz' as a synecdochic title is both a symbolic proof—if such proof were necessary—of the importance and legitimacy of jazz in the ethos of French modernism, and a reminder that jazz is as susceptible to artistic appropriation as any other cultural product. *Jazz* demonstrates no sense of debt, but rather the artist's understanding that freedom is by its nature transformative, and that, once received, it needs to be passed on.

# CHAPTER 6

# MAKING CROCODILES DAYDREAM
## Jazz and Literature

**All writing murmurs with an intense nostalgia for music . . .
writing is a desperate, pathetic attempt to decode the music
of the world.**
**Enzo Cormann**[1]

By 1930 the distinctive sounds and syncopated rhythms of jazz were fully
integrated into French cultural life. They were part of the background,
and were often in the foreground as well. Jazz was not only in the bars,
nightclubs and entertainment halls, but in people's homes too, through the
growing number of privately owned phonographs. Many of the young writers of the postwar generation turned to jazz, either simply as a new source of
excitement, or as an inspiration for new artistic codes.

To borrow a distinction from Yannick Séité,[2] the influence of jazz on
literature was in many cases no more than 'anecdotal' (texts using jazz as local
colour were abundant during the 1920s), but was often more 'fundamental'
—serving as inspiration for deeper reflection on the nature of the literary
act. Jazz was a cultural reality that poets, novelists and playwrights encountered in their attempts to invent their own imagined worlds. For the surrealists, as we saw, jazz was a music in the image of their rebellion, and a

similar attitude affected many other writers—even the young Pierre Drieu La Rochelle, who would later become a totalitarian collaborationist before his suicide at the end of World War II. In his 1920 poem 'Jazz', La Rochelle likens the music to the heartbeat of a world at war—'the greatest war in the world', in which the arrival of American troops coincides with the Russian revolution.[3] The linking of jazz to a moment of cataclysmic change is a poetic insight: it underscores the emotional impact of the music, and suggests a more general imperative for the creation of a new language capable of accounting for the extraordinary upheavals of the time.

There are many histories of the renewal that French literary language and form underwent in the course of the modernist period, but while they generally take into account the influence of nineteenth-century precursors of modernism such as Baudelaire, Rimbaud and Mallarmé, little attention has been paid to the impact of jazz. Yet widespread acknowledgment by major French writers of the significance of jazz to them suggests that it must be addressed. Because of the importance of the literary tradition in France and the continuing centrality of language in the nation's sense of its identity, an analysis of the interactions between jazz and French literary language can lead to a better understanding of how French cultural identity was regenerated and transformed in the twentieth century.

Writing to the American academic Milton Hindus from his Danish exile in 1947, Louis-Ferdinand Céline,[4] the author of the celebrated *Voyage au bout de la nuit* (*Journey to the End of Night*, 1932) and *Mort à crédit* (*Death on the Instalment Plan*, 1936), proclaimed Paul Morand (1888–1976) to be one of his masters, describing him as 'the first of our writers to have *jazzed* the French language'.[5] This was high praise indeed from the man who claimed, with considerable justification, to have revolutionised French literary language, and whose own debt to jazz was far from insignificant. Morand was just a few years older than Céline, but came from a privileged background. After World War I, he was part of the avant-garde that congregated around Proust, Cocteau and Milhaud, and was a frequenter of literary salons as well as jazz clubs. By the early 1920s, Morand had forged a reputation as a writer of real talent. Works such as *Ouvert la nuit* (1922) and *Fermé la nuit* (1923) combined a keen, almost journalistic observation of contemporary life with a rapid, jagged, broken-phrased discourse that imposed itself as new and confidently authoritative. For the likes of the young Céline, just back from the horrors of the war, Morand's stories mirrored the new society emerging in France, and were expressed in a language that rejected the cadences and syntax of high literary style, projecting a more individual and authentic voice.

Looking back at Morand from a contemporary perspective, much of the durable value of his work appears to be in his documentation of the interwar years. Although his literary career was eventually crowned by his election to the Académie Française—after a period of disgrace related to his ambassadorial service for the Vichy government during World War II—Morand has never obtained a place on the canonical list of France's significant twentieth-century writers. While not negligible, he is a minor figure, and his importance to Céline really only matters because of Céline's own status. Céline transformed the possibilities of French literary language through an iconoclastic, uncompromisingly radical recasting of the elements of his craft. It is Céline who must be credited with having 'jazzed' French literature, not Morand.

The one book of Morand's that does have an enlightening connection with the French jazz experience is *Magie noire* (1928), a curious collection of short stories devoted to the 'nègre' phenomenon, and spanning a geographical range including Haiti, the United States, Africa and France. His inspiration for these pieces came from his discovery of jazz in the postwar bars:

> Jazz has such sublime, such rending accents, that all of us understand that we need a new form to express our way of feeling. But what about the content? Sooner or later, I told myself, we shall have to answer this call from the darkness, and go and see what is behind this compelling melancholy that flows from the saxophones. How can we stay still while frozen time is melting in our hot hands?[6]

We can see that Morand's reaction to the powerful appeal of jazz was ambivalent. As with many of the young people of the postwar generation—there were similar responses from Leiris and the surrealists—jazz and all things 'nègre' represented for the European soul a reawakening of buried instinctual drives. It is these that Morand explores in the stories of *Magie noire*, with a mixture of fascination and the fear that the civilised humanity of Europe must inevitably give way to these forces of nature. In short, jazz was one facet of race, rather than an art form on which Morand might model his own writing. It affected his view of the world more than his expression of it.

In the prologue of *Guignol's band* (first published in 1944), Céline wrote that 'jazz has overthrown the waltz, Impressionism has killed *faux jour*,[7] you'll write 'telegraphic' or you won't write at all!'[8] By this time, he was already a major voice in the remarkable literary revolution that brought about the greatest transformation of French literary language since Rabelais. In his voluminous writings about his stylistic innovations, the dominant metaphor is that of music.[9] He often described himself as a failed musician, and returned constantly—even obsessively—to the image of his 'petite musique' as the secret of his literary magic.

Céline's musical interest in jazz was marginal. Indeed, over the course of his work he moved, in metaphorical descriptions of his craft, more towards classical music forms and towards a minimalist simplicity that was summed up in the image of the ancient southern French dance form, the rigadoon (*Rigodon* was the title of his last novel). His persistent metaphorical use of jazz to describe the stylistic and linguistic revolution in interwar French literature indicates, however, that Céline found in the ambient jazz culture of his formative years an important expression of the qualities he sought to impart to his writing. Jazz translated the vitality of popular culture unmediated by intellectual analysis, and was the vehicle for an energy that would allow Céline to override sacrosanct distinctions between literary language and popular speech, and to devise narrative strategies that would play directly on his readers' emotions. In Céline's work, an immense poetic achievement through which he 'musicalised'—or more accurately, 're-musicalised'—French literary language, jazz can be seen as a primary though increasingly indirect stimulus.

There is no evidence that Céline had much contact with instrumental jazz other than ragtime piano music. It was, rather, vocal music and, even more, dance that moved him. His novels are peopled with dancer figures, from the group of English girls at the Tarapout Club in *Voyage au bout de la nuit* to the Lili of his postwar work.[10] Lili is an incarnation of life and grace whose presence, in the apocalyptic chaos of Céline's last works, has almost redemptive force. Obsessed with a vision of humanity weighed down by the heaviness of individual egoism, social and political oppression, and barbaric international conflict, Céline saw in the controlled muscularity of dancers' bodies a miracle of lightness that he could admire unconditionally. It was this miracle that, as a writer, he tried to emulate.

The image of the dancer is not so much a reference to jazz *per se* as it is an expression of the common emotional and artistic ground that jazz and dance can share, through their directness and physicality. Just as dance can transform violence and crassness into transcendent, ethereal beauty, so in his use of language Céline seeks to subvert the ponderous fixity of the written word by infusing it with vibrancy and movement. Already in *Voyage*, but more systematically from *Mort à crédit*, he drew with increasing audacity upon a range of verbal registers that played havoc with the time-honoured traditions of novelistic prose. He used slang taken from many different sources—medicine, the army, crime. He invented new words by the dozen. Most pertinently, he delved into the structures and lexicon of popular speech: the emotion-driven, spontaneous communication of the common people. In so doing, he was attempting, quite deliberately, to renew the emotive power of the oral tradition that, in France, reached back to the time of the troubadours and beyond. Comparing himself variously to a bard or a minstrel, he linked the folk-song dimension of contemporary jazz culture to the pre-literary strata of the French narrative tradition, delivering to his readers, in a unique and always recognisable voice, stories, characters and settings that have the scope and charm of legends.

In *Guignol's band* there is an extraordinary passage in which a bomb-throwing, anarchist pianist, Borokrom, plays his instrument for the owner of a pawnshop. As a demonstration of Céline's linguistic virtuosity, this is an untranslatable *tour de force* of sound and rhythm, with images and snippets of phrases strung out along lines of Céline's signature three-dot ellipses.[11] But Borokrom's playing has a deeper analogical connection with the stylistic effects that Céline's writing seeks to achieve. The helter-skelter forward rush of the pianist's notes creates the movement of the prose, which, while made up of seemingly almost random fragments, has the coherence of a single voice—an amazingly athletic one—and the momentum of an unbroken flow of feeling. Significantly, the music that Borokrom performs is in waltz form —the traditional European form that the author in his prologue proclaimed to have been overthrown by jazz—but Borokrom's waltz (like Céline's prose) has all of the inventive capacities of jazz, and his playing, in its complete merging of musician with instrument, is unmistakably a jazz performance.

Unlike many writers before and after him, Céline was not in any way a jazz fan. With very few exceptions, he does not name pieces of jazz music or jazz musicians. He reveals no knowledge of jazz history. He was full of scorn for America, which he saw as a soulless, infantile society. And yet, even though his racism led him to belittle jazz sometimes as merely 'nègre', he found in it something truly novel. It was a 'new music',[12] a music for the very troubled times that he, as a writer, wished to confront. He seems to have understood the *spirit* of jazz, and to have found in its transformation of pain into art a deep commonality of purpose, and even technique, with his own creative impulsion. Without being directly influenced by jazz, he found in this music—the music of the time of his literary apprenticeship—a force that set dancers' legs in motion, and his own mind to dreaming. It is almost in jazz terms that he evokes the writer as a mediator of emotion:

> To render on the page the effect of spontaneous spoken life you have to twist language so that it is all rhythm, cadence, words, and it is a kind of poetry which produces the best spell—*the impression, the bewitchment, the dynamism*—you also have to choose your subject—Not everything can be transposed—You need 'live' subjects—hence the terrible risks—to read all the secrets.[13]

Céline's renewal of French literary language was pivotal, but he was not alone in his efforts. His own references to Morand are an indication that he saw himself as part of a wider movement, and any attempt at a comprehensive overview of France's twentieth-century literary revolution would necessarily take us back into the complex currents of modernism. Céline's dismemberment of classical French prose can be linked to similar preoccupations that we find in the work of the surrealists and Apollinaire, who were themselves the artistic inheritors of the experiments of cubism. In terms of the specific impact of jazz on his work, Céline was less explicit than many of the writers who preceded him, as well as less knowledgeable, and perhaps less conscious. There is no equivalent in Céline's writings to the effusions of a Cocteau, or a Morand; nothing that corresponds to the kind of enthusiasm for popular music that allowed the poet Robert Desnos to write jazz criticism for newspapers and the radio.[14]

Rather than being an opposing or contradictory writer of his time, Céline was one who managed to draw together, into the singularity of his own voice, a multitude of different energies. Thus, for instance, we can see a profound and significant structural convergence between Céline's project in *Voyage au bout de la nuit* and the key ethnographic journal that Michel Leiris was writing at the same time, *L'Afrique fantôme* (published in 1934). Much of James Clifford's description of this work could readily be applied to Céline:

> Its poetics is one of incompletion and process, with space for the extraneous. Interrupting the smooth ethnographic story of an access to Africa, it undermines the assumption that self and other can be gathered in a stable narrative coherence.[15]

Both Céline and Leiris chose modes of verbal expression that were more instinctive than intellectual. Leiris was more directly and more openly influenced by jazz than Céline, but it was Céline who, in the development of French literary narrative and style, became the principal channel through which the jazz influence passed to subsequent generations.

Céline's most significant literary disciple was Jean-Paul Sartre (1905–1980). The two writers did not get on: in his 'Portrait d'un anti-sémite' (1947), Sartre had insinuated that Céline had been a paid agent of the Nazis, a false accusation that threw the exiled Céline into a rage in which he described Sartre as a literary parasite, and more particularly as a 'tapeworm'. However, later in life, Sartre stated his belief that Céline was perhaps the only major writer of that generation.[16] It was not Céline who pointed Sartre towards the musical experience of jazz: he had had his own apprenticeship of it in his student days, and he maintained a level of familiarity with it that Céline never had. The importance of Céline was in the mediation between jazz and writing, in providing the formative model that allowed Sartre to transpose the liberating experience of jazz into literary expression and thought.

As a young man, Sartre became a gifted pianist and a charming singer, and he seems to have used these talents both for his own pleasure and as ploys of seduction: Simone de Beauvoir herself was much taken, on first meeting him, with his performances of such jazz standards as 'Old Man River'.[17] Jazz was to remain a significant point of reference for him throughout his whole career. In his early writings it already had some of the associations that it would retain: it was connected to sex and to the exotic; he felt it to be an expression of the mood of the times; and above all it was a form of release, of emotional freedom, and as such, was powerfully attractive:

> . . . [these tunes] capture our times, these strange jerky rhythms, these heavily voluptuous songs punctuated with squawking, with shrill cries, these phrases always in a minor key that seem to seek, vainly, to return to the major, display the ideal of our era: slim, supple, made-up women—their hair pulled back. Olive-skinned young men. Harsh lights. Sensual and complicated love affairs. Internationalism. Above all, I love that jazz instrument which imitates so well the human voice . . . One senses right away that one is in the presence of a machine, and I cannot tell you how strange one feels.[18]

For the young Sartre, jazz, like cinema, was part of a vicarious discovery of America, experienced through art with emotional directness, but linked to origins that were inevitably imaginary. After World War II, within the framework of a highly political Liberation in which he was part of an official French cultural mission, Sartre had his first real experience of the United States. It was confronting and exhilarating. In his celebrated piece 'Nick's Bar, New York City', jazz is described as the vehicle of American culture in all its immediacy and endless energy:

> Jazz music is like bananas, it has to be consumed on the spot. Heaven knows that in France there are recordings and also sad-sack imitators, but it's just a pretext to shed a few tears in good company. Certain countries have national forms of rejoicing, and others don't.
> . . . In France, the jazzmen are good-looking smooth-faced men with billowing shirts and scarfs. If you get bored listening, you can always look at them and take lessons in style.
> . . . Not the jazz at Nick's Bar. It is riveting, you can't think of anything else. Not the slightest consolation. If you come in as a cuckold, you leave as one, pitilessly.
> Jazz is the national entertainment of the United States.[19]

Towards the end of his life, Sartre showed that he had distilled his understanding of jazz into a small number of essential qualities: individualism, spontaneity, perpetual originality and self-renewal, and the capacity to unite musician, instrument and music in a single future-oriented act:

> . . . That's what makes real jazz! When Charlie Parker played, it wasn't somebody else, with a music that had already been played, already marked: no, it was Charlie Parker himself. You knew that he was an individual in that he was creating the piece he was playing, but even more, that the concert he was giving that day was individual in respect to other Charlie Parker concerts where the same piece figured . . .[20]

It is worth noting that in some of his later interviews Sartre acknowledged, with rare humility, a certain unwillingness to write about music in general. He ascribed this reticence to the fact that he did not feel able to talk about it with authority. An enthusiastic listener, curious about new developments and attentive to them, he was nonetheless constrained by what he felt to be his own inadequacies as a performer.[21]

In *La nausée* (*Nausea*, 1938) Sartre tried to come to terms with jazz as an active principle in his writing and thought. *La nausée* is presented as the journal of a historian, Antoine Roquentin, whose research in a provincial French city called Bouville (literally 'mud-town') leads him into an existential crisis, provoking him to question the meaning of his life and that of the society in which he lives. This crisis triggers the feeling of physical illness that gives the book its title. Roquentin's adventure is punctuated by a series of encounters with jazz. This narrative motif—based mainly, though not entirely,[22] on the Sophie Tucker song 'Some of these Days'—carries different layers of meaning for the protagonist.[23] By taking him outside the immediate time and place, the music serves as a momentary haven from his nausea. As an artistic form, it also helps him formulate his own ambitions as a writer. More particularly, as popular music, it provides a salutary repudiation of the stifling and rigid bourgeois world of Bouville.

The novel's account of 'Some of these Days' differs dramatically from historical reality. Roquentin imagines the singer as an African-American and the composer as a New York Jew, whereas in truth, Sophie Tucker was a blonde expatriate Russian, and the composer of the song, Shelton Brooks, was a black Canadian. It is possible that Sartre himself had this story wrong —it may have been an example of the writer's frequent mythologising of

America in the 1930s, or of his more general proclivity to cavalier treatment of facts in the interest of an argument.[24] However, Sophie Tucker's racial background had been so widely discussed in the press since the late 1920s that it is hard to believe that Sartre should have missed this detail.[25] Rather, we could consider the novel's presentation of 'Some of these Days' as an example of literary transposition. Sartre, in trying to give Roquentin an Everyman quality, instils in him the sort of commonly shared illusion signalled by the anonymous critic of *L'Édition musicale vivante* in 1928, in pointing out that Sophie Tucker was white:

> Record enthusiasts, who know foreign artists only by their voices, immediately compose in their imaginations more or less fanciful portraits. So it is that the warbling technique of negro singing has led many of our compatriots to commit unwittingly certain errors of appreciation concerning the stars from across the Atlantic ... [O]ne readily imagines that these melodies are escaping from the thick lips of coloured singers with crimped hair and white teeth, swaying before the microphone with all the stage charm of a Josephine Baker.[26]

In any case, within the context of the novel, the factual discrepancies do not affect the symbolic function of the music. On the contrary, Roquentin's imagined Negress and Jew form a powerful personification of the 'outsider' that helps the protagonist to make his life-affirming break from the whole stifling Bouville ethos.[27]

One detail in the presentation of 'Some of these Days' needs further attention. This is Roquentin's notation that he first heard the song whistled in 1917 by American soldiers in the streets of La Rochelle. What is different here, and new, is that the music, instead of being played by one of the various military bands credited with being the first real performers in France, is quite literally 'in the air'.[28] By foregrounding the music, Sartre pushes into the background the historical and political realities of the United States as a liberating military force. The American soldiers in *La nausée* are instruments of a more existential kind of freedom: the whistled tune is a metonymic figure for something ephemeral and aleatory; not so much a model to be followed, but rather a stimulus to the realisation that change and renewal are possible. Whether the young Sartre actually heard this particular melody in La Rochelle at the end of World War I ultimately matters less than the fact that as the author of *La nausée*, he chose to enshrine this fleeting memory as an expression of his idea of freedom. The tune floating on the air is clearly something foundational for Sartre's philosophy. It represents a privileged moment of insight, a 'prise de conscience' that allowed him to see the possibility and necessity of transcending the contingencies of time, place and tradition. It was an intimation of the chance to do something new.

Like Roquentin, Sartre chose as his mode of expression not music, but writing. There is an irony here because, in the cultural context of interwar France, the literary act was still very much a traditional one. To choose to write was, in one unavoidable sense, to situate oneself within that tradition. However, by setting himself under the flag of Céline, as he did with the epigraph of *La nausée*, Sartre was obviously trying to join the ranks of those who sought to subvert the notion of literature-as-tradition, and to generate forms of writing capable of transmitting the fullness of the freedom that he posited. On one level, he manifestly failed: Sartre had none of the stylistic or formal inventiveness of a Céline, and it is probable that when his literary contribution is judged by future generations, it will be found to be largely derivative and parodic. From another angle, however, his evolution as a writer moves very much towards his concept of the jazz musician, in whom the person, the instrument and the expression form a single entity, fully and freely engaged in all aspects of the present. There would seem to be a very close fit between Sartre's idea of the jazz musician and his idea of himself as a writer 'en situation', that is, working within a given set of historical circumstances. If his fiction fails to reach the kind of authority that Céline achieves, his written work as a whole offers unparalleled insight into the psychological, societal and political complexities of his era. In its optimistic belief that change was both necessary and achievable, this writing shares a great deal with the jazz musician launching into a solo whose outcome cannot be predicted but must be created.

In attempting to assess the relationship between jazz and the development of Sartre's philosophy, the notion of influence is perhaps less useful than the idea of appropriation. What goes in as jazz—that is, as a cultural 'Other' full of emotional connotations—is not just absorbed into an existing intellectual tradition, but *deliberately appropriated as an agent of transformation*, ultimately taking the form of writing that inflects and subverts ideologies. The legacy of Sartre's existentialism is, and will no doubt continue to be, the confidence in the human capacity to change direction and meaning. That legacy owes a considerable debt to jazz—not perhaps so much to the single tune that was snatched out of the air in 1917, but to what that tune symbolised: an affirmation of openness and spontaneity. It is these qualities of jazz that are so deeply interiorised in Sartre's thought and writings.

The success of Sartrean existentialist philosophy owed a great deal to the effervescence of youth culture immediately following the liberation of France in 1944–45. And one of the fundamental aspects of that culture as it developed in and around Saint-Germain-des-Prés was the unconditional adoption of jazz as its music. Sartre's writing and thought drew upon his own early discoveries of jazz and his admiration for Céline's 'jazzing' of literary language, and also depended to a considerable extent, for their diffusion, on the new wave of jazz enthusiasm that emerged after the war. One of the important manifestations of the new connection between jazz and French literature was the so-called 'Pataphysical movement, particularly in the work of Raymond Queneau (1903–1976) and Boris Vian (1920–1959).[29]

Queneau belonged to Sartre's generation and, like Sartre, was trained as a philosopher. He had been involved in the surrealist movement in the 1920s and, in his efforts to develop principles of linguistic renewal, had—once again like Sartre—been strongly influenced by Céline. Unlike his fellow surrealists and the other members of the 1920s avant-garde, Queneau seems to have missed the first wave of jazz. He was aware of its existence, but not of the extent to which it had already penetrated French culture. It was with the phenomenon of the 'zazous' during the Occupation that Queneau associated the fusion of jazz and a new form of youth culture that spilled into the Liberation period with such rebellious fervour. Although he did not have the whole picture, Queneau's insight into the magnetic power of jazz in the Paris of 1944–45 derived from his intuition of an important cultural shift. Literature and painting were the principal artistic vehicles for earlier generations of young people; this new generation was fascinated by cinema, theatre and jazz.[30]

Queneau's most obvious jazz-inspired work is his 1959 novel, *Zazie dans le métro*, but a number of his earlier writings reveal a similar engagement. This is true of the *Exercices de style* (1947), in which, along the lines developed by Céline, but with a quite different voice, he worked at infusing the literary language with the energies of popular speech. It is also true of his close involvement with the Collège de 'Pataphysique, founded in 1948 under the sign of Alfred Jarry (1873–1907). Jarry was a forefather of twentieth-century avant-garde theatre, and inventor of 'Pataphysics, that 'science of imaginary solutions' whose extreme playfulness does not exclude a highly serious defence of the human spirit. One of the offshoots of 'Pataphysics was the Ouvroir de Littérature Potentielle ('OuLiPo'), a loose-knit group of writers—still ongoing—who pit their inventiveness against a series of pre-established constraints.[31] All of these enterprises have evident analogies with jazz as a way of making music: they are based on the idea of testing imaginative creation against predetermined patterns—in much the same way that a jazz musician (at least in the mainstream tradition) will improvise on given melodies and harmonic structures. These similarities between writing and jazz helped to position Queneau as a kind of guru for the younger generation, a position that he shared with Sartre, though less publicly.

It is important to note once again that, in relation to literary/philosophical movements such as 'Pataphysics or the OuLiPo, jazz, while acting as a catalyst and even as a model, is only one of the factors involved. The modernist, avant-garde current that stretches back to Jarry embraces jazz and is enriched by it, but it also uses it for its own purposes. In Queneau's case, this is well illustrated in *Zazie dans le métro*. It is obvious that the name of the heroine—Zazie—is evocative both of the social rebelliousness of the zazous, and of jazz. It is possible to read this hilarious, energy-packed novel as the literary transposition of a kind of mad jazz solo, with Zazie in the role of the principal instrument, racing across the background portrayal of life in post-Liberation Paris. Zazie, in the novel, is identified as a representative of 'today's youth', and her adventurous causticity certainly typifies the postwar generation as Queneau saw it. But on another level Zazie embodies the spirit of Queneau's own linguistic performance, and the writer propels her into the story at high speed, sending her cutting through a storm of discontinuous events and colourful situations.

The novel ends in a destructive brawl of almost apocalyptic proportions. Yet the turmoil is less terrifying than the violence applied by the police who arrive to restore order. It would be easy to interpret this ending pessimistically: Zazie's Paris (read as the France faced by postwar youth) is torn between stimulation and confusion. American culture is omnipresent, and the city is overrun by English-speaking tourists. Even the native Parisians are quite uncertain of their identity, and are tossed about in a mess of their own incompetence and ignorance.

Zazie represents the force of poetic renewal that Queneau proposes as an antidote to the entropy of French society. In Zazie, stimulation and confusion are not in opposition; they are interdependent. Zazie herself is actually stimulated *by* confusion; she also creates it, disturbing the given order of things wherever her helter-skelter rush through Paris takes her. Constantly at the edge of peril, she escapes every time through sheer energy. Instead of being turned into a consumer of Americanism, for instance, she simply takes over the things she wants by inventing her own words for them, drinking 'cacocalo', and acquiring a pair of 'bloudjinnzes'. It is through her unquench-able emotional desire that Zazie becomes a believable incarnation of what Queneau seeks.

In the year that *Zazie* was published, Boris Vian, the 'prince of Saint-Germain-des-Prés', died at the age of thirty-nine. The coincidence is striking, because Vian himself had been the same kind of shooting star that Queneau creates in the figure of Zazie—a figure of perpetual, wilful youth, an exemplar of life lived in the here and now for all that it could offer. From an early age Vian had known that his heart weakness would probably prevent him living a long life. As a result, he threw himself into a frenzy of creativity that covered musical performance, the writing of songs, poems, novels, short stories and plays, translations both real and imagined, and a whole parallel career as a prolific journalistic and radio critic of jazz. To this day, Vian has remained a special cult figure for successive generations of French youth—his eccentricities and iconoclastic rebelliousness making him a kind of archetype of the individualism that is both the ideal of the young and an expression of their anxieties.

Vian came to jazz during his teens, joining the Hot Club of France in 1937. He acquired a reputation as a dynamic and inventive cornet player in bands led by Claude Abadie and Claude Luter. Although his heart condi-tion caused him to cease playing trumpet in the early 1950s, he continued to perform as a singer, and many of his own songs show strong jazz influence. From early 1946, Vian also became active as a jazz critic, both in specialist reviews such as *Jazz Hot* and *Jazz News*, and in more mainstream newspa-pers such as *Combat*.[32] In 1948 and 1949, as 'the famous French jazz expert', he even did weekly broadcasts, in very idiosyncratic English and with zany humour, for the New York public radio station WNEW.

It is therefore fair to say that, as a writer of fiction, Vian was more immersed in the world of jazz than any of his colleagues. At the same time, his literary career emerged from the same complex climate as the work of Sartre, de Beauvoir and Queneau, a climate in which existentialism and 'Pataphysics were important ingredients. He mixed with the *Temps modernes* milieu from early 1946—his first article for Sartre's review appeared in June that year—and his friendship with Queneau dated from the same period. When Vian joined the Collège de 'Pataphysique in 1952, he had already been a de facto practitioner for some time. Jazz, for Vian the writer, is *of* the essence, but it is one component among others.

Vian wrote under his own name six works that have been classified as novels,[33] of which one, *Trouble dans les Andains* (1966) was a posthumously published youthful 'exercice de style'. *Vercoquin et le plancton* (1946) contains a number of parodic allusions to jazz. Vian invents a series of bizarre English titles for jazz records: 'Until my green rabbit eats his soup like a gentleman', 'Toddlin' with some skeletons', 'Give me that bee in your trousers', 'Mush-rooms in my red nostrils', and so on. The text ends with an explosive zazou jitterbug party, where 'Les Bigoudis' ('Lady be good') de Guère Souigne (Gershwin) is played. The linguistic gymnastics displayed here anticipate the more systematic radical poetics of his subsequent novels. However, only *L'Écume des jours* (1947) has a sustained jazz theme. With its caricature of Sartre (restyled Jean-Sol Partre) and the existentialist movement, and its delirious manipulations of reality, it has echoes of both surrealism and the craziness of Jarry, and is an ideal case study for analysing more precisely the importance of jazz for Vian's creative processes.

*L'Écume des jours* is set in a Paris geographically transformed by the presence of jazz. There is a Louis Armstrong Avenue, a Sidney Bechet Street and a Gershwin House. Throughout the text, numerous jazz works are cited —'Black and Tan Fantasy', 'Loveless Love', 'The Mood to be Wooed'—and indeed the hero, a wealthy young engineer and dilettante named Colin, is completely obsessed with the music of Duke Ellington. His girlfriend and future wife, Chloé, not only bears the name of one of Ellington's most cel-ebrated arrangements, she only comes into existence, for Colin, because of Ellington. She is a projection, the incarnation of Colin's desire to be in love, a desire that melds the hormonal stirrings of adolescent sexuality with the intense aesthetic pleasure and sense of perfection that the young man derives from Ellington's music.

The love story, which constitutes the main thread of the novel, is condemned to inevitable failure. Immediately after her marriage to Colin, Chloé contracts a mysterious illness (she has a waterlily on the lung). Colin, in his vain efforts to save her, loses his fortune and his freedom and is forced into progressively more demeaning jobs. At the end of the novel, he is in a state of suicidal despair. In parallel to the Colin–Chloé story, the novel develops the sorry tale of Chick, Colin's best friend, who is an obsessive collector of works and memorabilia associated with Jean-Sol Partre. Chick neglects his girlfriend, Alise, and indeed everything else to feed his addiction. Alise, hoping to rescue Chick from his habit, murders Partre, tearing out his heart when he refuses to postpone publication of his next work. Chick, accused of tax evasion, is brutally shot by the police and his collection burnt.

There is undoubtedly something of the melancholy of Vian's own situation in the theme of decay around which *L'Écume des jours* is organised: the bitter understanding of a man whose genetic make-up contained the seeds of an inescapable early death. There is also, however, a more general message about freedom. Both Colin and Chick are guilty of allowing their freedom to become subjugated to external constraints, and the story can be interpreted as a moral fable about what happens when young people get caught up in stereotypes of romance or intellectual fashion.

What gives the novel its dreamlike charm is the playfulness of its composition—the spirit of improvisation that weaves through the text and keeps the reader constantly aware that the story is being performed, rather than simply written. It is on this level that the jazz influence is most evident. Vian plays with the fictional events and the words used to evoke them, and his text follows the results as far as his imagination will take him. One of his favourite devices is to take commonplace metaphors literally, and to follow the consequences through into the story-line. For example, on one occasion Colin is seeking to have a prescription filled—in French, to 'execute' a prescription. The pharmacist places the prescription in a guillotine, and we watch it die before our eyes.

In this activity of writing as a process of remodelling experience and language, imagination appears as a kind of weapon used by the author to defend himself and his reader against uncertainty and anguish. It is a way of altering the meaning of 'reality', and of bringing a kind of solution to what otherwise would be unresolvable. This is the 'Pataphysical goal of 'imaginary solutions', but it has much in common, too, with the jazz musician who plays in order to invent a world different from the one whose painfulness is too much to bear. Vian explodes commonplace expressions and clichés, precisely because they are part of the reality that he is seeking to transform. As with the jazz musician, the act of expression is identified with the act of imagining, and the act of imagining is a rebellion against the suffering and absurdity of human existence.

Boris Vian never set foot in America. Its realities were refracted through the prism of the jazz world. In addition to his fanatical attendance at jazz concerts by visiting American musicians and his encyclopedic collection of recorded American jazz, his jazz writings show him to have been an avid reader of *Downbeat*, *Melody Maker*, *Jazz Monthly*, and various other specialist publications. Jazz, as he lived it and used it, was a deeply American phenomenon and especially African-American. But in his system of values, it was jazz as a vehicle of freedom, rather than as an expression of America, that set the standard against which he evaluated most other things. (He once stated how much he would have liked the French president, Vincent Auriol, to welcome Charlie Parker at the Orly airport and to organise a ball at the Élysées Palace in honour of Art Tatum!)[34] In his literature, jazz sits easily with his commitment to 'Pataphysics and his sympathy for the liberating tenets of existentialism. It is part of the same conceptual framework and it has a similar role in his approach to the process of writing.

Vian's literature is the expression of a deeply personal world. It is less a depiction of a time and place than an evocation of a mood. That mood is darkened by the fatalistic intuition of a life doomed to frustration, but also by the gloom of an era whose sociopolitical realities seemed about to bring humanity itself to extinction. The sombre tone that one finds in Vian's songs —'Le Déserteur' (1954), 'La Java des bombes atomiques' (1955)—underpins his whole opus, which for all its wit and humour, is profoundly pessimistic. 'Le Déserteur', written as a protest against French involvement in the Algerian war—and banned by the government for that reason—ends on the expectation that the singer will be put to death for his beliefs. 'La Java des bombes atomiques' evokes universal destruction to the tune of a sweetly ironical hurdy-gurdy waltz. The exhilaration that Vian found in jazz came from the music's power: not to overcome the pain and tragedy of the real world, but to transpose that reality and to substitute its own qualities as an alternative. This was a form of escapism, but in Vian's vision of the world—

and it is a vision shared by many subsequent generations of young people—there was plenty to escape from.

Vian is often credited with contributing to the renewal of French fictional writing that, in the mid 1950s, led to the emergence of the so-called Nouveau Roman ('New Novel') school, whose leading writers were Alain Robbe-Grillet, Michel Butor, Nathalie Sarraute, Claude Simon, Claude Ollier and Marguerite Duras. The multiplicity of styles and visions evident among these artists makes any notion of 'school' extremely tenuous, but it cannot be denied that this new generation significantly re-energised French literature at a time when a shift towards audiovisual media was bringing about a deep and enduring cultural change.

Two of these novelists, Claude Ollier (born 1922) and Michel Butor (born 1926), acknowledge the direct impact of jazz on their writing. Ollier discovered jazz with Ellington's visit to Paris in 1933. Later, he discovered the be-bop musicians, whose mix of musical sophistication and emotional physicality became a permanent source of inspiration. He developed a particular affection for the work of Thelonious Monk, and in a number of his works introduced the figure of Monk as a kind of doppelgänger,[35] both as a homage and to mark his sense of closeness to Monk's way of creating his work from a combination of lyricism and rupture. Ollier likes to compare the blank page facing him to a keyboard, an instrument on which he can, in his own way, create new forms.[36]

Butor, a few years younger, had been caught up in the Saint-Germain-des-Prés jazz cellar scene. He attended concerts like that of Rex Stewart at the Salle Pleyel in 1947 and later, those of Duke Ellington and Charlie Parker. He especially appreciated jazz as dance music, and has continued to associate that side of the music with aspects of his own work.[37] Butor also claims to have been influenced by the improvisational nature of jazz, but for those familiar with the studied, elaborate layering of Butor's prose, a more apt analogy might be with the rich colouring of big band arrangements.

Among the groundbreaking writers of the contemporary generation, allusions to jazz are not infrequent, but recognition of influence is rarer. This is perhaps unsurprising, given that in France, as in America, jazz itself is now perceived more as a classical form than as an experimental one. There are a number of notable exceptions. The novelists Georges Perec, Christian Gailly (born 1943) and Jean Echenoz (born 1947), and the poet Jacques Réda (born 1929) are the most outstanding.

Perec (1936–1982), who died tragically early, is generally recognised as one of the most original and inventive postwar French novelists: his *La Vie: mode d'emploi* (*Life: A User's Manual*, 1978) is a masterpiece of world literature. Perec found in his experience of free jazz a model for exploring the relationship between freedom and constraint that informed his own writing. In a wonderfully revealing text, posthumously published and incomplete,[38] the novelist, with his customary wry humour, compares the situation of writers working after Joyce's *Finnegans Wake*—the fragmentation of story, characters, plot, and language itself—with that of jazz musicians now that free jazz has liberated the music from the ten years of 'soup' that followed the death of Charlie Parker. (In this 'soup', Perec included the Modern Jazz Quartet, the Jazz Messengers, West Coast jazz, and what he calls the 'pasteurisation' of Miles Davis and the 'geriatric decline' of Thelonious Monk!) The truly contemporary writer for Perec is, like the free jazz musician, poised at the edge of an existential abyss: behind him there is only the system that he must repudiate; before him, the urgent imperative to invent and build a bridge that will take him forward.

Gailly, himself a sometime jazz saxophonist influenced by Parker and Coltrane, attempts to reproduce, in his narrative voice, the rhythmic fluctuations of a jazz instrument. Two of his novels—*Be-Bop* (1995) and *Un soir au club* (2002)[39]—have explicit jazz settings, and offer real insight into the inner workings of jazz musicians' creative drive, as well as the difficulties of their daily lives. But for Gailly, jazz is also the metaphor for art-as-struggle, a way of confronting the entropic ebb of contemporary existence, and of refusing ready-made or reassuring notions of beauty.

For Jean Echenoz, too, jazz retains its capacity to inspire rebellion and change. Inspired by the more or less accidental acquisition of a Thelonious Monk 45 rpm record at the age of fourteen, Echenoz became, for a time, a real jazz fan. He listened passionately to Ornette Coleman, Coltrane and Mingus, as well as French musicians such as Portal. He wrote reviews for *Jazz Hot* and he even played in bands as a self-taught bass player.[40]

He named his second, and prize-winning, novel *Cherokee* (1983),[41] partly to signal his interest in post-be-bop jazz, partly in specific honour of Charlie Parker's famous up-tempo rendition of the Ray Noble tune, but mostly because of an incident that linked the music to his own ambitions as a writer. During an Ornette Coleman concert in Scandinavia, while the saxophonist was engaged in a particularly difficult improvisation, someone in the audience cried out, 'And now play "Cherokee"!' and Coleman, without hesitating, built the theme into his own improvisation, thereby demonstrating to those who were sceptical about the legitimacy of free jazz that he knew perfectly well what it was he had left behind. Echenoz, in his novel, wanted to show that he too could 'play "Cherokee"'—that is, include within the exploratory framework of an avant-garde and highly personal text, a demonstration of his ability to reproduce a canonical theme.

The canonical theme that Echenoz plays in *Cherokee* is that of a love quest condemned to failure: the familiar motif of the impossibility of fulfilment or permanence. In his rendering of it, he hybridises a number of cultural and literary forms: detective and adventure stories, comic strip characters, romance, and a multiplicity of narrative angles borrowed from cinema. The work is polyphonic in a way that is analogous to jazz. It sets a linear plot against dense textual imagery and verbal rhythm in a way reminiscent of Charlie Parker's approach to solo performance: a simultaneous development of melody and harmonic and rhythmic exploration. At the climax of the work—the point where all of the lines of force meet in a catastrophic shoot-out—the action is accompanied by the scripted sounds of a radio program devoted to a whole series of jazz pianists who followed in the footsteps of Bud Powell: Wynton Kelly, Ronnel Bright, Kenny Drew, Freddie Redd and Lou Levy. Just prior to this, Georges and two other characters have improvised a jazz performance as a kind of curtain raiser, using an incongruous assortment of instruments: saxhorn, double bass, and two whittled branches beating on an empty suitcase. The story's resolution and closure are accomplished within an explicit and carefully delineated jazz metaphor.

'Playing "Cherokee"' for Echenoz had the meaning of performing a literary *tour de force* as innovative and challenging as what Charlie Parker had done musically, and what Ornette Coleman had done after Parker. It affirms the way in which genius can become tradition, and acknowledges that tradition can be enlivened by new invention. His jazz experience was the source of this insight for Echenoz, and it has remained an underlying inspiration in all his subsequent work. He has consciously made it a habit—almost a signature—to refer directly in each of his novels to the jazz tradition.[42] More particularly, he has continued to draw on jazz in his creation of atmospheres and in the way he constructs the rhythm of his sentences—imitating swaying, syncopated, unbalancing effects that he has admired in the phrasing of various saxophonists, pianists and even bass players. His writing has an added dimension that makes it quite different from composition based solely on the spoken or written word, but complementary to it.

Echenoz has compared his shaking up of the rules of grammar and syntax to John Coltrane's transgressions of the conventions of melody and harmony. It is an expression of freedom that works precisely because the underlying rules and constraints are robust and widely accepted. Echenoz does not claim to be a revolutionary writer, and in this way he differs from some of the jazz musicians who have been most influential in his work. His approach to orthodoxy is more playful than aggressive, and is infused with as much respect as irony. But the pleasure that he derives from pushing linguistic constraints to their extreme limit is infectious. An Echenoz text has the exhilarating effect of the piano playing of Céline's character Borokrom, or (to use Echenoz's own analogy) of a performance by Roland Kirk, famed for his ability to play two wind instruments simultaneously and contrapuntally.[43] In this way, although the content of the story may be fragmented, the reader has an uninterrupted sense of a storytelling voice or voices unified by a recognisable 'feel'—a *style* where continuity is restored.

In some of his writing, the actual rhythm of the phrases is copied from snippets of jazz created by saxophonists, pianists and bass players. Without necessarily being able to identify which musical phrases Echenoz is emulating, the reader can gather the complex pleasure of how the narrative voice integrates the phonological variation, the evanescent images in kaleidoscopic succession, and the unpredictable shifts from extended phrases to abrupt endings or pauses. This is not the only kind of writing that Echenoz does. He also sometimes models his work on the intonations and modulations of speech. But in his 'jazz' writing, he claims to have the impression of using an actual musical instrument.[44]

In many ways, Jacques Réda embodies the most striking intersection of jazz and contemporary French literature, having established a major reputation both as a professional jazz commentator[45] and as a distinguished poet who, in 1993, was awarded the Grand Prize of the Académie Française. His early work, published in the 1950s, was rather self-consciously wrought under the double sign of surrealism and jazz, but it is in his later poems that there is the greatest convergence between his writing and his musical listening. Réda is above all a poet who walks and talks—who makes his way through the urban and suburban landscapes of Paris and its environs, and gives voice to his ruminations in word patterns modelled on oral communication. And it is as a *landscape* that Réda imagines his experience of jazz, seeing the music itself as a form of 'ambulatory' process in which discovery and expression are conjoined.[46]

Interestingly, in his maturity, Réda considers jazz as a particular musical form to have reached the end of its journey. He evokes the 'sparkling curve of its trajectory' from the 'proud and touching experiments of its beginnings' to the 'furious parkinsonian convulsions of its end'.[47] And yet, by virtue of the fact that the music has been so amply recorded—on acetate, vinyl, CD—it remains accessible to the poet as a permanent source of inspiration. In the end, for Réda, jazz is the preserve of two essential elements: the blues, which is both 'the human experience of separation' and 'an act of resistance and liberty',[48] and swing, which combines regular rhythm and syncopation in a way that binds dynamic forward movement of the music to the act of breathing.[49]

Céline, Sartre, Queneau, Vian, Echenoz and Réda are all iconic figures in French culture. The impact of jazz on their writing has been significant, and because each one of them has contributed to the renewal of literature in France, we must accept that jazz, to differing degrees and always in a rather diffuse manner, has had its role in that process of renewal. As a *current* of influence, jazz seems to have exerted its strongest attraction for French literature in the period between 1920 and 1960—predictably, at the time when the music itself was at its most vibrant and popular. Given that jazz music is no longer the vehicle of radical artistic transformation that it was in earlier decades, its persistence as a literary influence is remarkable.

The explanation lies in the fact that in its French literary incarnations, jazz is already something that has been appropriated. It is not perceived as foreign or exotic, and above all, its American roots are largely ignored. Rather, its presence is simply a part of the world in which the authors seek their inspiration and their understanding. Its potency lies in its essential freedom—a freedom translated sometimes as improvisation and spontaneity, sometimes as the right to transform the very elements of expression, and, most often, as a model for constructing an individual truth. The artistic visions of Céline, Sartre, Queneau, Vian, Réda and Echenoz are all, in this way, different.

But at the same time, each of these writers has been instrumental in reflecting some of the major social and cultural changes that have occurred over the past century. Their narratives are part of the intricate web of self-imagining that helps to create identity. In addition, each one of them has enriched the capacities of the French language itself and of narrative form. In this jazz has had an undeniable role.

It has not all been a one-way street. Although some of the writers discussed are not well-known outside France—writing that operates poetically always poses formidable challenges for translation—both Céline and Sartre have been extremely influential, not least in America. Although Céline has been somewhat forgotten in recent years, his impact on the likes of Ezra Pound, Henry Miller and Kurt Vonnegut is well documented. As for Sartre, his work has long since entered the literary canon. If French literature, in its self-renewal, owes a debt to jazz, it has at the same time enhanced its own original contribution to world culture.

# CHAPTER 7

# DANCING WITH DE BEAUVOIR
## Jazz and Feminism

**They were listening to Django Reinhardt's guitar,
they were dancing and drinking, and everyone
was laughing.**
**Simone de Beauvoir, *Les mandarins*[1]**

It is hard to imagine Simone de Beauvoir as a jazz fan. We are used to images of her that emphasise her seriousness: the severe hairstyles, the sensible if stylish clothing, the cultivated dignity of the celebrated intellectual. In her descriptions of her strict upbringing, in her long and tortuous relationship with Sartre, and in the elaboration of her pioneering feminist philosophy, there is a sense of dutiful earnestness. That earnestness does not sit readily with our customary associations with jazz. But a closer reading of de Beauvoir's life and memoirs tells a rather different story—one that reveals powerful passions coexistent with a sharp intellect. It is a story best approached obliquely, through the milieu in which de Beauvoir discovered what was perhaps most hidden in herself.

Omnipresent in the photographs of Saint-Germain-des-Prés during its golden era are images of a diminutive, red-headed, angular woman who often appears on the fringes of groups including people such as Boris Vian,

Sartre and Simone de Beauvoir. This is Anne-Marie Cazalis, and she cannot be dismissed as a simple groupie. A longtime friend of Juliette Gréco, Cazalis took pride in her status as the 'muse' of Saint-Germain-des-Prés.[2] Born in Algeria and raised in Bordeaux, she was the daughter of a well-connected Protestant pastor. At the time of the Liberation, Anne went up to Paris, where she discovered 'science-fiction, the origins of jazz, and all kinds of freedom'. If, in the end, her life and career proved less than what she had dreamed, and even though her own memoirs are filled with self-deprecating irony,[3] she was a pioneer of women's liberation, and jazz was a defining aspect of the freedom that she articulated.

Cazalis had won a minor prize for a collection of poetry, but she seems to have been driven less by any ambition to be recognised as a writer than by the ideal of creativity as a way of life. With Gréco and Marc Doelnitz—an art dealer's son who became an actor and cabaret performer—Cazalis was part of a trio who virtually ran the Saint-Germain-des-Prés nightlife. They were certainly its chief animators. For Doelnitz, who had met her on the Côte d'Azur at the beginning of the war, Cazalis was the 'intellectual' of the group, although this did not prevent her from waiting on tables in the jazz cellars.[4] It was Cazalis who first claimed the label 'existentialist' for the so-called and self-described 'troglodytes' of Saint-Germain, thereby conflating Sartrean philosophy with the youth culture of the Liberation years. With a keen eye for the value of publicity, she also stimulated the interest of the press, particularly the popular weekly *Samedi Soir*, whose feature articles in the spring of 1947—one with a front-page photo of Juliette Gréco guiding Roger Vadim down the narrow stone stairs of the Tabou club—were crucial to launching Saint-Germain as a socio-cultural phenomenon.[5]

There was a herd instinct at work among these young people. They were conscious of themselves as a group, and it was their rebelliousness as a group that gave them their identity. With minimal financial means, they cultivated their independence from their parents by doing things together: they went to the movies in groups, they listened to music and danced in groups, and they played together in each others' 16 mm films. Some of them learned how to smoke hash cigarettes by mixing with visiting American musicians, and they stayed up all night on their ritual crawls through the neighbourhood bars and cellars. But despite their brash defiance of convention and propriety, they were hardly intending to be revolutionaries: they were far more interested in having a good time than in changing the world. In many ways, like the characters in Boris Vian's novels, they were naive and innocent: Cazalis agreed with Sartre that the reason they liked the jitterbug so much was because it provided them with plenty of intense, healthy physical exercise, free of sexual innuendo.[6]

In one important respect, however, Cazalis *was* interested in changing the world, and that concerned the role and status of women in French society. She was aware that, with a single exception, the Parisian intellectual stage was occupied by males, notably Sartre and Camus. The exception was Simone de Beauvoir, whom Cazalis revered as an inspirational model after reading *L'Invitée* (1943, *She Came to Stay*). She claimed that it was because of de Beauvoir that she had been drawn to Saint-Germain in the first place. To a certain extent, she literally followed in de Beauvoir's footsteps: with Gréco, she actually rented the same room at the Hôtel de la Louisiane that Sartre and de Beauvoir had used during part of the Occupation.[7] It is not hard to see how the passionate contortions of de Beauvoir's first and very autobiographical novel appealed to the young freedom-seeking minister's daughter from straitlaced Bordeaux. In *L'Invitée*, de Beauvoir was trying to grapple with the complexities and confusions of her own emotions in respect to Sartre's uncontrolled physical infidelity, to explore the nature of relationships among women, and at the same time to probe and test her own powers as a creative artist.

It is likely that Cazalis would have identified equally readily with all four of the major female characters in *L'Invitée*: Xavière (based on Olga Kosakievicz, the capricious young woman who swept Sartre off his feet during his mescaline-addicted years),[8] who can dance all night and express her feelings without constraint, and the various incarnations of de Beauvoir herself: the repressed writer Françoise, the talented dancer–actress Paule, and the contrived, compliant Elisabeth. If the novel held no clear program for resolving issues confronting women in the new society that was emerging in France, the questions it raised were the essential ones: how to wrest identity from the male-dominated social structures of the past; how to redefine emotional connections among women without reference to men; and how to affirm, independently of men, the power of women to be artists in their own right. These questions were—centrally and critically—as physical and emotional as they were intellectual. As can be seen in the following passage from

'*She didn't speak English and I didn't speak French. We talked through our eyes...*'
*Miles Davis with Juliette Gréco at the Club Saint-Germain in Paris.*

*Anne-Marie Cazalis with French author Raymond Queneau in 1948.*

*Jean-Paul Sartre (left), Boris Vian (centre left) Michelle Vian (centre right) and Simone de Beauvoir (right) engaged in conversation in the Café Procope in Saint-Germain-des-Prés, Paris.*

*Boris Vian (left) and André Hodeir (right) at the Charles Cros Academy in 1958.*

*Jean Cocteau (left), Francis Crémieux (centre) and Norbert Gamsbon (right) gather around pianist Jean Wiéner during the recording of the* Boeuf sur le toit *memoirs in summer 1958.*

*Louis-Ferdinand Céline in 1932 – the year he published his celebrated novel,* Voyage au bout de la nuit.

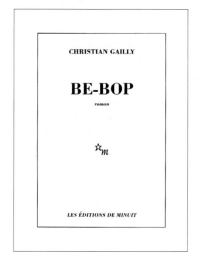

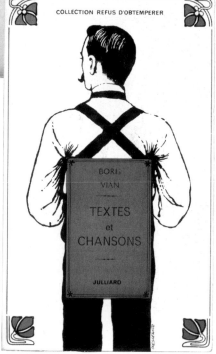

*Jazz influenced the writings of Boris Vian and many other French authors.*

*Actresses Nicole Courcel (front left) and Brigitte Auber (front right) dance to jazz music played by Pierre Merlin (left), Claude Rabanit (centre) and Claude Luter (right) on the set of Becker's Rendez-vous de juillet (1949).*

(Image Bibliothèque nationale de France, Paris)

*L'Invitée*, it was that link between physicality and freedom that made jazz so important:

> Elisabeth had left the table, she was dancing, her eyes swollen, her mouth tight. Something like envy passed through Françoise. Elisabeth's feelings might be false, her vocation might be false, her whole life might be false: her present suffering was violent and real. Françoise looked at Xavière. Xavière was dancing, her head slightly tilted back, her face ecstatic; she did not have a life yet, for her everything was possible, and this enchanted evening contained the promise of a thousand unknown enchantments. For this girl, and for this heavy-hearted woman, the moment held a bitter and unforgettable savour. And what about me? thought Françoise. Just a spectator. But this jazz, the taste of this whisky, this orange light—it wasn't just a spectacle, something should be made out of it. But what? In Elisabeth's untamed, tense soul, the music was being changed quietly into hope; Xavière was imbuing it with passionate expectation. Only Françoise found nothing in herself that was in tune with the plaintive voice of the saxophone. She searched for a desire, a regret; but behind and before her stretched only an arid and colourless happiness.[9]

Cazalis did eventually get to know de Beauvoir personally, but although de Beauvoir initially liked her, she frowned on her publicity-seeking and her tendency to gossip. She even ascribes to Cazalis most of the blame for the public misunderstanding of existentialism.[10] It is true that Cazalis has left little that would mark her as an important participant in those years of cultural ferment: she has recalled, with wry humour, a walk-on part with a single line in the first run of Sartre's *Le Diable et le Bon Dieu*, and a song that she wrote that was sung by Yves Montand[11]—hardly achievements to match those of her famous friend Juliette Gréco. At the same time, her subsequent career as a journalist for *Elle*, where her managing editor was the formidable Hélène Lazareff,[12] involved sustained serious reportage that ranged widely across a world undergoing revolutionary change. Cazalis deserves more attention than she has received. She states in her memoirs that she invented, in 1960, the term 'dans le vent', the French equivalent of 'in' or 'in fashion'.[13] Whether or not that is literally true, the phrase does sum up neatly the spirit of this woman of a perpetual present tense, who moved with her times with emancipated ease. She was insufficiently motivated or disciplined, no doubt, to transfer her experience into a more permanent form,[14] but she was none-theless a participant in the fertile intellectual life of postwar France, where the seeds of a more robustly philosophical feminism were about to be sown.

On the surface, the gossipy, jitterbugging flightiness and self-indulgent image of Anne-Marie Cazalis could not be further from the dignified, almost haughty restraint of Simone de Beauvoir. But such an impression underestimates the common ground that they shared. That common ground was made up of at least three important factors. The first—not gender-specific, but characterised by active and determined female involvement—was a desire that the social, political and cultural future should not be shaped by reference to tradition or the habits of the past, but should be the result of free and conscious choice. This was the existentialist ideal, and in this sense Cazalis was quite right to claim, for herself and her fellow 'cellar rats', as much right to the appellation 'existentialist' as was accorded to Sartre and de Beauvoir. The nightclubbing young folk of Saint-Germain-des-Prés did not have the intellectual ambition or rigour of the philosopher, but the fundamental demand for freedom that drove their lives was just as serious.

The second common factor was the demand that women, in particular, should be able to cut themselves loose from the ambient patriarchal struc-tures and to fashion their lives and identities without being trammelled by male power. This is what de Beauvoir had begun to articulate in *L'Invitée*, and for Cazalis, it had echoed urgently and strongly enough to take her from the serene certainties of her provincial home to the vibrant excitement of Saint-Germain-des-Prés.

The third factor was jazz, obviously a huge influence, as we have seen, in the life of Anne-Marie Cazalis, but also in Simone de Beauvoir's own development.

Jazz was to have a much greater impact on de Beauvoir than on Sartre, though it was he who originally made her realise its importance. As her memoirs reveal, music generally was an indispensable and permanent dimension of her life. From early childhood, it was all around her, and it is surprising that her major biographers do not pay any particular attention to the fact, because she herself returns to it constantly as a formative and transformative element in her personal and aesthetic development. Her entire work is strewn with extended references to musical experiences of one kind or another. Unlike Sartre, she was not herself musically gifted, but it seems to be precisely that lack of innate ability that stimulated her fascination:

> To decipher a sonatina amused me, but I hated having to learn it. I made a mess of my scales and exercises, and in my piano exams, I was always among the last. In '*solfège*', I was only attracted by theory: I sang out of tune and failed disastrously my musical dictation ... Doubtless, in order to reveal the truth of a piece of music, one needed to render its shades of meaning, not massacre them ... To create was something else again. I was full of admiration when someone brought something real and new into the world.[15]

While not naturally at ease with making music, she was enormously attracted to people who were. Her sister Hélène's singing talent, her friend Zaza's virtuosity on the piano and violin, helped shape what would become a lifelong and wide-ranging interest—though her admiration was sometimes tinged with envy.[16] By the time she was twenty, Simone was exploring the whole gamut of Paris's musical offerings, from the classical concerts of the Salle Pleyel and the experiments of the Ballets russes to the music halls and jazz clubs.[17] The first sound film, *The Jazz Singer*, was a major event in her cultural life.[18]

When she met Sartre in 1929, then, she was already familiar with a wide variety of musical styles: the high culture of the classical tradition, the more contemporary creations of Stravinsky and Prokofiev,[19] popular singers such as Maurice Chevalier, vaudeville, and the sounds of negro spirituals, blues and early jazz.[20] We have noted how Sartre's musical talent was an important factor in de Beauvoir's attraction to him. He in fact became her musical model and mentor, expanding her existing knowledge and helping to initiate her in the major developments and intricacies of musical history, including the techniques of contemporary composers and the spirit of popular music.

During the time she spent in Rouen on her first *lycée* teaching assignment, her attempt to keep her musical life going was both a preoccupation and a source of frustration. She listened assiduously to records of Bach, Beethoven and Stravinsky, and went dancing with Olga Kosakievicz to compensate for the provincial exile.[21] Her breaks in Paris allowed her to immerse herself in the swirl of the capital's nightlife. Her return to Paris residence was marked by several big events, such as the 1937 performances of the Cotton

Club of New York at the Moulin Rouge.[22] She also made regular visits to a variety of clubs—above all the Bal Nègre in the rue Blomet, which was the centre of Caribbean and African-American jazz music and dance in the immediate pre-war period.[23]

In *La Force de l'âge* (*The Prime of Life*, 1960), de Beauvoir remarks that her musical self-education was especially intense during the period of the 'drôle de guerre' and the early part of the Occupation (1939–41).[24] Interestingly, there is little reference to music at all in her writings that deal with the later part of the Occupation: she does note various sorties to the theatre, but while she had gone to hear Piaf in early 1940, there is no sign that she followed any of the well-known singers of the Occupation years—Trenet, Solidor, Chevalier or Piaf—or indeed any other form of music. Did she continue to listen to records? Perhaps. Certainly she was, during this period, absorbed in her own writing—she was composing *L'Invitée*, which overflows with allusions to music, and perhaps this fact helps to explain the unique absence of reference to music in her memoirs of this time.

Music, for de Beauvoir, is associated with the discovery of something *that does not come naturally to her*. It is an expression of an 'otherness' that she learns to appreciate and describe without being able to perform it. However, we can observe that the process through which she learned to analyse and contextualise music is directly analogous to the way in which she gradually became able to analyse and contextualise the people and events of her time. Her writing, which is in so many ways an articulation of the 'other', can thus been seen as a kind of extension of the process of her apprenticeship in music.

What about jazz in particular? As with Sartre, it seems to have entered de Beauvoir's consciousness during her student days. At that stage, it had two very different connotations for her, the one quite deeply personal, the other associated with her embryonic perceptions of global politics. On the first level, it concerned the release of a physicality, which previously had been shut off by taboos. On another level, jazz brought with it the astonishment and attraction of American culture:

We could only perceive this country through a distorting lens. We didn't understand it at all, but with jazz and Hollywood films, it had entered our lives. Like most young people of our era, we were passionately moved by negro spirituals, work songs and the blues. We liked everything—'Old Man

River', 'St James Infirmary', 'Some of These Days', 'The Man I Love', 'Miss Hannah', 'St Louis Blues', 'Japansy', 'Blue Skies'. The plaint of humanity, lost joys, broken hopes had found to express themselves a voice which defied the politeness of conventional art, a voice which had brutally surged from the heart of the night, shaking with rebellion. Because they had been born of vast collective emotions—the feelings of each and of all— these songs touched each of us in that most intimate part of ourselves which is also the part that we share with each other. They inhabited us, they nourished us in the same way as certain words and cadences of our own language, and through them, America existed within us.[25]

America appeared to her as a quasi-Nietzschian space beyond good and evil: its capitalism and racism were sources of horror, but it nonetheless exercised irresistible fascination. In the interwar ethos in which contemporary sociopolitical realities were a dominant preoccupation, it was America that most strongly symbolised the attraction of those new and somewhat frightening realities. It was through the 'otherness' of jazz that de Beauvoir recognised, took into account and came to terms with both the 'other' within herself (that is, her own sensuality and sexuality) and the vast cultural 'other' represented by the United States. Jazz was thus a catalyst for opening up de Beauvoir's understanding of the whole spectrum of life, from the most intimate to the global.

Over the next decade, the dynamics and meaning of jazz changed for her: partly through her relationship with Sartre, but also through her own professional career and her growing independence and maturity. By 1939, when she was frequenting the Bal Nègre, she had learned enough about herself and about the world to have achieved greater distance and a different perspective. She now saw the white women who attempted to dance with the black dancers as symbolic of a whole society still stiff with the puritanical constraints that she had experienced ten years earlier. Her descriptions were not kind:

We were exceptions at that time: very few white women mixed with the black crowd, and fewer still ventured onto the floor. Beside the lithe Africans and the pulsating West Indians, their stiffness was painful and if they tried to escape it, they ended up looking like hysterical zombies.[26]

While she consistently described the music and dancing of the blacks as 'obscene', de Beauvoir not only admired it, but came to think of it as the bewitching symbol of a transgression that had to be undertaken.[27] Moreover, the music itself, first seen as a broadly American phenomenon, was now more subtly—and more accurately—perceived as an integral part of an experience that was specifically African-American. Through jazz, de Beauvoir's knowledge and understanding of America had become more three-dimensional, and more politically astute. From being a quasi-magical force of personal liberation, it had become an instrument for comprehending the world.

Or it had become so for at least that part of the world that, for Sartre and herself, was the main area of interest after the Liberation: the United States of America. We have seen how Sartre, in a snap judgment, identified jazz as an American icon. For her part, de Beauvoir was to take a more systematic approach. During the two or three years prior to the work that would propel her onto the world stage as a revolutionary feminist thinker (*Le deuxième sexe* (*The Second Sex*), 1949), she made three trips to the US, initially in the professional framework of university and public lecture tours, and then with the more personal agenda of developing her relationship with Nelson Algren, the Chicago writer who became her lover.[28] During the first visit, especially, which lasted for four months, her rather eclectic curiosity about jazz started to become a thirst for much more precise knowledge.

In New York, she consciously and successfully sought out informants. She was taken to the best clubs, and she met both musicians and knowledgeable fans. Algren showed her the clubs of Chicago, and with other friends she explored the jazz scenes of San Francisco, Los Angeles, Las Vegas, Santa Fe, San Antonio and New Orleans. Her notes about these experiences betray some hesitancy and uncertainty in the formation of her taste and opinions, and some of her conclusions may appear naive or limited. Thus, for instance, she was for a time exclusively fixated on New Orleans style and on black jazz, and rejected be-bop as a perversion introduced by white American jazzmen. It is nonetheless clear that de Beauvoir was accumulating listening experience in a determined and autonomous fashion, independent of Sartre's formative influence. That emerging independence may have been in part a reaction to Sartre's affair with Dolorès Vanetti,[29] which certainly encouraged her budding relationship with Algren, but it was also a product of her personal discovery of America. Jazz was an integral part of her exploration of race relations, and, as she began more explicitly to associate the oppression of African-Americans with that of women, it became a key link in her reflections on gender relations.

The function of jazz in the development of de Beauvoir's thought can be summarised as follows. Beginning on the personal level as pleasure—release from the stiffness of her upbringing, a salutary transgression—jazz was also a window onto American culture. Even more, it seems to have represented the flow of a new kind of energy, which de Beauvoir identified as both American in origin and deeply vitalising for herself. Next, within the American framework, jazz became a means of establishing an important insight into the divided nature of American society. On the one hand, it connoted a black culture that she saw both as oppressed and as vibrant with positive energy; on the other hand, jazz revealed more clearly its cultural opposite: the exploitative capitalism of white America. Finally, it led her to the discovery of what she describes, in the introduction to *Le deuxième sexe*, as the 'profound analogy'[30] between the oppressed situation of blacks and that of women.

From a relatively abstract starting point, de Beauvoir's thinking and writing can be seen to become more grounded, more *embodied*—personally, socially and politically. This is a shift that can be measured very clearly by the different expressions of her feminism that are found in *Pour une morale de l'ambiguïté (The Ethics of Ambiguity)* and in *Le deuxième sexe*. In the first work, women are compared to black slaves of the eighteenth century.[31] While this comparison clearly identifies the disempowerment of women, it is marked by temporal distance, and the writing style is theoretical if not recondite. In the later text, the point of comparison is the living present-day African-American community whose realities have been experienced directly and personally by the author.

It would be excessive to claim that *Le deuxième sexe* is uniquely or directly derived from jazz. The work is very much constructed according to an existentialist model, and while we have pointed out that existentialism itself has a debt to jazz, it also has its own set of rules and processes, to which de Beauvoir adheres quite closely. *Le deuxième sexe* catalogues the historical, mythical, sociological, psychological and gender constraints that impinge on women, as distinct from human beings in general, and men in particular, in order to establish the level of awareness necessary to mount an ongoing struggle for liberation. The development of this model can be traced back through de Beauvoir's earlier writings. In *Pour une morale de l'ambiguïté*, first published in 1946–47, for instance, there is a prototypical form of the later work's main argument. The existentialist line is already clear in the essays of *L'Existentialisme et la sagesse des nations* (*Existentialism and the Wisdom of the Ages*, first published in 1945–46), and indeed the link between de Beauvoir's existentialist perspective[32] and her emergent feminism is evident in her first novel, *L'Invitée*, and can be followed through the subsequent novels, *Le Sang des autres* (*The Blood of Others*, 1945) and *Tous les hommes sont mortels* (*All Men are Mortal*, 1946).

Another significant factor that contributed to *Le deuxième sexe* was auto-biographical. The work was written over a period of almost three years, from mid 1946 through early 1949. This was a time of intense agitation: in de Beauvoir's own life, in her perceptions of the human condition, in the regeneration process of postwar French society, and indeed in the world-wide political situation. It was a time of intellectual, sexual and artistic revolution, and de Beauvoir, notwithstanding her very controlled manner, was fully engaged in it. Within the French context, she was acutely aware of the internal political wrangles that, by mid 1947, had led to the dissolution of the fragile unity constructed on the Resistance, and of the circumstances leading to the onset and development of the Cold War. Perhaps more pertinently, she experienced severe doubts about her relationship with Sartre, which had been a stabilising force for almost fifteen years, when he threw himself into his obsessional love affair with Dolorès Vanetti; her own affair with Nelson Algren was more a source of distraction than of any recentring. From this angle, the writing of *Le deuxième sexe* required de Beauvoir to sur-mount considerable personal difficulties, but it also allowed her to establish the basis for a philosophy capable of giving coherence to a life often beset by confusion.

In many ways, de Beauvoir's work is very organic, with no obvious gaps between its autobiographical, literary and philosophical strands. It is there-fore unsurprising that the impact of music in general and jazz in particular, which we have documented in her memoirs and novels, should have con-tinued to underpin her more explicitly philosophical writing.

De Beauvoir was to visit the United States several times during the late 1940s, and these experiences allowed her to develop and refine her project.[33] Back in France, her involvement with jazz continued through her friendship with Boris Vian and his circle. As we have seen, Vian was without question France's central jazz figure at this time: player, composer, critic, writer, and the driving force of the Saint-Germain-des-Prés youth movement. De Beauvoir had met him in early 1946, and was to remain close to him and his family for a decade. Beyond the problematic public identification of jazz with existentialism, jazz was a very important factor in de Beauvoir's life—something she felt the need to master in her own right—and she acknowledged that she learned a great deal from Vian, who shared with her his immense knowledge of the history of jazz and its musicians.

De Beauvoir, like Sartre, and unlike other French writers such as Céline and Vian, never sought to model her writing on the rhythms or forms of jazz. Nonetheless, her choice of literary forms—whether one considers the straight autobiographies, the autobiographical novels or the journalistic style of her American travel writings—is congruent with the immediacy and direct personal expression associated with jazz performance. There is significance, too, in the fact that her taste in jazz was for the 'classical' New Orleans style rather than for the progressive and fragmented lines and harmonies of be-bop. Her experience of jazz enhanced her willingness and ability to create a literary universe characterised by quite revolutionary thought; it did not impinge on her very traditional use of language.

Jazz remained a source of relaxation and pleasure—usually taken with a glass of whisky—for a long time in de Beauvoir's life. It is also a thematic presence in later novels such as *Les mandarins* (*The Mandarins*, 1954), in which the music is used to capture the mood of postwar Paris, triggering memories of youth, happiness and freedom for de Beauvoir's generation but also providing a much-needed insight for the younger generation, who had grown up in the rigours of the Depression and the Occupation and thus had no recollection of how to be free and unencumbered. With time, however, the presence of jazz as an active ingredient of life faded. De Beauvoir had a nostalgic evening with Algren in Paris in March 1960, listening to records that he had brought: Bessie Smith, Charlie Parker, Mahalia Jackson. But, at the following New Year, when she organised a 'réveillon' for friends, her notes seem symptomatic of a growing distance from the music: 'I had prepared some jazz records, but they weren't used: we just chatted.'[34]

There is another poignant moment in *La Cérémonie des adieux* (*Adieux: a Farewell to Sartre*, 1981). Jazz is brought up in her conversation with the ageing, almost blind Sartre, only to be immediately dropped:

There was jazz too (says de Beauvoir). Imagine, we didn't mention it when we talked of your love for music. Jazz meant a lot to you.

Him: Yes, a lot.[35]

The conversation branches off onto America, and never returns to the subject of jazz.

In personal terms, this may well have to do with growing older, for de Beauvoir always associated jazz with her youth and the idealism and rebelliousness of the postwar era. Her work, however, stands as an important illustration of the music's impact on French culture: it provided a powerful injection of energy that she absorbed and ultimately appropriated, transforming it in ways that allowed her to shape and alter her own culture.

Both de Beauvoir and Sartre appropriated jazz, but, although the music was for both of them associated with freedom, they embraced it for different reasons and with different results. For all her stumbling beginnings and for all his musical facility, she probably got more out of it than he did. It is present in her writing to a greater degree, and while he used it to inform and illustrate his philosophy, she derived from it a program of action, or at least the basis for developing such a program. There can be no doubt, however, that both of them made major contributions to French culture in the postwar period. Sartrean existentialism, less in its precise detail than in its general faith in humanity's capacity to build a decent future, was an active element in the rebuilding of national confidence and identity; de Beauvoir's nascent feminism has helped to ensure that the concepts of humanity and identity have not continued to be distorted by the exclusion of half the species.[36] At the same time, no less than Sartre, de Beauvoir has helped to position French culture as a base for creating unexpected meanings and possibilities of jazz culture, and bringing these ideas into the international dialogue.

It would be absurd to claim that the de Beauvoir story gives a neat or complete account of the relationship between jazz and the emergence of French feminism. While the importance of jazz in her own life and in connection with her work is undeniable, it is not at all evident that jazz played any significant or direct part in subsequent developments of female emancipation. The progressively more enlightened legislation—from women's right to vote (granted in 1944), through equal rights as workers (the 1970s and 1980s), to the full panoply of legal rights in the 1990s—sometimes owed a debt to battles waged by women who acknowledged de Beauvoir as a pioneer. But not always. Often, battles won had to be refought and won again, and this process of restarting from scratch continues for each successive generation. Perhaps the most that one can say is that in those domains where women's freedoms owe something to Simone de Beauvoir, they also, albeit indirectly, owe something important to jazz. De Beauvoir's work announced the right of women to determine their destiny: it did not achieve that right.

By the early 1950s, the Saint-Germain-des-Prés phenomenon had lost most of its novelty and its dynamism.[37] But many of the jazz clubs would continue to function for years to come, attracting members of the younger generation to the sites to which Vian, Gréco, de Beauvoir and Sartre had given mythical status. And jazz continued to be experienced as a force of liberation. Françoise Sagan turned up in Saint-Germain-des-Prés on the heels of the success of her *Bonjour tristesse* (1954). This bombshell novel, with its unprecedentedly frank revelations of a young woman's sensuality and desire, was written under the acknowledged influence of de Beauvoir's *L'Invitée* and Sartre's *L'Âge de raison*. Interestingly, *Bonjour tristesse* itself contains hardly any reference to jazz at all: nothing more than an evocation of jazz trumpets on the car radio; a mournful clarinet when the heroine, Cécile, is dancing with her boyfriend in a Saint-Tropez nightclub; a moment when her father asks her to teach him the 'be-bop'. It seems to be something external, with no inherent connection to her awakening sensibilities and sensuality. Cécile is a child of the southern French summer, and her erotic awakenings are almost exclusively a factor of the sun, the sand and the sea.

Any influence of jazz in the creation of this work must therefore be seen as purely indirect, via the impact of de Beauvoir on the young Sagan's psyche. Such an influence can nonetheless be reasonably posited, especially in view of the fact that in her second novel, *Un certain sourire* (1956), jazz and sensuality are explicitly linked, as are music and love. Repeating the device used famously by Proust, and almost as famously by Sartre, Sagan writes into her narrative a song motif—'Lone and Sweet'—that the heroine Dominique associates with her amorous adventures, first with Bertrand, then with Luc. And more specifically, when she goes with Bertrand to the Kentucky to hear a bop band and to dance, she links the jazz to something elemental:

Contrary to what I had expected, we danced very well, we were relaxed. More than anything else, I loved this music, the energy it gave me, the pleasure my whole body had in following it . . .

'The music,' I whispered to Bertrand, 'Jazz music is accelerated freedom.'[38]

The music is not only a source of energy and pleasure, for the protagonist. It speeds up, almost like a drug, her sense of freedom from responsibility. This feeling is then transformed into a conviction of necessity and inevitability:

'Listen. The trumpet, it's not only carefree, it's necessary. He absolutely had to go right to the end of that note—didn't you feel it? Necessary. It's like love, you see, physical love, there's a moment where you have to . . . where it can't be any other way.'[39]

For those familiar with Sartre's work, this text will be reminiscent of Roquentin's quest, in *La nausée*, for a reliable guide to meaning in life. But the forward-driving momentum, which Sagan associates with a music that reaches its fulfilment only when it has exhausted its every possibility, is not a product of literary influence. It is the symbolic expression of the way in which she conceives of life itself.

One could readily see most of Sagan's writing as being, in this way, 'marked' by jazz. It is far from the measured, composed, reflective prose of de Beauvoir: more immediate in its personal inspiration, more rapid, more clearly showing the rough edges of improvisation. Indeed, Sagan's links with jazz may be more readily found in her life—her compulsive gambling, her love of fast cars, her serial romances—than in her writing. The 'acceleration of freedom' that she found in jazz became a principle on which she modelled her existence. In her 1984 book of memoirs, she wrote in praise of speed:

The taste for speed has nothing to do with sport. In the same way that it is tied in with gambling and chance, speed is tied to the joy of life and, consequently, to that vague death wish that always accompanies the said joy of life. In the end, that's all I believe in: speed is neither a sign, nor a proof, nor a provocation, nor a defiance—it's a burst of happiness.[40]

It is difficult to reconcile the idea of happiness with the life that Sagan has led, or with the ravaged expressions captured by late photographs of this woman. Sagan's story evokes that of Billie Holiday, and it is certainly not by chance that the first chapter of her memoirs is devoted to that singer, whom she knew and admired. It is almost as if, in Lady Day's raw and terribly diminished last performances, Sagan was watching herself.

Despite this, Françoise Sagan remains a significant player in the unfolding drama of women's emancipation in France. The 20-year-old rebel, who startled the literary world with *Bonjour tristesse* in 1954, made possible a level of self-revelation that had previously been taboo. In so doing, she opened doors for future generations of women, including those who, like contemporary film-maker Catherine Breillat (*Romance*, *À ma soeur!*), continue to push back the borders of female self-expression. More of a risk-taker than the mentor she admired, Sagan was indebted to Simone de Beauvoir, but not limited by her debt. That her rush forwards into freedom should ultimately have been self-destructive is perhaps less important than the fact that she named, and claimed, the power to determine her own direction.

# CHAPTER 8

# 'IN ONE WORD: EMOTION'
## Jazz and Cinema

**Everyone loved what I did with the music on that film.**
**Miles Davis, *Miles: The Autobiography*[1]**

From the French perspective, cinema and jazz, as art forms, were born of the same modernist parentage at virtually the same time. Their closeness as the major arts of the twentieth century was historically symbolised in the title of the first sound film, produced in 1927: *The Jazz Singer*. The star of this film, Al Jolson, does not sing jazz, and there is something insulting to the history of jazz in this presentation of a white man in black-face imitating African-American singing. However, the enormous impact of the film was undeniable, both in the United States and in France. Two years later, the King Vidor production of *Alleluia*, with an all-black cast, featured some jazz and blues, as well as a number of extended scenes portraying the cast singing negro spirituals; it too enjoyed great success in France. For the young Simone de Beauvoir, these two films were major formative events.[2] Michel Leiris, in a wildly enthusiastic review of *Alleluia*, discovered in the film a new form of sanctity—a sanctity infused with eroticism, alcohol, scandal, adventure and ecstasy:

> The mystical power of the black race . . . inflicts a harsh lesson on the white
> race which is artistically drained and faded (capable now only of technical

progress). The strength of its song, music and dance overwhelms us through their rhythm, their frenzy and their erotic and ritual majesty.[3]

From their very beginnings, cinema and jazz seemed destined for a fertile partnership. Both forms offered ample potential for the kind of personal expression inherent in the modern sensibility,[4] and both opened dramatic new possibilities of interchange between visual and auditory experience. When the Lumière brothers put on the world's first cinematographic projection to a paying audience in 1895, the gadget they were showing off, the 'cinematograph', was at once a machine for recording images, a box for developing exposed film, and a projector. It was in every way an instrument for seizing the present moment and expressing its immediacy. Similarly, the content of the films of the first Lumière program promoted the value of the 'here and now': in the last sequence of the original program, a boat is shown leaving a harbour. In another, Louis Lumière supervises the demolition of an old wall—a dramatisation of society's intention to set aside the old in order to make way for the new.

The Lumières left no indication that they foresaw just how significant their invention would be, either as a new way of examining and knowing the world or as a new form of entertainment. One of the spectators of their first show, the stage magician Georges Méliès, had a better understanding of how the cinema could be used to create a world of fantasy that would appeal to a paying public, and he did that with great success over the following decade. But Méliès, too, was unaware of the full implications of his work. It is ironic that these pioneers should have remained unconscious of what had already been demonstrated embryonically in the first Lumière program and in Méliès's rudimentary editing strategies: namely cinema's potential for the radical manipulation of time and space. It was this quality that made cinema one of the most important instruments of modernism: a tool of a collective imagination that no longer accepted the framework of narratives and metaphors established over previous centuries, replacing it with a spirit of discovery.

Despite cinema's apparent artistic affinities with jazz, historical differences began to emerge quite early as cinema developed more in the direction of storytelling than with an agenda of personal discovery or expression. The seeds of this are visible already in Méliès, though it could be argued that the old magician's often zany scenarios have a lot in common with the inspirations of jazz. The arrival of the Hollywood model over the period between 1915 and 1930, however, marked a clear change of direction for cinema. Increasingly sophisticated camera and editing techniques, and from 1927, the use of sound, were put in the service of narratives carefully composed along stereotypical generic lines. In many ways, the overwhelmingly narrative function of Hollywood films (and those that follow the Hollywood pattern) is not at all modern: it is retrogressive, looking back to the realist settings, characters and plot-lines of the nineteenth-century novel. This is a form that depends on its capacity to wrap the world in a sense of completeness: time passes in a reassuringly chronological fashion (albeit sometimes with flashbacks of memory); people behave in ways that are, if not always predictable, at least ultimately explainable; and events are organised in patterns that rarely challenge the given order of the social and political world.

The more cinema grew in this direction, the further it distanced itself from the spontaneous, poetic, open-ended possibilities of its origins. The history of Hollywood's domination of world cinema needs no retelling here.[5] It is important to note, however, that during the silent era, European cinema retained some of its capacity for poetic expression, and it is for these qualities that many still value the work of directors such as Eisenstein, Lang and Gance. Arguably, this approach to cinema continues as one of the factors distinguishing the European tradition from Hollywood. It has been promoted by such significant film-makers as René Clair and maintained in the French so-called 'poetic realism' school of the 1930s, as well as in the New Wave and the renaissance of Italian and German cinema after World War II.

In France, attempts to combine jazz and cinema were slow and sporadic. As was the custom elsewhere before the advent of the soundtrack, projections were accompanied by live music, including jazz. However, this link was largely fortuitous, and does not represent any kind of serious artistic integration. In the handful of interwar French films that contain jazz,[6] the music plays only an incidental role, although it was sometimes performed by prominent musicians of the time. The Ray Ventura band in *L'amour à l'américaine* included Stéphane Grappelli, for example, and Django Reinhardt provided the music for *Naples au baiser de feu*. It is possible in some instances to ascribe significance to the use of jazz. In Renoir's *Chotard et compagnie*, it is used to underline the cultural sophistication of Paris in contrast to the film's provincial setting. In Duvivier's *Pépé le Moko*, jazz is introduced (displacing the dominant North African theme music) as a signal of the sexual attraction between Pépé and Gaby, the film's femme fatale. A form of ragtime, with drums—produced by a mechanical piano—is also used to accompany the sequence in which the mortally wounded Pierrot executes the treacherous Régis. In general, however, the jazz music used in the cinema of this period is no more than part of the social backdrop.

After World War II, two French scientists opened the way to a more organic use of jazz in cinema, seeking to exploit the sonorities and rhythms of the music as an integral dimension of documentaries revealing the hidden secrets of the biological world. Jean Painlevé used recordings of Duke Ellington for *Le vampire* (1945)—a film about bats in which the scientist includes scenes from Murnau's *Nosferatu*—and *Les assassins d'eau douce* (1947), which dramatises the evolution and habits of microscopic underwater creatures. Jacques Cousteau called upon André Hodeir to compose the music for his underwater documentary *Autour d'un récif* (1949), in which musical motifs are synchronised with the unpredictable movements of fish and other underwater animals.[7] Perhaps unknowingly, Painlevé and Cousteau were applying an aesthetic principle enunciated by René Clair at the beginning of the sound era and reiterated in 1950: namely that sound, in cinema, should not be considered as an aspect of realism, or simply as a way of colouring an atmosphere. Clair believed rather that the soundtrack offered a multitude of creative possibilities and that its relationship to the image needed to be constantly explored, along with the rest of the film-maker's creative processes.[8] André Bazin, the founder of modern film criticism and a progenitor of the French New Wave school of film-making, saw a link between the music chosen and the 'supernatural grace' of these image sequences, which were generated more by chance than by any predetermined program.[9] By giving jazz such prominence in their work, Painlevé and Cousteau were pioneering the more conscious experimentation of the film-makers of the next generation.

French cinema of the 1940s and 1950s acknowledged the importance of jazz as a social phenomenon. There were more than two dozen films that contained significant treatments of jazz[10] before Louis Malle's 1957 landmark work, *Ascenseur pour l'échafaud* (*Lift to the Scaffold*). A few were actual documentaries (on Django Reinhardt, Sidney Bechet, etc.); some simply featured episodes in which well-known musicians appeared (in this way, Sidney Bechet performed, usually with the André Réwéliotty band, in a series of crime films in the mid 1950s). In *Rendez-vous de juillet* (1949), Jacques Becker went further. In his portrayal of the Saint-Germain cellar culture (with the Claude Luter band, augmented by former Duke Ellington trumpeter Rex Stewart), he evoked the importance of jazz for the young people of the time and also linked the music to the thematic explorations of the work. The story of the film develops loosely around the lives of half a dozen young people, creating a criss-crossing structure that reflects the polyphony of the jazz. In turn, the music serves to give a sense of unity to the diverse lines of the narrative. Becker thus borrows some of the formal qualities of jazz to make a new model of cinematographic storytelling.

As the French 'New Wave' began to crest in the late 1950s, jazz became an almost standard component in films. A wide range of the music was exploited: live and pre-recorded, black and white, American and French. In *Sait-on jamais?* (1957), Roger Vadim worked closely with John Lewis and the Modern Jazz Quartet to generate a cohesive harmony between the sober sequences of images and the thoughtful limpidity of Lewis's music. In *Les liaisons dangereuses* (1960), he again used jazz extensively but this time called on the less controlled energies of Thelonious Monk, Barney Willen and Art Blakey's Jazz Messengers, both to mirror the intensity of the dangerous love stories, and as a vehicle for the explosive climax.

Marcel Carné's use of jazz in *Les tricheurs* (1958) offers a panoramic view of the whole contemporary jazz world, from recordings of Dizzy Gillespie, Coleman Hawkins, Oscar Peterson, Stan Getz and Gerry Mulligan, to Maxim Saury's New Orleans band playing in a sequence filmed in the Cave de la Huchette. Jean-Pierre Melville turned to Martial Solal for the jazz that permeates *Deux hommes dans Manhattan* (1958), an imitation of American B-grade noir thrillers that followed the vein he had begun to explore with *Bob le flambeur* in 1955 and which was to reach its richest expression in *Le samouraï* (1967). Édouard Molinaro (*Des femmes disparaissent*, 1959; *Un témoin dans la ville*, 1959; *Une fille pour l'été*, 1960), Claude Chabrol (*Les cousins*, 1959), and François Truffaut (*Tirez sur le pianiste*, 1960) all followed the trend. Even Jacques Rivette, in *Paris nous appartient* (1961), where most of the soundtrack music is completely unrelated to jazz, felt the need to include jazz as atmospheric music in a brief sequence set in a Saint-Germain-des-Prés café.

The use of jazz in films had several possible meanings. As a social phenomenon, jazz was at the height of its popularity in France, and its presence in the films is on one level just an acknowledgment that it was a dominant sound of the time. For many of the film-makers, however, it was also an emblem of America in all its complexity: the bustling energy, the lavishness, the swaggering power, the glamour of beautiful women and big cars, the violence and gangsterism, and of course, the cinema itself. In the postwar period, a vast array of work had flooded from Hollywood onto the French screens—which had been inaccessible to American material during the German Occupation—and provided an inexhaustible source of wonder, excitement and inspiration for French film enthusiasts.

For some of the New Wave French film-makers, jazz was also an object of aesthetic interest: they saw in its spirit of creative improvisation a reflection of their own desire to make personal films expressing an individual sensibility and vision of the world. Although it would be difficult to prove that jazz was a precondition for the French New Wave, it was an indisputable part of the context in which the major tenets of France's cinematographic revolution took root. The heightened levels of individual responsibility associated with the concept of the 'auteur'—the idea that a film director is, like any writer, the 'creator' of his or her work—may not have derived in any direct way from jazz, but the music provided exemplary support in an ethos that demanded artistic autonomy.

Two film-makers whose work illustrates most comprehensively the symbiotic interaction between jazz and French cinema are Louis Malle and Jean-Luc Godard. Their individual bodies of work are very different. However, each can be seen as the expression of a philosophy of art that is related to jazz in two essential ways. First, the film-making in both cases has some of the spontaneity, rhythm and physicality of jazz as performance. Second, their cinematographic practice is closely analogous to jazz in its assertion of both the artist's freedom and his or her ownership of the creative act. Malle engaged with jazz as a source of direct and ongoing personal inspiration; whereas Godard's interest in the music was fleeting and evident only at the very beginning of a career that, nonetheless, invites comparison with the exploratory art of the great jazz musicians.

Louis Malle (1932–1995), like many of his generation, discovered jazz during its postwar blossoming, when he was in his mid teens. Along with literature and cinema, it remained one of his great passions. His success with Jacques Cousteau, *Le Monde du silence* (1956), which won the Palme d'Or at Cannes, made it possible for him to make his own first feature film. In that work, *Ascenseur pour l'échafaud*, he managed to combine all three passions in what is now acknowledged as a cinematographic masterpiece. It won the 1957 Prix Louis-Delluc for best French feature film,[11] as well as the Académie Charles-Cros prize for its music. Malle drew on the iconoclastic brilliance of the young novelist Roger Nimier and obtained the services of Miles Davis for the soundtrack, bringing literature, jazz and cinema together in an unprecedented way. The experience with Davis was pivotal in Malle's self-conception as a film-maker.[12]

The story of *Ascenseur pour l'échafaud* concerns an ex-paratrooper, Julien Tavernier, who has set out to murder his lover's husband by faking the husband's suicide. It hinges on a double series of misadventures through which he becomes a police suspect for another crime, which he has not committed. The real suspense of the film, however, is generated by the nocturnal peregrinations of Julien's lover, Florence Carala, the murdered businessman's wife (played by Jeanne Moreau). Unaware that Julien has been trapped in the office lift and not knowing even whether he has successfully dispatched the husband, she spends the night searching for him. The Miles Davis music plays most effectively into the obsessiveness of her interminable and fruitless search, lighting up her growing desperation from within.

It was almost an accident that Malle was able to call upon Miles Davis, who happened to be in Paris at the time, playing with a group at the Club Saint-Germain. Through the good offices of Boris Vian and Marcel Romano (the program manager at the club),[13] Malle met Davis, whose work he had known and admired for many years. Davis tells of watching the first prints of the film and writing down musical ideas to be used in the score.[14] Malle, on the other hand, claims that after he had showed Davis the film twice, the music was recorded in a single improvised session that ran from ten or eleven at night until five the next morning.[15] That Miles Davis should wish to remember the event more as an act of musical composition is consistent with a jazz musician's need for legitimacy; conversely, Malle's memory of the event as a complete improvisation underscores the value he placed on freedom as an aesthetic virtue. From Malle's point of view, the music was the result of a spontaneous emotional experience, rather than the product of any structured process. Whether or not it is entirely accurate, the story has the advantage of tying the creation of the music to the time frame of the film's action, which also takes place in a single night.

Davis used the band from the Club Saint-Germain, with his compatriot Kenny Clarke on drums, and three French musicians: René Urtreger on piano, Barney Wilen on saxophone and Pierre Michelot on bass. The sustained tightness of the playing, achieved after a very small number of takes, bears witness not just to the quality of the musicians, but to the degree to which jazz was already a truly international language. The music, both the slow ballads and the up-tempo sections, appears to have been elaborated around the chord grid of 'Softly as in a morning sunrise', a jazz standard that would have been well known to all of the musicians concerned. The soundtrack of *Ascenseur pour l'échafaud* became and has remained a classic. This is especially interesting because the music offers no pretence of development or completion. It is always, clearly, music conceived in fragments, music that seems to reach back towards the image sequences that inspired it.

To the extent that he had deliberately chosen to create a thriller in the style of the American B-grade movies, Malle was simply continuing the stereotypical use of jazz as associated with criminality and sex. However, from very early in the film, the plot takes second place to other thematic strands. The deep subject of *Ascenseur pour l'échafaud* is neither in the plot nor in the psychology of the characters, but in the climate of existential desolation that permeates the images and the music. This film contributed significantly to Jeanne Moreau's emergence as a major star, largely because of the way in which Malle uses her to personify the uncertainties and foreboding shadows that he saw at the time. Although he maintains the crime thriller plot in the foreground, *Ascenseur pour l'échafaud* is full of allusions to social and political realities bleaker than anything portrayed on screen: the Algerian war, the disaffection of the young, the corrupt practices of big business, the breakdown of fundamental social cohesion. It is these things, much more than the events of a thriller, that Miles Davis's jazz translates and echoes, tapping into emotional anxieties and amplifying the symbolic power of the image sequences.

At the time he made *Ascenseur pour l'échafaud*, Malle was just twenty-four, and very much at the beginning of his artistic career. Davis was seven years older, and had already established his reputation among the very greatest of jazz musicians: he was on a par with Parker, Monk, Gillespie, Mingus, Coltrane. What he brought to Malle's film was revolutionary: instead of being simply an accompaniment or a way of building atmosphere, his music imposed itself as an independent creation that gave a new dimension to the work as a whole. As Malle described it: 'In the film, there is a kind of general tone, a kind of mood that Miles's music maintains from beginning to end and which gives the film its unity.'[16] At the outset, Malle believed that, except for the music, his film was already complete before he met Davis. In fact, through its deep emotional connection with the rhythms and emotions of the images, the music actually probes and lays open the more reflective and personal elements of Malle's work, clarifying and liberating what otherwise might have remained latent. In this sense, Davis does not add music *to* the film, he plays *with* it, as if it were another musical instrument. The final version of the film is almost like the recording of a jam session duet between jazz and cinema.

One of the key underlying elements of the film is Malle's attempt to come to terms with what he thought about America and the increasing presence of American culture in France. In choosing to create a pastiche of an American B-grade thriller, the young director was following the trend set by Melville with *Bob le flambeur* in 1955, a trend continued by Godard and Truffaut and one that picked up on French audiences' enthusiasm for this genre in the postwar years. *Ascenseur pour l'échafaud* is full of images of the Americanisation of French culture: there are glitzy bars, hyper-modern office buildings, a motel, omnipresent American cars, and pistol-carrying characters evoking a mood of violence and criminality.

Malle did not quite know whether to accept and admire this, but the prominence given to the jazz on the soundtrack demonstrates that what most inspired him in the American cultural presence was neither material progress nor a particular artistic genre, but rather the fundamental demand for artistic freedom that permeates the trumpet-playing of Miles Davis. We can infer that it was partly through the vulnerable but courageous solitude of this voice that Malle learned the power of treating film direction as an individual creative act.

Malle's subsequent output, which saw him working in Mexico, India, the United States and Britain almost as much as in France, has frequently caused critics puzzlement and frustration because of its eclecticism and unpredictability, which some have interpreted as an absence of a defined, readily recognisable style.[17] But while it has little unity of theme or genre, Malle's work is underpinned by a number of important recurrent preoccupations: a tension between alienation and belonging, between individual freedom and social responsibility, between an autobiographical impulse and the desire to document the broader sociopolitical realities of his time. As *Le Monde* put it at the time of his death, he was '. . . above all conscious of the need to confront the reality of the world, to probe the real in order to extract from it the material of his art, and to constantly reassess his own role as film-maker . . .'.[18] Malle's oeuvre reveals an ever-deepening preoccupation with the problem of how individuals can live, think, create and fulfil themselves in a society whose most fundamental structures are flawed by moral uncertainty. And these were very much the anxieties of his time.

One of the consistent criteria against which he tested his art was jazz, which remained both a lifelong love and, in some way, a measure of artistic authenticity—an anchor to the values that mattered most to him as he extended his film-making in ever new directions. Although he employed many different kinds of music on his soundtracks, there are a number of films where jazz plays a critical role, and taken as a group these 'jazz' films offer an illuminating map of Malle's whole body of work. They also illustrate the more general impact of jazz on French cinematographic culture.

*Le souffle au coeur* (1971) was a major turning point: here, for the first time, Malle undertook a film that was openly autobiographical. Up until then, while he had often given quite personal dimensions to his adaptations of literary texts,[19] it was as if he was using literature as a way of maintaining distance as well as a vehicle for experimenting with different narrative strategies. After his monumental documentary work in India in the late 1960s (*Calcutta* and *L'Inde fantôme*), which had brought him face to face with the overwhelming challenges of humanity's diversity and paradoxes, Malle looked inward and, in *Le souffle au coeur*, undertook to tell some of his own story.

Against the background of the looming French defeat in Indochina in 1954, Laurent, the youngest son of a wealthy Dijon family, undergoes the sexual awakening of adolescence in a repressive Catholic school. At this already vexed time of life, he is unsettled by the knowledge that his beautiful, carefree and immodest mother has a lover. When it is discovered that Laurent himself has a heart murmur, his mother takes him to a spa, and a reservation mix-up leads to their sharing a suite. This in turn leads to an episode of incest, which generated enormous controversy when the film was released.

With the exception of the actual incest, Malle admitted that most of this material was literally autobiographical. Laurent shares Malle's passion for jazz and literature. He reads voraciously among modern and contemporary writers—everything from Proust to Camus and Boris Vian. And as well as having spirited discussions with his school friends about the relative merits of different styles of jazz, he is shown on many occasions listening to contemporary jazz, especially Charlie Parker and Dizzy Gillespie. Jazz is the music in which Laurent can both lose himself and find himself: it is sometimes a refuge from his emotional confusion, but most often it is a medium that, almost like a religious epiphany, reveals and affirms his very identity as a person.

Laurent is troubled as an individual—to the point of thinking seriously about suicide—but part of his difficulty lies in the world in which he is trying to grow up. It is not just his family that is unstable. The priest who acts as his confessor has an obvious sexual interest in him, making a mockery of religion as any source of certainty. The frequently reported news from the war in Indochina is all about French losses, signalling the collapse of France as a colonial power; and throughout the film, the idea of nationality as a basis for identity is systematically ridiculed. On the cultural level, values are no clearer. At one point, Laurent's brothers bring him a present consisting of Proust, Tintin and Dizzy Gillespie. This gift symbolises a cultural mix every bit as startling as what the boy is encountering in the sexual world: a combination of high intellectuality and popular comic strip culture, and of French and foreign productions.

Malle also confessed his physical fascination for his own mother, and the film's ample illustration of this adolescent obsession demonstrates the degree to which the film-maker was attempting to bring his personal experience more directly into his art. The incest event is an important symbolic statement by Malle the film-maker, implying that the new level of personal engagement he was seeking to achieve had for him the force of breaking a taboo, of committing a serious transgression. *Le souffle au coeur* marked a new willingness to place what was most vulnerable in Malle's own experience at the core of his stories.

The story of an adolescent's initiation is the vehicle for the film-maker's own story of how, in order to come to terms with the important issues of his time, he first had to come to terms with himself: with his family, and with his own sensibility and experience. To be authentic, he could not separate himself from the world that he wanted to portray. Malle, in *Le souffle au coeur*, clarifies a principle of personal responsibility that becomes a constant in his subsequent work. In acknowledging the inspiration of jazz, and particularly of Charlie Parker, he was paying homage to a music in which he saw the same kind of risk-filled expression of individual and collective experience to which he aspired in his cinema.

*L*acombe Lucien (1974), like *Le souffle au coeur*, marked a new direction. This film, with its story of a young peasant boy who by a stroke of fate ends up working for the Gestapo rather than for the Resistance, which he had intended to join, brought Malle into head-on conflict with official versions of France's history in World War II. Lucien's story, based on fact and fictionalised with persuasive detail by the novelist and screenwriter Patrick Modiano, was a direct affront to those Resistance groups who, from de Gaulle to the French Communist Party, had sought to rebuild France's postwar morale by playing up their own role and playing down the extent of the nation's collaboration with Nazism. Malle was not the first to challenge this tendentious view of history, but because of its public impact, *Lacombe Lucien* signalled the real beginning of a battle for French history that would still be blazing two decades later.[20]

The music of *Lacombe Lucien* is taken from recordings of Django Reinhardt. Over the opening credits of the film we see the protagonist, who is going home to his farm during a break from his hospital orderly job, wheeling through the sunlit undulations of the southern French countryside. The accompanying jazz is the very upbeat 'Minor Swing', recorded in 1937 by the original quintet of the Hot Club de France, with Stéphane Grappelli on violin. In defiance of anachronism—the spectator is informed from the very first image that the action is taking place in the summer of 1944—Malle used the music for its optimistic colour, to underline Lucien's happiness.[21] The music is also used to convey the physical luminosity of a part of France that has been relatively untouched by the war—deceptive luminosity, to be sure, an ironical calm that precedes the violence that is about to unfold. This moment is, in a sense, Lucien's pre-war innocence, which will be lost when, on his return bicycle trip, a puncture lands him in the arms of the Gestapo and their French collaborationists.

Through the rest of the film, we hear the wartime quintet, with various clarinettists replacing Grappelli's violin. Malle selected these pieces for their moodier, gloomier tonalities, and the music is used as something that the film's characters listen to as part of their daily lives. There is, however, another dimension to the inclusion of Django Reinhardt in the film, which reinforces Malle's subversive approach to the history of the period. Through the highly emblematic figure of Django, Malle creates a sense of continuity that goes beyond the music itself. Django's career as noted earlier, begun in the 1920s, not only continued throughout the war, but also flourished for some time afterwards and became a canonical part of French cultural tradition. This unbroken line of music suggests, symbolically, that the story of Lucien also has to be taken as part of a continuity. In some ways this is obvious, but in the context of France's postwar reconstruction, the whole period of the Occupation and the Vichy government was routinely presented as a parenthesis, as something situated outside the history of the 'real' France. It was Malle's attack on this myth that got him into so much trouble, and his use of Django's jazz is integral to his critique.

But it was also central to Malle's own project, the quest for authenticity that was perhaps his greatest motivation. *Lacombe Lucien* pursues the autobiographical current that Malle had begun to explore in *Le souffle au coeur*. This time, however, he sets it in the specific historical context of World War II, which was both the time of his own childhood and, since the death of General de Gaulle, a focus for renewed national fixation on uncomfortable memories. While de Gaulle was still president (until 1969), the legend had been maintained of a French population overwhelmingly supportive of resistance against the Occupation, but with his departure, re-examinations of the war period surfaced everywhere. Malle's film was a leading example of this new consciousness. For Malle himself, *Lacombe Lucien* opened the process through which he would eventually be able to face the repressed guilt of his inadvertent childhood betrayal of a Jewish school friend, the episode that forms the climax of his 1987 film, *Au revoir les enfants*.

The prominence given to French jazz in *Lacombe Lucien* shows that it is not the mere historical authenticity of the music that is at stake in the film, but the fact that Frenchness itself is being examined as a precarious and problematic notion. Malle's gaze here is not clinical or objective: he is questioning his own identity as strongly as that of the national community. As with *L'Ascenseur* and *Le souffle au coeur*, the jazz soundtrack forms the sounding board against which he plays out his search for meaning.

P*retty Baby* (1978) was Malle's first American film, and a new departure. Although Malle had been a frequent visitor to America, there were serious risks involved for a European director trying to make a film within the American system, where directors rarely managed to maintain their artistic independence in the jostling battles between scriptwriters and producers. But Malle succeeded in making *Pretty Baby* very much as his own project. Using a story set in the whorehouse quarter of 1917 New Orleans, he sought to undertake a symbolic re-evaluation, in a directly experiential context, of his whole relationship with American culture. The film marked the beginning of Malle's 'American period', a nine-year stretch in which he would make a further half-dozen films, including two documentaries, before returning to France to make *Au revoir les enfants*.[22]

*Pretty Baby* is a film about fundamentals—the fundamental nature of Malle's fascination with America, the fundamental links between art and sex as manifestations of the creative drive—and this explains why Malle turned to the music of Jelly Roll Morton as his particular jazz reference in this work. Malle had been attracted for ten years to the idea of making a film based on the Alan Lomax recordings of Jelly Roll Morton,[23] although his personal musical interests had long since shifted from New Orleans towards modern jazz.[24] In *Pretty Baby*, Morton and his music become the symbol of a return to the source. The film opens on the plaint of a solo trumpet, sounding across the Mississippi at twilight: a clear echo of the legendary Buddy Bolden who, in the annals of jazz, stands as a sacred ancestor, whose trumpet, it was claimed, on a still night could be heard a dozen miles away.

The plot of *Pretty Baby* is based on two real-life stories that Malle melded: the professional initiation of a 12-year-old child prostitute, Violet (played by Brooke Shields), and the project of a photographer, E. J. Bellocq (Keith Carradine), to capture portraits of the working women of New Orleans. Violet, temporarily abandoned by her mother, also a prostitute, seeks refuge with Bellocq when the brothel is closed down. A deeply ambiguous relationship develops between the saucy uninhibited girl and the fussy, rather effeminate photographer, until Violet is eventually reclaimed by her mother, now turned into an honest married woman. As usual with Malle, the plot is more a vehicle than an object in its own right, and the underlying story of *Pretty Baby* is that of a pivotal moment in the history of America and the history of jazz.

The 1917 setting in New Orleans is that of the critical moment of America's entry into World War I and onto the world stage. The brothels of Storyville were closed because they represented, in the eyes of the authorities, too great a temptation for the thousands of soldiers training nearby for imminent deployment in Europe. Despite the persistent myth, it was not the closure of Storyville that *caused* the dramatic exodus and subsequent spread of the New Orleans jazzmen who would transform the future of American music. However, the historical moment was one of a veritable change in American civilisation, and it is this moment that the film portrays. The story of Violet's mother's conversion to the status of an 'honest woman' (and ultimately Violet's own redemption) symbolises America's emergence from its original chaos of opulence, energy and unselfconscious amorality, having discovered the sudden need for respectability concomitant with its new position as a world power.

In the film, the Jelly Roll Morton figure—the brothel pianist, Claude—represents the turning point in the history of jazz that saw it shift from a local to a national music. He also epitomises an art that is, in its very essence, protean. It is an art willing and able to wed itself to any circumstance that will support it—and is hence perfectly at home in the brothel. But it is also aware of its own transience, and is able to move on without looking back when the situation requires it. When the authorities close the brothel, Claude simply packs his bags and leaves. This is art as kinesis, subject to the forces of history but able to move with them. In contrast, the art of the photographer, Bellocq, comes across as a symbol of stasis. Bellocq's still images are an attempt to capture the beauty he sees amid the tawdry and abusive activities of the brothel. He is also, in a way, not just trying to seize moments of time, but to stop time altogether. This is evident both in his photography and in his relationship with Violet, whom he would like to keep forever in her little-girl-not-yet-woman state.

In the tension between the photography and the jazz, we can identify Malle's own unresolved artistic ambivalence. Bellocq represents the filmmaker's desire to portray a disappearing world, to rescue its ephemeral beauties from the turbulence and ugliness surrounding them. Malle's nostalgia is present here, too: the sense of loss of something precious, so neatly represented at the end of the film when Violet's new stepfather photographs his family with a box brownie camera, thereby consigning to oblivion in a split second all the patience, care and craftsmanship embodied in Bellocq.

**M**alle returned to France in 1986 to make *Au revoir les enfants* (1986), the hauntingly autobiographical story of the concealment, and ultimate betrayal, of Jewish children in a provincial Catholic boys' school during World War II. There is no jazz, strictly speaking, in this film, but there is one poignant sequence when, during an air raid alert, Malle's schoolboy alter ego, Julien, and his Jewish friend play a joyful and defiant boogie-woogie duet on the school piano. By association, at least, jazz remains the emblem for Malle of deep emotional experience. This was made clear in the second film made after his return, *Milou en mai* (1989), in which the filmmaker took stock of his thoughts and feelings about the land of his birth.

*Milou en mai* reconstructs a provincial view of the revolutionary events that shook France in the spring of 1968. 'May '68' has entered the national memory as a moment of great historical importance: the point at which the old order of things—represented by the towering figures of General de Gaulle in politics, André Malraux in arts and culture generally, and Jean-Paul Sartre in philosophy—was confronted and rejected by an unlikely but potent coalition of disaffected students and oppressed factory workers. A great deal of mythology has grown up around these events, sustained in adulthood by the once-young people who lived through them, and they still have strong symbolic resonance. This was even more the case when Malle made *Milou en mai*, two decades later. Malle claimed to have little interest in the political ramifications of the 1968 revolution, but was fascinated by what he saw as its 'imaginative, dreamlike side, the desire to think up a different society'.[25]

What he shows in *Milou*, however, is anything but forward-looking. Set in the dilapidated estate of an archetypal French provincial family, the film details a process of decline. Milou, the main character (played by Michel Piccoli), already well into middle age, is the one member of his generation to have remained at home, where he lives with his aged mother. The death of the mother at the beginning of the film sets in train the narrative proper: the return of the rest of the family, the revelation of savagely conflictive relationships among couples and within the family at large, and the inevitable squabble over the inheritance. It is a comedy of sordid manners, whimsically told, with Milou at the centre of a whole way of life that frays to nothing before his eyes.

This family drama is overlaid by a tragicomic portrayal of the events of May 1968, increasing the sense of dissolution. The film could easily have closed on the shot of Milou alone with his bicycle in the shadow of the hall of the empty house. Malle's choice to include a final moment in which this broken man dances, in a blissful dream, with the ghost of his mother, is a happy-ending concession to his audience that the film as a whole does not justify.

This, once again, is the typical late Malle mix of rueful realism and nostalgia. Milou dancing with his mother's ghost in a house emptied of its furniture is an analogue of Malle promenading his camera around a France rediscovered with deep affection, but found to be emptied of its substance. Like Milou, Malle is resigned rather than rebellious, but certainly he sees May 1968 as an ending, and if it is the beginning of anything new, it is not something for which he has any appetite. The bemused irony that gives the film its tone and meaning is nicely summed up in one of the frank exchanges between Milou and his forthright granddaughter, Françoise, during a discussion of the sexual revolution. She asks him: 'Grandpa, what's the Pill?' He replies: 'Progress.'

When Malle was in the process of creating Milou's character, he noted in the margin that 'Milou is Grappelli's violin'.[26] Stéphane Grappelli was eighty-two at the time of the making of *Milou en mai*, still very active as a musician, but working within a form and style that had been established many decades earlier. The music is dextrous, tuneful and inventive, but its freshness is that of an autumn breeze. Grappelli, very much like Miles Davis before him, performed his improvisations over previously shot image sequences. And to this extent Malle was reaffirming his faith in the ability of authentic artistic styles to transcend the vicissitudes of sociopolitical change. It is nonetheless impossible to escape the impression that Grappelli's violin, like the character of Milou and like Malle's whole project in the film, is directing its energies and its inventiveness to the evocation of a world that already, however regretfully, belongs to the past. The retrospectivity is reinforced by the spectator's almost inevitable memory of Grappelli's role in the Django Reinhardt music at the beginning of *Lacombe Lucien*. One might say it is doubly reinforced, because of the backward-looking nature of the earlier film. There is virtual self-quotation in the scene where Milou rides his bicycle home to the accompaniment of Grappelli's violin, just as Lucien rode home to the tune of Django's 'Minor Swing'.

Against the feeling of loss, Malle offers, through the Grappelli music and his own images, the time-defying construct of artistic inscription. This is a classical view of art, one that rejects the paradigm of progress. Grappelli's soundtrack—which includes an ironic, jazzed-up version of the 'Internationale'—is part of an integrated view of life that also takes in Milou's niece, Claire, playing Bach and Debussy on the piano, and his sister, Camille, singing Mozart. It is also a reference point that allows us to measure progress and perhaps, with Malle, to question its benefits.

Malle was aware of the Chekhovian resonances of *Milou en mai*, and he had seen Michel Piccoli's much lauded performance of *The Cherry Orchard* at the Bouffes du Nord in the early 1980s.[27] It is fitting, if not predictable, that Malle's last film, *Vanya on 42nd Street* (1994), should deal with the rehearsal by a group of New York actors of Chekhov's *Uncle Vanya*. Most of the film is devoted to a performance of the play, with its world-weary portrayal of a society in decay. This is Malle territory *par excellence*. However, the film goes beyond the play. The opening sequence is shot in the streets of New York, the camera picking out the actors from the crowd as they make their way to the run-down theatre where they are to perform; and throughout the film, intervals are created where we see the actors relaxing out of their roles, engaging with each other in free-ranging conversations about life.

It is into these interstices of 'life' (as opposed to the 'art' of the performance) that Malle introduces the jazz that leads to the film's most profound insight. The music, composed especially for the film, is played by a young contemporary quartet led by Joshua Redman, with Brad Mehldau on piano. It is used to enhance a warm homage by Malle to these actors as artists and as people. The presence of André Gregory and Wallace Shawn, the stars of *My Dinner with André* (1981), already creates a sense of family reunion. But what *Vanya on 42nd Street* reveals most illuminatingly is that it is the constantly renewed commitment of artists—the reiterated engagement of their humanity in the cause of art—that keeps alive the possibility of transforming gloom into catharsis. It is the actors' willingness to perform, and the tireless dedication to rehearsal that this entails, that allows Chekhov's work to live and that brings vitality back within the walls of the crumbling theatre. This is the film-maker seeing art as process rather than product, and that too is Malle territory.

The spectator never sees the group of musicians, but the film is a tribute to them as well, and it places them symbolically in a lineage that not only links them to the wisdom and experience of the mature actors, but also respects them as representatives of a new generation. That Malle should have given such an important, even definitive, role to a group of young jazz musicians was a poignant reaffirmation of his lifelong belief in jazz as the ultimate sign of creativity. In *Malle on Malle*, he made a statement that can be considered almost an epitaph of his whole life and work:

> In the end, I guess, my films always had a lot to do with where I was at that point in my life. I'm still very enthusiastic and excited by the medium. Film-making is incredibly difficult and contains so many elements you must keep under control. I like to think that I am getting better at mastering what I do, but there's still room for improvement. After all these years, I'm still finding out about the medium and discovering new possibilities. The longer I live, the less I trust ideas, the more I trust emotions.[28]

A jazz artist would not have expressed it differently. Malle's reputation as a dilettante and pleasure-seeker was in sharp conflict with the questioning, committed and rebellious artist that he felt himself to be. As heir to a great industrial dynasty—the Béghin sugar empire—he had a lot to put behind him in order to fulfil his artistic vocation, and in the view of many commentators, he failed in that enterprise. It would be fairer to say that his successes were intermittent and imperfect. However, by achieving in his own work a climate in which rejection of past patterns, tradition and ritual was integrated with sustained openness and curiosity towards the future and the 'other', Malle was one of the transformative influences on the culture of his day, and the role of jazz in that process was crucial.

The process of transformation can be seen even more clearly in the work of Jean-Luc Godard (born 1930), who is a much more extreme example of the personalised qualities of French cinema production. More than any other individual in contemporary French cinema, Godard is an icon of creative freedom. Across his entire body of work, only his first film, *À bout*

*Sidney Bechet, having taken up residency in France in 1949, is photographed in a bistrot near the Notre-Dame-De-Lorette Church in Paris in 1960.*

*Pianist Martial Solal (left), winner of the Jazz Academy's Django Reinhardt award, watches while Honorary President, Jean Cocteau (right), experiments on the drum kit. Paris, June 1955.*

*Martial Solal entertains the guests at the celebration of the donation of the Delaunay Collection to the National Library of France in May 1986.*

(Image Bibliothèque nationale de France, Paris)

*French free jazz musician, Michel Portal (front), performs with Henri Texier (behind) in January 1985.*

*Benny Carter (left) sits with Charles Delaunay (right) at the celebration of the donation of the Delaunay Collection to the National Library of France in Paris, May 1986.*

(Image Bibliothèque nationale de France, Paris)

*French jazz pianist Michel Petrucciani on stage at a concert in 1994 in Nevers.*

*The grave of Michel Petrucciani lies a few meters from that of Frédéric Chopin in the Père-Lachaise cemetery in Paris.*

*Joachim Kühn (left) and Ornette Coleman (centre) listen while philosopher Jacques Derrida (right) takes the stage at the La Villette Jazz Festival in July 1997.*

*de souffle* (*Breathless*, 1960) uses jazz directly in a sustained way, with a score especially composed by Martial Solal. On the other hand, his whole cinematographic aesthetic can be seen as being very close to some of the developments of jazz, particularly the music of the be-bop, post-be-bop and free jazz eras. Godard's film-making, in its own way and on its own terms, participates in the same kind of questioning of art and the role of the artist that we find expressed in the jazz experimentations of Parker, Gillespie, Monk, Coltrane and Coleman.

On every level, *À bout de souffle* served as a way for Godard to explore both his sense of America and his understanding of what cinema was about. Godard began his cinematic career as a critic and his enthusiasm for American cinema was so great that cinema, for him, virtually was the United States and vice versa. By the time of his first feature, however, that association had become complicated. He still admired American cinema, but capitalism and militarism, for which he had a growing hostility, were also associated with the United States. America was a geopolitical superpower, with a continuing presence in postwar France; it connoted freedom, but also threats to that freedom.

*À bout de souffle* is a parody of an American B-grade thriller—parody as homage rather than mockery. Nonetheless, negative allusions to the US presence in France are pervasive: it is the theft of a US army officer's car at the beginning that sets the protagonist's adventure in motion, and American cars are a motif throughout the film. The ambiguous tension between the two cultures is most potently brought to life by the relationship between Michel Poiccard (Jean-Paul Belmondo), the French gangster who models himself on Humphrey Bogart, and Patricia Francini (Jean Seberg), the American student who sells the *New York Herald-Tribune* on the Champs-Élysées. Patricia is enormously attractive to Michel, but simultaneously frustrating and perplexing, and ultimately she is the person who betrays him.

On a psychological level, Michel has doubts about Patricia, provoked by her sexual and professional confusions. Her will for independence, for personal freedom of choice and for control over her destiny is very much identified with her Americanness. Michel wants the same things, but for himself. His psychology is very much that of the traditional European male, and his mindset has little space for the complexities of a female like Patricia, whose refusal to be a traditional female is evident in her cropped hair, boyish clothes and general androgyny. That Godard should have chosen a French jazz score rather than the American jazz that his film-making colleagues were using underlines the ambivalence of his choice of genre, and the inter-cultural conflict weighing on his protagonist's romance. The use of any sort of jazz implicitly acknowledges the importance of America as a source of creativity, but Godard's choice of French jazz would seem to assert that the freedom he is expressing is his own—or at least that he wants it to be.

The way in which the jazz score is integrated into the soundtrack and into the film more generally demonstrates that Godard was seeking to reach beyond the France–America question, but not by skirting around it: rather, by going through it. On the most obvious level, music follows a romantic pattern, with different kinds of motifs associated with each of the major characters. This is an almost Wagnerian use of the leitmotif. Thus the music associated with Michel in his gangster role, and introduced over the credits, consists of portentous chords followed by a dynamic, up-beat melody. This is a turbulent, frenetic music, driven by the need for action and reflecting the excitement, confusion and violence of the gangster's world. With Patricia, the music is slower and dreamier. A change of pace and mood is established with the first images of Paris, even before we meet Patricia on the Champs-Élysées. In contrast to the extreme linearity of the 'Michel–gangster' theme, the second motif is altogether more rounded: it is softer, gentler, more reflective. It cannot be said that this music is actually supposed to represent Patricia—its sweetness does not match up very well with the edges in her character. Rather, it seems to correspond more to Michel's image of Patricia —the way he would like her to be, an evocation of a world fashioned by love and languor, of Paris as a city of romance, a refuge from the dangers of his life as a gangster.

As well as being associated with the characters, the music also draws attention to one of the underlying principles of Godard's cinematographic aesthetic: that is, the tension between continuity and discontinuity—or put differently, between narrative and a less structured, even unstructured, flow of disparate images and sounds, springing from an immediate engagement with the external world. Both themes are rendered differently at different times, and both are used to reflect the continuity–discontinuity tension. There are changes in orchestration and tempo, there are variations and improvisations, and there are startling disjunctures between the soundtrack and the images, which have a disconcerting effect on the spectator. For instance, the Michel theme, in its linearity, its forward-moving pulsion, corresponds well to the idea of rapid, event-based narrative. But at the same time, its very speed has it verging constantly on the edge of breakdown.

The Patricia theme, on the other hand, promises a different kind of narrative—one based on desire and love—but its fragmented presentation also leads to a sense of breakdown. In this respect, the music reflects what Godard does with his camera and his editing, although it doesn't necessarily accompany the images in any strict way. He uses extended uncut sequences that subvert rather than support ideas of continuity (for example, the much discussed bedroom scene), or discontinuous shots (including the famous jump cuts) that actually enhance the excitement of the narrative and hence, paradoxically, increase the feeling of continuity.

It is clear that only the most modern jazz could serve Godard's purpose. The extreme crossing of rhythms, coupled with the intricate melodic lines and the frequent tempo changes, represents the kind of eddying of contemporary life that he is also seeking to render through the construction of his image sequences. Aesthetically, in this first film, Godard's creation is very much a cinematic equivalent of be-bop and free jazz.

Whether one can speak of a direct influence of jazz on Godard is, however, debatable. While the experiments of be-bop and free jazz in their quest to probe every reach of musical and instrumental possibility are obviously important, they are only part of a broader exploration on Godard's part of what can be done with sound. There is plenty of music other than jazz in the film: Michel sings 'Buenas Noches Mi Amor' in the opening sequences; we hear Chopin on the radio in the bedroom; we hear American prairie music and western music in the cinema, and Latin-American music in the Montparnasse sequence. On their last morning together, and as an emblem of their separation, Michel and Patricia are playing a record of a Mozart clarinet concerto. And in addition to the music, there is a whole range of other sound—the bustle of the city, and especially its motor vehicles—that, in combination with the highly stylised dialogue, turns the soundtrack into a composition in its own right. (Technically, Godard shot the images of *À bout de souffle* without sound and treated the soundtrack as a separate undertaking).

In his extraordinarily prolific career, Godard has rarely used jazz again, and when he has, it appears as a music thoroughly associated with the decadence of the bourgeoisie. In *Pierrot le fou* (1965), jazz is used in the party scene near the beginning, when Ferdinand becomes so disgusted with a society entirely given over to materialist consumerism that he decides to make his break from it permanently. In *Je vous salue, Marie* (1985), jazz plays during the scene where the student, Ève, yields to her pompous professor's seduction game. It seems that jazz, for Godard, has strong associations with an Americanness with which he has become increasingly impatient. In *Éloge de l'amour* (2001), the United States is the object of a savagely satirical sequence. It is branded as a country whose inhabitants have neither identity nor culture, and who nourish themselves by feeding, like greedy vampires, on the lifeblood and memory of others. The spirit of freedom to which the young Godard had responded so enthusiastically in American cinema and music has lost its power to inspire creative dreaming.

Godard never turned his back on music. Indeed, his films offer, albeit in the collage form characteristic of his work, an almost encyclopaedic history of music in the Western tradition, from the baroque to the contemporary, and from folk forms to modern pop and rock-and-roll. Critics have often remarked that Godard, in his approach to cinema, works with his visual and sound materials in much the same way that musicians work, emphasising rhythmic and emotional characteristics rather than psychology or story-line.[29] And it is true that his work invites at least as much analogy with musical form as it does with, say, painting and poetry. The composer Antoine Duhamel, who worked with Godard on *Pierrot le fou* and *Weekend*, paid tribute to Godard's passion for music and the extreme precision of his musical knowledge.[30]

But Godard and jazz? There are areas of overlap: the importance of improvisation, the use of contrasting rhythms, and above all, the conception of cinema as an instrument of personal expression, particularly expression of anger, rebellion, and resistance to the commodification and commercialisation of life. Godard shares with the great jazz musicians the ontological difficulty of maintaining an individual identity in a fragmenting world, and the notion of art as a lifelong process of self-development and exploration. As in good jazz, Godard's film-making integrates chance not simply as a theme or an attitude, but as a structuring device that forces the work to remain open to new ideas, new experiences and new feelings. But does this comparison lead us to conclude that Godard's work owes some significant debt to jazz? Probably not, other than in the very general and rudimentary terms that he explored in *À bout de souffle*, where his efforts to forge a new cinematographic language can as readily be explained in a modernist context as by specific reference to jazz. In contrast to Louis Malle's, Godard's personal engagement with the music was a temporary one, a kind of obligatory rite of passage that he traversed with many others of his generation, something that he passed through and left behind. Not unlike Céline, Godard is an instinctive mediator of the cultural currents of his time, and it is almost by osmosis that he seems to have absorbed so much of the aesthetic of jazz into his own cinematographic work.

Paradoxically, however, as an emblematic film of the New Wave, *À bout de souffle* has become a permanent testimony to the historical intersection of jazz and cinema in France. It highlights a profound correspondence between a music born of personal freedom, pain and commitment, and France's film-making practice, which has felt an urgent need to reclaim those qualities. And to the extent that a great deal of contemporary French cinema is rooted in the values of the New Wave, one can see that the impact of jazz—as a set of aesthetic values—is an enduring one. Even though Godard's project develops in ways that outreach any useful analogies with the jazz experience, Godard's name remains a potent symbol of the dynamic creativity embodied in the conversations between jazz and the French modernist experience.

This connection was celebrated by Bertrand Tavernier in his 1986 film, *Round Midnight* (*Autour de minuit*), thus far the only real feature-length 'jazz film' to be made in France. Tavernier (born 1941) belongs to the post–New Wave generation of film-makers, and during his teenage years he participated in the jazz craze that swept through France: collecting records, reading Boris Vian's chronicles in *Jazz Hot* and haunting the nightclubs and concert halls to hear the likes of Miles Davis, Duke Ellington, Memphis Slim and the Modern Jazz Quartet.[31] He has described *Round Midnight* as the result of a long effort 'to make a totally free, genuine, and uncompromising film that would testify to my passionate love for jazz, especially be-bop'.[32]

Tavernier's passion for jazz is evident throughout the film. Much of the work is taken up with pseudo-documentary footage of jazz sessions, recorded live. It features an impressive array of important contemporary musicians, mostly African-Americans but with a few French and other Europeans, shot largely in a reconstructed setting of the Paris club of the late 1950s, the Blue Note. The fictional narrative used to draw these sequences together is meagre: it is the story of the last trip to Paris by a tenor saxophone player who is an alcoholic junkie, Dale Turner, and of the unexpected friendship that develops between him and a younger French commercial artist, Francis. Francis takes upon himself the duty of filming Dale's Paris sojourn as well as the impossible task of restoring him to health. Dale, played by eminent saxophonist Dexter Gordon, is an amalgam of the pianists Bud Powell and Lester Young. He is accompanied by a range of other musicians, who behind their fictional names reveal a collection of the best in the jazz world of the 1980s: Herbie Hancock, Ron Carter, Freddie Hubbard, John McLaughlin, Wayne Shorter, Pierre Michelot. In the course of the film, other significant musicians are evoked, especially Thelonious Monk, who wrote the title song, and the legendary Charlie Parker.

But jazz is only one dimension of *Round Midnight*, which Tavernier also uses as a basis to take up and explore, in his own way and for his own generation, some of the themes already broached by Godard, particularly the jazz–cinema–France–America nexus. Like Godard, Tavernier began his artistic life with a great deal of enthusiasm for American culture, but, also like Godard, he has shifted towards a much more critical attitude towards the United States. As a film-maker, he has been engaged—directly and, over the years, increasingly politically—in the defence of the French cinema industry against the domination of the world's screens by Hollywood. In *Round Midnight*, by characterising both jazz-making and French film-making as restorative acts, he formulates a sharp critique of America. In blunt terms, America is what puts Dale and his music to death, and France is what restores them to life.

This is illustrated in the film's New York sequence. The ironically named white entrepreneur Goodley (played by Tavernier's old friend Martin Scorsese) manages Dale as pure 'product', and conceives of his job as making sure that the product is properly packaged and delivered to the consumers in return for an appropriate amount of money. The relationship is based on values of professional competence and efficiency, and its complete lack of any human dimension is as marked as Goodley's total disregard for any artistic objectives in his management of Dale's music. This sequence is in stark, even caricatural, contrast to the deferential reception afforded to the African-American musicians in France.

It could be argued that Tavernier's portrayal of the happy life of the expatriate musicians in Paris is insufficiently self-critical. It would seem that the film-maker, here, is simply reproducing the historically received wisdom whereby black American musicians, writers and painters have always been given a warm welcome in France, valued for their work and quality as artists without any reference to their racial origin. In the same intercultural stereotype, African-Americans value France and the French as part of a liberating experience that allows them to think and create outside the oppressively racist discrimination of their homeland. Such attitudes have rightly been vigorously challenged,[33] and Lester Young himself was angrily sarcastic about the myth of France as a refuge from American racism.[34]

The caricature serves Tavernier's polemical needs, perhaps the more so because of his obvious awareness of the immense differences of scale between France and the United States, represented iconographically in the disparity of size between the towering Dale and the tiny Francis. But the friendship between Francis and Dale is also an image of a more significant cultural exchange. Dale comes to depend on Francis for his very life. What Francis, symbolically, has to offer is the beauty of a well-tended, welcoming civilisation.

Most profoundly, for Francis, the totally new sounds and rhythms of jazz allow him to rediscover the creative well-springs of his own (that is, the French) artistic tradition. It is important to stress that it is the *making* of the music, or the music-in-the-making, the live performance of jazz, that entrances him. And it is in this that we can see the inspirational link, for Tavernier, between jazz and cinema, with film-making conceived of as a kind of individual performance, the expression of an individual sensibility and vision—thus linking back to the inheritance of the New Wave and an ongoing cinematographic alternative to Hollywood.

Tavernier's portrait of Dale Turner, in this context, is a generic portrait of the artist and of the compulsion that can drive artists to subordinate and sometimes sacrifice themselves to the demands of their art. Interviewed by Ken Burns for his monumental TV series on jazz, Tavernier speculated that jazz musicians took to dope because the music was so 'demanding', requiring people to live 'on a tightrope'.[35] A similar sense of risk underlies his own film-making career.

In the end, the political pugnaciousness of *Round Midnight* gives way to a more melancholic resignation to the contingency of the human condition and the limits of art. The tragic nub of the film, in its exploration of cinema through the lens of jazz-making, is its conclusion that art can provide no lasting transcendence. And in this, Tavernier shows himself to be as much a child of Proust, or of Camus, as of Lester Young and Bud Powell. Like the narrator of *À la recherche du temps perdu* with his literary cathedral, Tavernier is forced to acknowledge that his cinematographic opus, like everything else, will be subject to the destructive erosions of time. Like Sisyphus, the artists of *Round Midnight* (Dale Turner, Francis, and Tavernier himself) have only their hill and their stone, and the destiny that forces them to invent and constantly reinvent, emptying their own substance into compositions of sound or image in an effort that will ultimately exhaust them and that can offer others only a transient sense of plenitude.

# CHAPTER 9

# NON-STOP AT LE JOCKEY
## Americans and Jazz in Paris

It is not certain that works of art have ever been expected. When they happen to be received favourably, one discovers that they were not the real object of the hospitality.
**Pascal Quignard, *Les Ombres errantes*[1]**

Exploration of the impact of jazz on French culture inevitably leads to broader reflection on the intercultural relations between France and America. In his brilliant survey *Not Like Us: How Europeans Have Loved, Hated, and Transformed American Culture Since World War II*, Richard Pells argues compellingly that there has never been a moment when the Old World and the New were not culturally intertwined, but acknowledges that deep bonds have almost always been accompanied by conflict, controversy and suspicion. Today, the negatives seem to loom larger than the positives, and cultural relations seem to be governed more by misunderstanding than by understanding. Cultural diplomacy has a longer history in France than in America, where it was developed overtly only during World War II. Since then, however, it has become an integral part of America's dominant presence in the world. Jazz itself was used for a while, after 1955, as a weapon in this cultural muscle-flexing, when the State Department sent the likes of Benny

Goodman, Louis Armstrong, Dizzy Gillespie and others on a series of European concert tours.[2]

And yet jazz retains its potential to play the role of a connector between the two cultures, both as an activity and as a symbol. The story of jazz in France is a story of how an outsider became an insider. In the history of French culture, this is not a new phenomenon—there are many similar examples of transformative influence, from the impact of the Italian Renaissance to that of German romanticism and philosophy in the nineteenth century. That jazz has been a force of similar scale, however, is itself significant. Its contributions to the renewal of art and thought have resulted not only in new forms of creation, but in an ethos of dynamism that has helped to prevent France from settling too comfortably into its centuries-old cultural traditions. The French love of jazz has also played a critical ongoing role in the elaboration and maintenance of jazz as an international language and culture. But it has done so as part of its own adaptation to the pluralisms of modern cultural identity and as part of a self-regenerative process.

At no time during this process was there any serious attempt on the part of the French to deny the essential American and African-American nature of jazz music. A few commentators anxious to defend the national integrity of French culture tried to find historical links between the new music and European and French traditions.[3] There have also been conservative and xenophobic forces in French society that interpreted jazz as a threatening invasion. Generally, however, the fundamental Americanness of jazz has not only been consistently acknowledged by French culture, but enthusiastically embraced. Between the wars, with very few exceptions—the Reinhardt–Grappelli combination is the most obvious—French jazz musicians modelled themselves on their American counterparts; French bands played American tunes and even sang American lyrics, with a sometimes delicious accent.

But it is important to stress that 'Americanness', in the development of a jazz culture in France, has almost always been perceived as something quite different and separate from the United States as a discrete sociopolitical or cultural entity. It was rather a more diffuse image of a 'new world'. And this is why James Lincoln Collier, when he berates his fellow historians for over-rating the importance of Europe (and particularly of France) to jazz in general, is missing the point.[4] He is talking about a cultural phenomenon entirely coextensive with the United States as a historical presence in the world. Americans often conflate jazz with 'America', and 'America' with freedom: Dave Brubeck, for instance, has explicitly stated that jazz, for him, is America. He went on to say that 'all over the world jazz is accepted as the music of freedom'—thus amalgamating his idea of jazz with a kind of elementary patriotism.[5] For the French, as André Hodeir put it, jazz was something else: it was an 'essence' that, once assimilated, was no longer limited by its historical origins.

No doubt, when James Europe was directing the ragtime improvisations of his military band in the concert halls of Nantes or Aix-les-Bains, there was an unavoidable association in the ears and minds of French listeners with the presence on French soil of a liberating army. And when Darius Milhaud drew on jazz for *La Création du monde*, it was surely at least in part because of his admiration for the vitality and bustling energy that he had found when visiting America. The confidence and the economic and military power of the transatlantic world exercised real fascination and magnetism in the 1920s French imagination, and jazz was part of that, along with American cinema, which was making ever greater inroads into the French theatres. The real associative power of jazz, however, was as a vehicle of freedom: freedom of personal and immediate expression for anyone with access to an instrument; freedom to dance in ways that released both men and women from social and cultural habits; and more symbolically, freedom to refashion the world. The America of jazz, as received so positively into French culture, perhaps has more in common with the mythical non-conformism of America's founding Pilgrims than with the realities of the contemporary United States. For the French, jazz was the music and the dream of possibility that echoed and re-enlivened the dreams and myths of their own long history of social and political restlessness.

The fact that jazz so readily found a welcoming home in France had as one of its important outcomes a constant flow of American—and particularly African-American—musicians to France, where their presence helped the local jazz scene to expand and evolve. The positive reception of jazz also demonstrates the significant degree to which French culture itself, for all its centuries of tradition and accumulated artistic creation, has been resilient enough and open enough to absorb some of the immensity of the jazz phenomenon. In short, the French encounter with jazz has been a kind of mutual seduction that has led to an enduring and largely happy relationship.

In the 1920s, as the jazz age was taking root in Paris, the mutually appreciative nature of this relationship was highly visible. At this time, France experienced a massive influx of American middle-class tourists: hundreds of thousands of them annually. As Levenstein points out, this was a new breed of tourist, far removed from the previous generations who had sought opportunities to explore France's prestigious culture. Those who crowded into the ocean liners bound for Europe in the 1920s had less noble motives. For the most part, they spoke no French, not even enough to order the alcoholic drinks made more attractive by the Prohibition laws that had been passed back home in 1920. They were in Paris for pleasure and fun. The cost of living was extremely low for the dollar-bearing invaders, and as well as the unchecked flow of champagne and spirits, the men could find ready sexual gratification among the city's 70 000 prostitutes. Women could do likewise with a willing throng of gigolos, and female hedonistic tourism was just as prevalent. For a decade, Paris was the ideal escape holiday. It was cheap, fast, prestigious and safe. The tourist hordes not only made nuisances of themselves in the famous cafés of Montparnasse, where the owners and waiters tolerated their clients' rowdy behaviour in the name of postwar economic recovery; they also flocked to the jazz clubs of Montmartre, where many of them encountered black jazz for the first time.[6]

The tourist bubble burst with the advent of the Great Depression, and the wave of American presence in France ebbed away to almost nothing by the late 1930s. Although the phenomenon was to some extent repeated after World War II, it must be doubted whether Paris's mass exposure to American consumerism made any long-term contribution to intercultural understanding, other than to reinforce the French stereotype of Americans as essentially barbaric, and the American view of France as fundamentally decadent. The tourists certainly had a role in jazz music's taking root in France, through their patronage of the bars, clubs and music halls where it was being played. Budding French musicians also benefited from the influx of money, as their lobby groups and unions fought for and obtained protectionist legislation to ensure that local talent was given a fair opportunity for employment.[7]

A far greater and more enduring impact came through another group, namely that 'lost generation' of American writers, painters and musicians who believed that France would provide them with a liberty of expression unavailable to them in their homeland. By the mid 1920s, 25 000 Americans had elected to take up residence in Paris: by the end of the decade this number had risen to 40 000.[8] This 'deep' Americanisation of Paris was unprecedented and would never again reach such proportions. (By comparison, from the late 1950s to the 1980s fewer than 8000 American expatriates lived in Paris.)[9] Paris was affordable for Americans, but above all, its established reputation of encouraging artistic independence made it an attractive alternative to many who found that their own country had become less welcoming to their work. Prohibition was only one symptom of what many saw as encroaching repression: Joyce's *Ulysses* was banned in America as obscene but could appear freely in Paris. Politically, the fears of the nascent communist movements in the world and the anti-Wilsonian isolationism dominating Congress militated against freedom of thought and expression.

The adventures and exploits of the American expatriates in the Paris of these years are legendary. Given the range and quality of the artists involved —composers such as Aaron Copland and Virgil Thompson, poets such as E. E. Cummings, William Carlos Williams and Ezra Pound, the sculptor Alexander Calder, the novelists William Faulkner, John Dos Passos, F. Scott Fitzgerald, Ernest Hemingway and Henry Miller—it is not hard to understand why. One must also note the importance of Paris for black writers of the Harlem Renaissance—Langston Hughes, Countee Cullen, Gwendolyn Bennett, Jessie Redmon Fauset, Claude McKay. In fact, it is virtually impossible to think of a single significant American artist of that era who did not spend formative time in France.

If Paris achieved mythical status in the minds of the American expatriates it is because, with all its dirt and leaky plumbing, it was a reality more authentic and more attractive than what they had left behind. The people who gathered around Gertrude Stein, or Sylvia Beach and her Shakespeare and Co library–bookshop, or who met in salons like those of Natalie Barney, or attended the parties of Cole and Linda Porter in their lavish rue Monsieur apartment, or ate in the restaurants and bistros scattered around Montparnasse and Saint-Germain, were full of dynamic energy and unpredictable discoveries. Metaphorically, this amazing generation of men and women was an incarnation of the jazz that they heard all around them in the streets of Paris.

The jazz music that they encountered was not necessarily the best jazz —nowhere near what was being played in cities all over the United States. The music may not even have been good. With the exception of visitors such as Bechet and Armstong, not a single great musician graced the Paris jazz scene. When Budd Freeman went there in 1928, he returned home almost immediately, having found that 'the music would be bad'.[10] Robert McAlmon, a publisher and a long-term Paris resident, described Gypsy's Bar (frequented by Joyce, Wyndham Lewis, Djuna Barnes and A. J. Liebling) as having a three-piece orchestra that 'played American jazz very badly'.[11] It would, however, be wrong to denigrate all of the jazz being played in France. Louis Mitchell was no amateur, nor was Arthur Briggs. Furthermore, some of the early French players had already established a deserved reputation by the late 1920s, and the 1930s brought the entirely original sound of Django Reinhardt and the Quintet of the Hot Club de France.

Two Americans whose lives and careers were most affected by the Paris jazz age were the photographer Man Ray (1890–1976)[12] and Josephine Baker. Their stories offer an illuminating illustration of a magical historical moment.

When Man Ray went to Paris in 1921, it was in order to seek a greater degree of freedom than he had been able to find in his native New York. Even though he had already been self-consciously active in the American avant-garde, first as a painter and then as a photographer, his encounters with Marcel Duchamp and Francis Picabia sharpened his appetite for a context in which he could radically renew his identity and his work. He loved jazz. He delighted in hanging out in the clubs where jazz was played, and rubbing shoulders with the black patrons, which was not an option in New York. Jazz was part of Paris, the same Paris where he could hear James Joyce read selections from the as yet unpublished *Ulysses* and where he could take his own photographic techniques into new artistic territory.[13] At the time of his death, Man Ray was more of a celebrity in France than in his native country, and if he did achieve lasting status as a pioneer of the American avant-garde, this could not be separated from his time in France, where he produced the great bulk of his best work. In an important way, Man Ray the *American* is a product of 'jazz-age' France.[14]

After her triumph in *La Revue Nègre* in 1925, Josephine Baker dreamed of becoming a French star. And she did. Like Ada 'Bricktop' Smith, she had her own club for a while in the late 1920s, but it was in the music halls that she consolidated her fame. She did not have much of a voice: it was light, without resonance, only just in tune, and in fact rather squeaky if surviving recordings are anything to go by. Nor was her French particularly good: despite evident efforts to master the finer points of the French vowel system, her pronounciation remained erratic at best and at worst heavily anglicised. But the audiences loved her: her enthusiasm and dramatic presence on stage set her apart. In retrospect, the success of some of her most popular songs seems ironic. 'La Petite Tonkinoise', first sung in 1906 and performed by Baker in 1930, is a piece of the silliest colonialist sentimentality that recounts the delight and pride of a young Indochinese girl whose French lover has elevated her to legitimate companionship. Scarcely less vacuous is 'Si j'étais blanche', which has a punchy jazz backing, but whose lyrics avoid any serious social or racial comment: the narrator would like to be white in order to be able to choose a wider range of finery, and at the end of the song wonders if she needs to be white to be more attractive to her man. Baker's signature tune 'J'ai deux amours' (I have two loves—my country and Paris), written for her in 1930, leaves any listener who has read her biography wondering why on earth she might have hankered for her native land, which was never kind to her. In 1936 she made a bruising attempt to return to America. She was massacred by the New York critics, and dismissed as 'just a slightly buck-toothed young negro woman whose figure might be matched in any night-club show, and whose dancing and singing might be topped practically anywhere outside of Paris'. She was also snubbed by both the white and black communities. Having become used to an environment where race was not an issue, she was shocked by the harshness of her American reception. After this, she adopted France as her permanent home, and as the core of her identity. When she died in 1975 it was as a French citizen and as a French Resistance heroine of World War II, with full military honours at her funeral.[15]

As William Shack has pointed out, Josephine Baker was not acknowl-edged by other musicians as a jazz performer, and it is true that her voice was in no way a jazz instrument. But Shack also rightly notes that Baker was the subject of a prodigious public cult. Her hairstyles and eccentricities were adulated and mimicked by the fashionable Parisian classes.[16] The direction of Baker's reputation had been set at the time of La Revue Nègre, and what-ever musicians may have thought about her singing, her dancing was received unequivocally as a jazz *phenomenon*, in its freedom and in its strongly sexualised physicality. Even today, in any discussion of the history of jazz in France, Josephine Baker's name is always in lights.

A. E. Hotchner in his biography of Ernest Hemingway recounts a late-in-life return to Montparnasse by the author of *A Moveable Feast*. Hemingway reminisced about Le Jockey: 'the best nightclub that ever was . . . Best orchestra, best drinks, a wonderful clientele, and the world's most beautiful women.' He went on:

> Was in there one night with Don Ogden Stewart and Waldo Peirce, when the place was set on fire by the most sensational woman anybody ever saw. Or ever will. Tall, coffee skin, ebony eyes, legs of paradise, a smile to end all smiles. Very hot night but she was wearing a coat of black fur, her breasts handling the fur like it was silk. She turned her eyes on me—she was dancing with the big British gunner subaltern who had brought her—but I responded to the eyes like a hypnotic and cut in on them. The subaltern tried to shoulder me out but the girl slid off him and onto me. Everything under that fur instantly communicated with me. I introduced myself and asked her name. 'Josephine Baker', she said. We danced non-stop for the rest of the night. She never took off her fur coat. Wasn't until the joint closed she told me she had nothing on underneath.[17]

This episode captures just about everything that made Paris such a fertile and liberating place for Americans. The simplest aspect of this story—a white man dancing with a black woman in a public place—so natural and uncomplicated (apart from the macho joust between the two males) would have been impossible in the America of the time. The outrageously blatant sexuality of the naked body wrapped in fur is another symbol of a freedom no doubt desired, but totally repressed in the United States. But what most deeply affected Hemingway here has less to do with Paris as a place where it is possible to escape taboos and limitations, than with something more positive: Paris as a place where wonder-provoking things can happen without being sought, and where such unanticipated happenings can turn, at least for a time, the whole of life into an extended dance.

These two Americans dancing together in Paris are not just any Americans. They are certainly not the middle-class consumer–tourists evoked by Levenstein. They are more striking even than the scandalous couple Nancy Cunard, the steamship heiress, and Henry Crowder, the black jazz pianist who was her trophy lover. Josephine Baker and Ernest Hemingway symbolically draw together the emancipative force accompanying the

African-American birth of jazz and its arrival in France, and the surge of white American creativity that characterised the work of the 'lost generation'. Arguably, it is this combination that established America as a cultural superpower after World War II.

The French–American intercultural exchange retained much of its amicability and potency during the second wave of the French jazz age. It was during World War II that New York displaced Paris as the undisputed epicentre of Western culture, and it is therefore not surprising that the American expatriate phenomenon of the interwar years did not repeat itself in Liberation France. When Chester Himes and James Baldwin took up residence in Paris, they were exceptions to the general norm. On the other hand, the enthusiasm of both black and white American musicians for France continued unabated, and the French reception of American jazz became even more ardent than it had been before the war. Well into the 1950s, French love of jazz could legitimately be conflated with a broader attraction to American cultural energy. The flow of American films into the theatres of a nation that had been largely starved of images for five years nourished a new generation of 'cinéphiles'. Many of the highly creative and entrepreneurial people who had found haven in New York during the war —scientists, artists, writers, publishers, intellectuals, political thinkers— returned with the determination to reinvest their positive experience of America in the renewal of their own social and cultural landscape.[18]

It was not a one-way process. During this same period, many Americans continued to display an almost deferent curiosity about French cultural productions. Sartrean philosophy, De Beauvoir's feminism, the challenges of the 'absurdist' work of Camus, Ionesco and Beckett, the bold techniques of French New Wave cinema—all of these things were the subject of serious discussion and debate in universities as well as in wider cultural forums. We have seen how the postwar renewal of French culture drew on the inspirations of the jazz experience. Indeed, the whole fertile transatlantic cultural exchange was infused with the spirit of jazz.

Unfortunately, those levels of shared excitement and passion no longer exist. The amicability that allowed different kinds of spontaneity and creativity to mingle and play off each other seems almost absent from the highly politicised cultural relations between France and America today. What has happened? Is it pure coincidence that the meteoric decline in the popularity of jazz since the heady days of the 1930s corresponds to the paradigm shift which has seen the United States become simultaneously the centre of consumer-capitalist ideology and a global military superpower? Ken Burns' monumental celebration of jazz, like his earlier panegyric on baseball, is a fine document, but it is redolent with nostalgia for an earlier, seemingly less complicated American way of life. Over the same period, France, in its pursuit to maintain some vestige of its former power and influence, has shut itself into a defensive and caricatural anglophobia that threatens to stifle its own creative channels.

Would it be an exaggeration to portray jazz as a common language or common cultural space in which France and America could understand and better accept each other's cultural identities? That was certainly more the case up until the 1960s than it is today.[19] Jazz was born out of the toil and pain of a subjugated people, but from its first cries, it protested its right to be different and free. As such, it had a universalism and an integrity that found ready echo in French culture's traditional celebration of diversity and of its own particularities. If the French continue to promote their own reception of jazz as something special and different from jazz cultures in other places, including other European countries, it is perhaps partly because their own need to be different is endemic. More profoundly and more paradoxically, jazz as it has been experienced and mythologised allows France to continue its cultural love affair with an America that—for the time being at least—has been eclipsed by a United States that threatens not only political but also cultural hegemony.

The complexity of this relationship was neatly illustrated in an event that occurred in 1997 at the Paris La Villette jazz festival, when the festival's major attraction, the African-American free jazz exponent Ornette Coleman, invited the philosopher Jacques Derrida to share the stage with him for an improvised jazz–text music duo. In fact, it was an anticipated happening that did not happen, not quite a fiasco perhaps, but one of those unfortunate circumstances in which symbolic expectation is thwarted by reality. The audience, or at least a small part of it, intolerant of this unaccustomed form, did not even allow Derrida to get into his stride. Those trying to shout him down were met with invective treating them as a 'shithouse audience', and the slanging match among the 1000-strong crowd finally drove Derrida off the stage, his part of the performance pathetically foreshortened and unfulfilled.[20] While the incident shows that the French jazz fans were not yet ready for such hybrid creativity,[21] the *intention* of the Coleman–Derrida performance is revealing.

Coleman and Derrida, culturally, are not only both major figures, but archetypes of controversy, whose standing has been established at least as much in the international arena as within their own communities, and perhaps more so. They are 'outsiders' who, paradoxically, have come to be seen as highly representative of the cultures they have attempted to reform. Coleman, as the principal voice of the free jazz, 'New Thing' movement, had reclaimed for jazz its territory of radical creativity. Derrida was not just France's leading revolutionary philosopher, but a thinker whose theories of deconstruction and difference had helped to redefine, globally, the parameters of epistemology in the humanities and social sciences.

By coincidence, the two men were the same age, born in 1930. More significantly, in their conversation, both defined themselves by their difference from the mainstream cultures of their respective countries, and by their choice of radical means to express their alienation. Coleman was a product of the oppressed black minority of Fort Worth, Texas, and seems to have been driven to extremes of originality by some inner force. These extremes had often led to his being considered an object of ridicule by fellow musicians and the public alike. Derrida, as an Algerian Jew, had a similar experience of exclusion, and just as Coleman had taken the well-trodden path of jazz as a form of expression and escape, completely changing the path as he did so, Derrida chose the stereotypically French path of philosophy, but also in a manner that subverted the pathway itself.

During their dialogue, Coleman recounted an anecdote in which, as a young man, he had expressed to his mother his distress about having to make his living by playing in gaming houses and brothels; her response—'Do you want to be paid for your soul?'—struck him with the power of a second baptism. From then on he had felt liberated: to make music with and for his soul, and without reference to the world of commerce and corruption. It was this incident that Derrida set at the heart of the meditation intended for his duet performance with Coleman. In doing so, he articulated, in his own medium of the spoken word, the essence of the affinity he felt with Coleman—the quest for an authenticity and uniqueness free of the trammels of power and commercialism:

Soul and the music of the soul, what is it? What does it mean? How do we recognise it, soul? Beyond all the psycho-theologico-spiritualist discourse? By the fact that it can't be sold or turned into capital pre-emptively; it's the failure of capital, it's the ultimate revolution, it's unsellable from birth, when it happens, when it's created, and when it's not calculated, and when it suddenly shifts its ground in a blast of saxotelephone of which neither the eye nor the ear had warning, even though so much work, as with Coleman, had gone into writing . . .[22]

Derrida's conviction that all individual speech acts are bound to be a form of repetition within the context of existing verbal language coincides with Coleman's belief that within the flux of musical language there is no fixed frontier between jazz improvisation and written composition. Coleman defends—with Derrida's wholehearted accord—an idea of the musical act as a form of discovery as well as of personal expression, a notion of invention that resists hierarchical distinctions between improvisation and inscription, but on the contrary highlights the dynamics of creativity inherent in the tension between composition and improvisation.

In his conversation with Derrida, Ornette Coleman expressed his impression of Paris as a particularly welcoming place:

. . . [W]hat I like in Paris, is that you can't be both a snob and a racist here, because it's not cool. Paris is the only city I know where racism never exists in your presence; it's something you hear about.[23]

Despite Derrida's quick rejoinder underscoring the realities of French racism, however concealed, it remains evident that, for Coleman and for other African-American musicians before him and since, France is experienced as a place where one's art can be practised without reference to skin colour or social oppression.

It is, of course, drawing a long bow to portray this encounter between Coleman and Derrida as a historical representation of France's relationship with jazz. On one level, these two men are simply a couple of 70-year-old revolutionaries exchanging, with the help of an interpreter, the stories of their trials and conquests. Moreover, within their respective societies, both are marginalised, and even within their areas of specialisation—jazz and philosophy—each is far from being considered as representative. The failure of their artistic encounter as a public event is a measure of the danger of positing any idealised synthesis between jazz and French culture. And yet the affinities are undeniable. Derrida's voice has established itself across the world as one important expression of a philosophy of difference: the promotion of the value of diversity in politics and social organisation as well as in culture. It is a voice of resistance to forms of globalisation based on commodification, ungoverned capitalism and market-driven economics. For his part, Coleman has created his story and his art from a different position of resistance, one that draws its strength from the broad American traditions of liberty, as well as from the history of African-American struggle against racist oppression.

The conservative reactions of an audience of so-called jazz lovers at La Villette—in reality a group entrenched in the comforts of its listening habits—provoked an interruption of intercultural dialogue mirroring the suspension of Franco-American understanding on the larger scale. On the other hand, the willingness of Derrida and Coleman to engage their creativity, their freedom and their vulnerability in an adventurous exchange signals something much greater and much more hopeful than an off-the-cuff indulgence.

For Ted Gioia, the history of jazz is at a point where 'the music's past threatens to dwarf its present'.[24] The same, alas, is true of cultural relations between France and America. The Derrida–Coleman duet underlines the difficulty of meaningful intercultural dialogue in the complex and fraught realities of today's world: we could hardly be further from the enchanting image of Hemingway dancing with Josephine Baker in Le Jockey Bar. But it is also evidence that, in the spirit of the jazz that generated it, dialogue can always begin anew—provided that there is the courage to go to the heart of things.

# Notes

## Introduction

1   5th edition, Columbia University Press, New York, 1993.

2   The soundest scholarship on this topic is provided by Merriam and Garner in 'Jazz: The Word'. The debate was already being summarised in one of the first attempted comprehensive histories of jazz, André Coeuroy's *Histoire générale du jazz: strette, hot, swing*.

3   Frank Tirro attributes the earliest sighting to the San Francisco *Bulletin* in 1913. See his *Jazz: A History*, p. 88.

4   Cited in Lomax, *Mr Jelly Roll*, pp. 62–3. Morton, in establishing his claim, made an interesting distinction between ragtime and jazz: 'Ragtime is a certain type of syncopation and only certain tunes can be played in that idea. But jazz is a style that can be applied to any type of tune. I started using the word in 1902 to show people the difference between jazz and ragtime.'

5   Born in the Greek islands to a Greek mother and an Irish father whose marriage did not survive the family's return to Ireland, Hearn was adopted out. After a Catholic education, which he detested but which gave him a solid knowledge base and strong language skills, he went to New York at the age of 19. Profoundly marked by his study of the French modernists, Hearn declared himself to be devoted 'to the worship of the Odd, the Queer, the Strange, the Exotic, the Monstrous'. (Bisland, *The Life and Letters of Lafcadio Hearn*, p. 328.)

6   Merriam and Garner, 'Jazz: The Word', p. 381.

7   Henry Edward Krehbiel would later become the long-time music editor of the *New York Tribune*. His *Afro-American Folksongs* was a seminal study, and it bears many marks of Hearn's influence. Krehbiel was also well known for the 1921 English version of Thayer's celebrated *Life of Beethoven*.

8   Bisland, *The Life and Letters of Lafcadio Hearn*, pp. 188–9.

9   Ibid., pp. 358–9.

10   Ibid., p. 336.

11   Henry Didimus, quoted in Marshall and Jean Stearns, *Jazz Dance: the Story of American Vernacular Dance*, p. 19.

12   Bechet, *Treat it Gentle*, p. 48.

13   See Blesh, *Shining Trumpets*, pp. 157–8.

14   Ibid., p. 217 ff., and passim.

15   John Hasse gives a well-documented account of these developments in *Jazz: The First Century*, pp. 15–22. See also Gioia, *The History of Jazz*, p. 45 ff.

16   Badger, *A Life in Ragtime*, p. 293.

17   Sullivan, *New World Symphonies*, p. 219.

18   See Starr, *Bamboula! The Life and Times of Louis Moreau Gottschalk*, p. 15 ff.

19   Ibid., pp. 79–96.

20   Starr rightly points out that the contemporary tendency to identify improvisation as belonging uniquely to jazz overlooks one of the main attractions of nineteenth-

century musical performance. Improvisation was a standard component of presentations by most major musicians. When they delighted their salon audiences, Chopin and Liszt—and Gottschalk—were continuing a tradition established by the likes of Mozart and Beethoven.

21　Starr, *Bamboula!*, p. 36.
22　See Russell, *Black Genius and the American Experience*, p. 14.
23　Stearns and Stearns, *Jazz Dance*, p. 22.
24　See Jordan, Jazz Changes, pp. 11–23. See also Blake, *Le Tumulte Noir*, pp. 13–23.
25　Cited by Levenstein, *Seductive Journey*, p. 341, note 65.
26　For valuable coverage of the creation of *Parade*, see Roger Shattuck's classic, *The Banquet Years: The Origins of the Avant-Garde in France 1885 to World War I*, pp. 151–8.
27　*Jazz Hot: Revue du Hot Club de France* (octobre 1945), no. 1 (nouvelle série).
28　Collier, *The Reception of Jazz in America: A New View*.
29　Ibid., p. 77.
30　Ansermet, 'Sur un orchestre nègre', pp. 171–8. This article is discussed in Chapter 1.
31　Goffin's works are discussed in Chapter 2.
32　Particularly notable was the work of Daniel Filipacchi and Frank Ténot, who launched *Jazz Magazine* in December 1954 and were equally responsible for organising major jazz concerts and expanding the radio space of jazz that had been established by the American Sim Copans. See Ludovic Tournès, *New Orleans sur Seine*, pp. 138–40 and 154–66.
33　In his summary of the 'Jazz in French Culture' colloquium held in Seysses, France, 29 July–1 August 2003.
34　Stovall, *Paris Noir: African Americans in the City of Light*. See also the posthumously published work by William A. Shack: *Harlem in Montmartre: A Paris Jazz Story between the Great Wars*.
35　Blake, *Le Tumulte Noir*.
36　Tournès, *New Orleans sur Seine*.
37　Jackson, *Making Jazz French: Music and Modern Life in Inter-war Paris*.
38　Ibid., p. 14.

## Chapter 1: A Different Music

1　Cited in Badger, *A Life in Ragtime: A Biography of James Reese Europe*, p. 195.
2　See, for example, Little, *From Harlem to the Rhine*, pp. 126–35; Collier, *The Making of Jazz*, pp. 314–15; Stovall, *Paris Noir*, pp. 10–23; Kenney, '*Le Hot*: the Assimilation of American Jazz in France, 1917–1940', pp. 5–6; Badger, *A Life in Ragtime*, pp. 165–71; Shack, *Harlem in Montmartre*, pp. 11–25; Jackson, *Making Jazz French*, p. 17. The French historian Gérard Conte appears for his part to have largely followed the Americans: 'Jim Europe et les Hellfighters', *Le Jazz Hot*, octobre 1968, pp. 8–9.
3　Badger, *A Life in Ragtime*, pp. 191, 305, 313.

4   See Nouailhat, *Les Américains à Nantes et Saint-Nazaire 1917-1919*, pp. 38–44.

5   This account draws largely on material extracted and collated from Little, Stovall, Badger and Shack.

6   There was widespread celebration of Lincoln's birthday across the places in France where American troops were quartered. See the *New York Herald* (European Edition), 13 February 1918, p. 4.

7   Nouailhat, *Les Américains à Nantes et Saint-Nazaire 1917-1919*, pp. 178–80.

8   Little, *From Harlem to the Rhine*, p. 128.

9   Stovall, *Paris Noir*, pp. xiii–xiv. Jeffrey Jackson shares this view: *Making Jazz French*, p. 17.

10  Badger, *A Life in Ragtime*, p. 167.

11  Conte ('Jim Europe et les Hellfighters') regretted being unable to find 'a single pertinent document concerning this tour which is without doubt the very first in the history of jazz in France'. He believed that there might be interesting information in provincial daily newspapers, but until now no one appears to have followed up on this idea.

12  The announced program was as follows: *Première partie*. 1. Marche 'Sambre et Meuse' (Goudet); 2. Stars and Stripes (Souzat [*sic*]); 3. Indian chant (Ganne); 4. Negromance (Europe); 5. Songs of the South, par l'orchestre; 6. Plantation Echoes; 7. Songs, New York Inf., quintette; 8. Echoes of old Broadway (Kern), Sergeant Noble Sissle; 9. March Clef Club (Europe) orchestre. *Deuxième partie*. 1. Marche 'American Expeditionary' (Mikell); 2. Ouverture 'Morning-Normand Night' (Soupe); 3. Negro Oddities, par l'orchestre; 4. Cornet solo 'Old Kentucky Home', le quintette; 5. Santa Lucia by Sextette (Verdi); 6. Songs: Jeanne d'Arc, Camp Heiling Day (Mikell); 7. Drum Dult Oyon Drumer [*sic*] (Herbert-Stephen-Wright), Sergeant de Broit; 8. Marseillaise, Star Spangled Banner, par l'orchestre. According to Sissle (Badger, p. 167), the concert also included, at its climax, the 'Memphis Blues'.

13  *Le Populaire*, lundi 11 février 1918, p. 2.

14  *Le Populaire*, mercredi 13 février 1918, p. 2.

15  Ibid.

16  Ibid.

17  Ibid.

18  Ibid.

19  Ibid.

20  *Le Phare de la Loire*, mercredi 13 février 1918, p. 3.

21  Some evocative newsreel footage of dancing by Europe's band members has been preserved in Jean-Christophe Averty's *Jazzband: une histoire du jazz français*, with Pierre Bouteiller: Three-part television series for France 3 and Canal+, 1993, Part 1: 1917–1940.

22  Much of this music has been reissued on 'Lieut. Jim Europe's 369th US Infantry "Hell Fighters" Band: The Complete Recordings', Memphis Archives MA7020, 1996; 'James Reese Europe featuring Noble Sissle', IAJRC Records, 1012, 1996.

23    Badger, *A Life in Ragtime*, p. 195.
24    Quoted by Badger, pp. 193–4.
25    Tim Gracyk, in the liner notes of 'Lt. Jim Europe's 369th U.S. Infantry "Hellfighters" Band: The Complete Recordings', classifies Europe as 'a significant pre-jazz artist, a transitional figure'.
26    Badger, *A Life in Ragtime*, p. 9.
27    The title is borrowed from a contemporary account of the impact of the New York Infantry Band.
28    Badger, *A Life in Ragtime*, p. 196.
29    See Nouailhat, *Les Américains à Nantes et Saint-Nazaire 1917-1919*, p. 133 ff., 201–16. Cf. Stovall, *Paris Noir*, p. 18.
30    Ibid., passim. Also Badger, *A Life in Ragtime*, p. 212.
31    *Le Journal d'Aix-les-Bains*, samedi 23 février 1918. Also *L'Avenir d'Aix-les-Bains*, 23 février 1918.
32    *L'Avenir d'Aix-les-bains*, 23 février 1918, p. 1.
33    *Le Patriote républicain*, samedi 2 mars 1918, p. 1.
34    Thus it is not surprising that the *New York Herald*'s report of the American arrival in Aix should give prominence to Europe and his band, declaring: 'If you ever danced all night to the music of Europe's players, you will not wonder that the soldiers marched untiringly a good part of the morning. There's one thing certain, even if Aix is not the musical center of Europe, Europe is the musical center of Aix from this morning on.' (17 February 1918, p. 1).
35    *Le Petit Savoyard*, 9 mars 1918, p. 2.
36    *The New York Herald* (European Edition), 25 and 26 August 1918.
37    Jazz was also performed by the band of the 329th Regiment, and by a group from the Casino de Paris. The latter was no doubt Louis Mitchell's Jazz Kings.
38    *Le Temps*, 26 août 1918, back page.
39    See Badger, *A Life in Ragtime*, pp. 214–15.
40    Tournès, *New Orleans sur Seine*, pp. 14–16. For more on Mitchell, see Shack, *Harlem in Montmartre*, pp. 4–5 and passim.
41    Ward and Burns, *Jazz: A History of America's Music*, p. 72.
42    Rye, 'The Southern Syncopated Orchestra', pp. 217–32, passim. See also Blake, *Le Tumulte noir*, pp. 63–5.
43    The article has been reprinted in Ansermet, *Écrits sur la musique*.
44    Jackson has a good discussion of the issue: *Making Jazz French*, p. 25 ff.
45    Interview quoted in Mouly, *Sidney Bechet: notre ami*, p. 43.

**Chapter 2: Settling In**
1    Levenstein, *Seductive Journey*, p. 275.
2    For an insightful history of Montmartre as a cultural landscape, see Hewitt, 'The Changing Landscape of Montmartre'. See also Jackson, *Making Jazz French*.
3    See Shack, *Harlem in Montmartre*.
4    Goddard, *Jazz Away from Home*, p. 16; Stovall, *Paris Noir*, p. 47.

5   See Hansen, *Expatriate Paris*, p. 268.

6   Stovall, *Paris Noir*, p. 38. Cf. Goddard, *Jazz Away from Home*, pp. 19–20.

7   Stovall, *Paris Noir*, pp. 39, 46.

8   Wiéner, *Allegro appassionato*, p. 43. See also Martin and Roueff, *La France du jazz*, p. 36.

9   Panassié, *Douze années de jazz*, p. 11.

10  'Jazz à deux pianos', quoted in Wiéner, *Allegro appassionato*, p. 109. For Roland-Manuel, see Martin and Roueff, *La France du jazz*, p. 196.

11  Jackson, *Making Jazz French*, p. 120.

12  Désormière, 'Une séance de musique moderne', *Courrier musical*, 1 janvier 1922, p. 18.

13  Wiéner, *Allegro appassionato*, p. 106.

14  Louis Vuillemin, 'Concerts métèques . . .', cited in Wiéner, *Allegro appassionato*, pp. 66–7. Vuillemin's racist title, 'les métèques', is used pejoratively to describe the Jewish Wiéner and his fellow musicians as 'half-breeds'.

15  Ibid., pp. 67–8.

16  For a discussion of some of the very early French bands that sought to imitate jazz, see Hélian, *Les grands orchestres de music-hall en France*, p. 30 ff. Cf. also Jackson, *Making Jazz French*, pp. 20–1.

17  Louis-Victor Mialy, 'Le légendaire Léo Vauchant vous parle', *Jazz Hot* (décembre 1969) no. 256, pp. 26–8.

18  Kenney, '*Le Hot*: the Assimilation of American Jazz in France, 1917-1940', p. 10.

19  Delaunay, *Delaunay's dilemma*, p. 52.

20  Jordan reports on weekly program guides in *L'Antenne* and *Radio Magazine* (Jordan, *Jazz Changes*, p. 139). See also Jackson, *Making Jazz French*, pp. 49–51, 151.

21  Ward and Burns, *Jazz: A History of America's Music*, pp. 73–4.

22  Cf. ibid. p. 106.

23  Klein, 'La Revue Nègre', pp. 366–8.

24  André Davon, 'Bonjour Josephine', *Nouvelles littéraires*, 28 mai 1959, p. 1.

25  Ibid., p. 10.

26  Well documented by Jordan, *Jazz Changes*, pp. 150–1.

27  See Hansen, *Expatriate Paris*, p. 216.

28  Cited in Hansen, *Expatriate Paris*, p. 217.

29  Klein, 'La Revue Nègre', p. 369.

30  Cf. Ward and Burns, *Jazz: A History of America's Music*, p. 156.

31  Daven, 'Bonjour Joséphine', p. 10.

32  Tournès, *New Orleans sur Seine*, p. 25.

33  Blake, *Le Tumulte Noir*, p. 94.

34  Levinson, 'Paris ou New York', p. 2.

35  Klein, 'La Revue Nègre', p. 373.

36  This is discussed further in Chapter 5.

37  Cf. Ward and Burns, *Jazz: A History of America's Music*, p. 157. See also Bechet, *Treat it Gentle* and Mouly, *Sidney Bechet, notre ami*.

38  Delong, *Pops: Paul Whiteman, King of Jazz*, p. 68.

39  Ibid.

40  McCarthy, *The Dance Band Era*, pp. 96–7. Also, Brierre, *Le jazz français de 1900 à aujourd'hui*, p. 21.

41  The name was spelled 'Grappelly' until about 1960.

42  Brierre, *Le jazz français*, p. 21 ff. Also Tournès, *New Orleans sur Seine*, pp. 26–9.

43  Jean-Christophe Averty (with Pierre Bouteiller): *Jazzband: une histoire du jazz français*, three-part television series for France 3 and Canal+, 1993, Part 1: 1917–1940.

44  Goddard, *Jazz Away from Home*, p. 138. The others are Philippe Brun, Alix Combelle and Django Reinhardt.

45  Louis-Victor Mialy, 'Le légendaire Léo Vauchant vous parle', p. 23.

46  Ibid.

47  This is the line of inquiry pursued in the second part of this book.

48  See 'Main d'oeuvre étrangère', *Jazz Tango* (novembre 1930), no. 2, p. 3.

49  Huddleston, *Paris Salons, Cafés, Studios*, p. 18.

50  Jeffrey H. Jackson gives a good account of resistance to jazz in 'Making Enemies: Jazz in Inter-war Paris', p. 199. These ideas are more widely developed in his book, *Making Jazz French*.

51  Panassié, *Douze années de jazz*, pp. 55–78. See also Delaunay, *Delaunay's Dilemma*, p. 68.

52  In this article, published in *Le Disque vert* in 1920, Goffin praised the ability of jazz to cut through conventional attitudes to music and to stimulate the feelings and senses directly. See also Goddard, *Jazz Away from Home*, p. 59 ff.

53  Tournès, *New Orleans sur Seine*, passim, provides interesting analysis of the connection he sees between Panassié's right-wing ideological leanings and his inability to appreciate jazz beyond the traditional form that it reached in the Chicago era.

54  Panassié, *Douze années de jazz*, pp. 95–106. See also Delaunay, *Delaunay's Dilemma*, pp. 60–7; Tournès, *New Orleans sur Seine*, pp. 40–50; and Jackson, *Making Jazz French*, pp. 159–90.

55  Tournès, *New Orleans sur Seine*, p. 47 and passim.

56  See Jordan, Jazz Changes, p. 266 ff.

57  Alexandre Stavisky was a high-profile confidence trickster whose frauds involved very large amounts of money and significant police and government figures. The mystery and suspicion surrounding his supposed suicide triggered widespread unrest. The protest marches by right-wing groups on the French Parliament on 6 February 1934, during which numerous people were killed and wounded, led to further riots in subsequent days and months.

58  *La revue musicale* (mars 1931), cited by Panassié in *Douze années de jazz*, pp. 66–7.

59  Panassié, *Douze années de jazz*, pp. 214–15.

60 Stéphane Mougin, 'Après Duke Ellington', *Jazz-Tango Dancing 36* (septembre 1933), p. 3.

61 This account of Django Reinhardt's childhood is drawn largely from Delaunay, *Django mon frère*, pp. 33–4.

62 Tournès, *New Orleans sur Seine*, p. 48.

63 Delaunay, *Django mon frère*. Cf. also Delaunay, *Delaunay's Dilemma*, pp. 101–3, and Panassié, *Douze années de jazz*, p. 139 ff.

64 Pesquinne, 'De l'improvisation dans le jazz', pp. 177–88; and 'Le blues, la musique nègre des villes', pp. 273–82.

65 Désormière, 'Une séance de musique moderne', *Courrier musical*, 1 janvier 1922, p. 18.

66 Pesquinne, 'Le blues, la musique nègre des villes'.

67 Coeuroy, *Histoire générale du jazz*, pp. 118–19.

## Chapter 3: Revival and Revolution

1 Vian, *Jazz in Paris*, p. 98.

2 Charles Delaunay, *Django mon frère*, pp. 97–8.

3 Tournès, *New Orleans sur Seine*, p. 61. Lewis had come to France with Noble Sissle. He eventually returned to the United States, undertook study at the State University of Vermont, and in 1970 wrote a thesis, in French, on Proust and music. Cf. Delaunay, *Delaunay's Dilemma*, pp. 75–6.

4 Tournès, *New Orleans sur Seine*.

5 Ibid., p. 87.

6 In the wake of the Allied invasion of North Africa (November 1942) and the capitulation at Stalingrad (February 1943), German regulation of life in occupied Paris toughened substantially. All public dancing was banned.

7 Tournès, *New Orleans sur Seine*, p. 88. See Jordan, Jazz Changes, p. 343 and passim. Rebatet, as early as 1930, had revealed himself to be something of a jazz fan, although he despised black jazz musicians. For instance, he attacks Armstrong's 'naïve and impoverished anarchy' and praises the sober humour of Ted Lewis. Cited in Panassié, *Douze années de jazz*, p. 67.

8 Delaunay, *Django mon frère*, pp. 182–9.

9 Ibid., pp. 114, 115.

10 Ibid., p. 114.

11 Coeuroy, *Histoire générale du jazz*, p. 195.

12 Delaunay, *Delaunay's Dilemma*, p. 150.

13 Tournès, *New Orleans sur Seine*, pp. 63–71.

14 Delaunay, *Delaunay's Dilemma*, pp. 150–1. This practice was notably followed on Django Reinhardt's recordings and on radio.

15 Information kindly provided by Anne Legrand, curator of the Fonds Delaunay at the Bibliothèque de France.

16 The word *zazou* was coined in 1938 by the singer Johnny Hess, who had picked it out of the scat singing of the visiting Cab Calloway. In his 'Je suis swing', it

was part of the catchy refrain: *Je suis swing, je suis swing/Zazou, zazou, c'est gentil comme tout.*

17   See for example, Halls, *Politics, Society and Christianity in Vichy France*, pp. 287, 307.

18   See Tournès, *New Orleans sur Seine*, p. 89. The yellow star was imposed in May 1942 and it provoked considerable resistance among young people. In many French cities, people took to wearing yellow insignia of various kinds inscribed with ironic words such as 'Auvergnat' or 'Goy'. The 'jazz' and 'zazou' stars are part of this broader movement of resistance to what many felt to be a shameful act. See Marrus and Paxton, *Vichy et les juifs*, pp. 222–3.

19   Coeuroy, *Histoire générale du jazz*, pp. 220–1.

20   Ibid., p. 24.

21   Cf. Delaunay, *Django mon frère*, p. 122 ff.

22   Cited by Noël Arnaud in *Les vies parallèles de Boris Vian*, special number of *Bizarre*, 39–40 (1966), p. 36.

23   Cazalis, *Mémoires d'une Anne*, p. 78.

24   Vian, *Autres écrits sur le jazz*, p. 55.

25   'Will I be alone in telling future generations that IT never existed? That no existence preceded its mythical essence and that certain myths are like mayonnaise in restaurants with unbeatable prices: the fewer the eggs, the more it rises.' (Cau, *Croquis de mémoire*, p. 48).

26   Cazalis, *Mémoires d'une Anne*, p. 84.

27   *Samedi Soir*, 25 octobre 1947, p. 9.

28   Delaunay, *Delaunay's Dilemma*, pp. 165–6.

29   Ibid.

30   Jordan, Jazz Changes, p. 414.

31   Paris: Errol Buckner, 1948.

32   Dorigné, *La guerre du jazz*, p. 28.

33   Ibid., p. 123 ff.

34   Ibid., p. 78.

35   Ibid., p. 16.

36   See Tournès, *New Orleans sur Seine*, pp. 124–6.

37   *Jazz Hot* (juin-juillet 1937), no. 18, pp. 3–4.

38   Delaunay, *Delaunay's Dilemma*, p. 171.

39   Vian, *Autres écrits de jazz*, pp. 242–3.

40   See *L'Aurore*, 21 février 1948, p. 2.

41   In a 'cutting' competition, musicians try to demonstrate their superiority by playing longer, louder, more imaginatively, etc. The term dates back to the very beginnings of jazz.

42   Recounted in Billard, *Louis Malle: le rebelle solitaire*, pp. 87–8.

43   Tournès, *New Orleans sur Seine*, pp. 129–32. The fair was held twice more, in 1952 and 1954. Despite increased popular success (up to 90 000 people attended the last one), the costs proved too great for the organisers, who were obliged to abandon the idea.

44    See Stovall, *Paris Noir*, p. 155.

45    Mouly, *Sidney Bechet, notre ami*, p. 97.

46    Jacques Nosari, 'Bousculade à l'Olympia pour Sydney [*sic*] Bechet', *Le Figaro*, 20 octobre 1955, p. 4.

47    *Le Monde*, 21 octobre 1955, p. 8.

48    Tournès, *New Orleans sur Seine*, p. 287.

49    See the list established by Hippenmeyer, *Jazz sur films*, which includes documentaries not mentioned by Tournès: *Jazz Jamboree, Piédalu député* (1953); *L'Inspecteur connaît la musique, Blues, Série noire, Un ange comme ça* (1955); *Ah! Quelle équipe!* (1956).

50    See Brierre, *Le Jazz français de 1900 à aujourd'hui*, pp. 65–6; also Tournès, *New Orleans sur Seine*, pp. 255–6.

51    Gréco, *Jujube*, p. 132.

52    Stovall, *Paris Noir*, p. xiv. Stovall is rightly sceptical about France's good reputation in matters of race, and there are various anecdotes of unhappy experiences, including that of Lester Young, reported by Postif in *Les grands interviews de Jazz Hot*, pp. 183–4. But however problematic the stereotypical perceptions, they were very widely shared.

53    Delaunay, *Delaunay's Dilemma*, Preface.

54    See Tournès, *New Orleans sur Seine*, pp. 376–8.

55    Stovall, *Paris Noir*, p. 213.

56    Tournès (*New Orleans sur Seine*, pp. 460–4) provides very useful statistics for concerts given by American and French musicians, both separately and mixed, and they show that the degree of collaboration reached its peak in the mid 1950s. There was a similar pattern for recordings on the Vogue label.

57    This story is reconstructed principally from the Miles Davis and Juliette Gréco autobiographies, together with some supplementary sources: Davis, with Quincy Troupe, *Miles: The Autobiography*; Gréco, *Jujube*.

58    2 août 1947, p. 9.

59    Davis, *Miles: The Autobiography*, pp. 126–31.

60    There is an extended discussion of this music in Chapter 7 on jazz and cinema.

61    Davis, *Miles: The Autobiography*, p. 218.


**Chapter 4: French Jazz Comes of Age**

1    Michel Petrucciani, as quoted in *Jazz Magazine* (février 1989), no. 489, p. 5.

2    Ken Burns, *Jazz* (TV series, 2001), no. 8.

3    See, e.g., Gioia, *The History of Jazz*, p. 141 ff.

4    This attack on the racist Governor of Arkansas led to Columbia Records' refusal to publish a version containing the lyrics, which Mingus promptly issued on another label.

5    Tournès, *New Orleans sur Seine*, pp. 383–5. Also Brierre, *Le jazz français de 1900 à aujourd'hui*, p. 161.

6    Brierre, *Le jazz français de 1900 à aujourd'hui*, p. 161.

7    Tournès, *New Orleans sur Seine*, p. 381.

8    Ibid., pp. 243–4.

9    Brierre, *Le jazz français de 1900 à aujourd'hui*, p. 130.

10   Ibid., pp. 125–9.

11   Hodeir's major works include: *Introduction à la musique de jazz* (1948); *Hommes et problèmes du jazz* (1954); *Toward Jazz* (1962); *Les mondes du jazz* (1970). The English translation of *Hommes et problèmes du jazz* (*Jazz: its Evolution and Essence*) is recognised as having had an important influence on jazz criticism in America.

12   This is a viewpoint shared by Tournès, *New Orleans sur Seine*, pp. 263–83.

13   Martial Solal, 'Solal par Solal', *Jazz Magazine*, (novembre 1998), pp. 34–6.

14   Ibid.

15   *Jazz Magazine*, (octobre 1998), pp. 32–5.

16   Cited in Yves Buin, 'Michel Portal: un choix courageux', *Jazz Hot* (mars 1966), p. 18.

17   Ibid.

18   Cited in Buin, 'Michel Portal: un choix courageux', p. 19.

19   Tournès, *New Orleans sur Seine*, pp. 401–2. Jean Georgakarakos had some success in this respect, with the creation of the record label BYG in 1969, through which he issued performances of a score of free jazz artists, both American and French.

20   See Brierre, *Le jazz français de 1900 à aujourd'hui*, pp. 137–8.

21   Using onomatopoeic word-plays in French both to imitate musical instruments along the lines of famous jazz solos and simultaneously to construct stories, the Double-Six had a period of international fame from 1960 to 1965.

22   Tournès, *New Orleans sur Seine*, p. 417.

23   Ibid., pp. 418–21; Brierre, *Le jazz français de 1900 à aujourd'hui*, pp. 149–52.

24   Félix W. Sportis, 'Delaunay's Dynasty' (Interview with Delaunay's sons Jean-Louis and Eric), *Jazz Hot* (mai 1993), p. 13.

25   Reported in the special feature on Petrucciani in *Jazz Magazine* (février 1999), pp. 3–13.


## Chapter 5: Folk Hot or Modern Cool?

1    Goffin, *Aux frontières du jazz*, pp. 23–4.

2    One of the best evocations of the vitality of this period remains Roger Shattuck's *The Banquet Years*. The whole era that separated the Franco-Prussian War (1870–71) from the beginning of World War I was one of prodigious social and political change. France, having discarded the authoritarianism of Napoleon III, enthusiastically (albeit sometimes haltingly) accustomed itself to the ways of democracy. The French colonial empire was at its height, and the French presence in the Pacific, Indochina, Africa and the Middle East meant not only an important role on the world stage, but also a constant flow of artefacts and

knowledge of many exotic cultures. The colonial dimension was critical to the modernist experience.

3   It remains difficult to confine the 'Belle Époque' to a precise period. Jean-Baptiste Duroselle (*La France de la "Belle Époque"*) limits it to the 1900–1914 period. Not infrequently, the term is used to cover the whole time between the inception of the Third Republic to World War I.

4   Among the more persuasive contributors to these discussions are Kern, *The Culture of Time and Space 1880-1918*; Karl, *Modern and Modernism: The Sovereignty of the Artist 1885-1925*; Berman, *Preface to Modernism*; Sowerwine, *France Since 1870: Culture, Politics and Society*; and Danius, *The Senses of Modernism: Technology, Perception and Aesthetics*.

5   Papal infallibility was declared in 1870 by the first Vatican Council, under Pope Pius IX.

6   See Kern, *The Culture of Time and Space 1880-1918* for a brilliant analysis of these changes.

7   Karl (*Modern and Modernism*, p. xvi) rightly points out that fears of modernism were intrinsic to its development.

8   This was the first of several 'world fairs' or 'universal exhibitions' held in Paris. Others took place in 1867, 1878, 1889 (the Eiffel Tower year), 1900 and 1937.

9   Baudelaire, *Oeuvres*, p. 693.

10  See Dewitte, *Les mouvements nègres en France 1919-1939*, p. 253.

11  Jody Blake documents these practices in *Le Tumulte Noir: Modernist Art and Popular Entertainment in Jazz-Age Paris, 1900-1930*, pp. 23–35.

12  Gobineau's *Essai sur l'inégalité des races humaines* was published in the mid 1850s; Drumont's book appeared in 1886.

13  Louis Ferdinand Céline, *Death on the Instalment Plan*, tr. Ralph Manheim, New Directions, New York, 1971, p. 82.

14  Dewitte, *Les mouvements nègres en France 1919-1939*, pp. 144–5, 246. Cf. also Clifford, *The Predicament of Culture*, p. 136.

15  Dewitte, *Les mouvements nègres en France 1919-1939*, pp. 25–47.

16  Ibid., pp. 74–5.

17  Aragon, *Aurélien*, p. 30. *Aurélien* is a fresco of Parisian upper-class life in the early 1920s with an epilogue set during the 'débâcle' of 1940.

18  Dewitte, *Les mouvements nègres en France 1919-1939*, p. 222 ff. In the late 1920s, the Bal Nègre of the rue Blomet was especially modish. See Berliner, 'Dancing Dangerously', pp. 59–75.

19  Cited by Dewitte, *Les mouvements nègres en France 1919-1939*, p. 241: '(L)'art nègre est le sperme vivificateur de l'Occident'. *La Dépêche africaine*, no. 17 '15 octobre 1929'.

20  Fréjaville, *Au Music-Hall*, Chapter 1, passim.

21  See Duvau, 'Music-Hall 1900', in Académie du cirque et du music-hall, *Histoire du music-hall*, p. 91.

22    A 'pétomane', or 'fartiste', is a professional entertainer who uses flatulence as his chief means of expression. There were several famous ones who made a good living in the music halls, the first and best-known being Joseph Pujol (1857–1945).

23    Jeffrey Jackson gives an insightful analysis of the economic and commercial factors at work in the implantation of jazz through music hall culture. See *Making Jazz French*, p. 35 ff.

24    Bernanos, *Le crépuscule des vieux*, p. 66.

25    *L'Esprit nouveau et les poètes* (1917).

26    Jean Cocteau, quoted in Criel, *Swing*, Preface.

27    Cocteau, *Le Coq et l'Arlequin*, p. 54.

28    Huddleston, *Paris Salons, Cafés, Studios*, p. 20.

29    Cocteau, Le Coq et l'Arlequin, p. 63.

30    Wiéner, *Allégro appassionato*, p. 47.

31    Cf. Criel, *Swing*, presentation pages.

32    Darius Milhaud, 'Impressions d'Amérique', *Le Courrier musical*, 'mars 1923', p. 115.

33    Maurice Ravel in *Contemporary Music*, quoted in Goddard, *Jazz away from Home*, p. 130.

34    Cf. Le Boterf, *Harry Baur*, p. 60 ff.

35    *Jazz: l'actualité intellectuelle*, no. 1, 1928.

36    See Jordan, '*Amphibiologie*: Ethnographic Surrealism in French Discourse on Jazz'; also Stovall, *Paris Noir*, p. 42 ff.

37    Berliner, 'Dancing Dangerously'.

38    Soupault, *Le nègre*, p. 163.

39    Tournès, *New Orleans sur Seine*, p. 30.

40    *Documents* ran from April 1929 to August 1930. There were 15 numbers in all.

41    *Documents* 4, septembre 1929, pp. 221–5.

42    Leiris, 'Civilisation', *Documents* 4, pp. 221–2. Cf. also Jordan, who gives an insightful account of Leiris's interest in jazz: '*Amphibiologie*', pp. 172–8.

43    In 1931, Leiris participated as 'secretary–archivist' for the Dakar–Djibouti expedition, which collected vast amounts of ethnographic material. See Clifford, *The Predicament of Culture*, pp. 136–8, 165–74.

44    Leiris, 'Saints noirs', in *Zébrage*, pp. 21–2.

45    Leiris, *L'âge d'homme*, pp. 161–2.

46    Ibid., p. 161.

47    See, for instance, Aragon, *Aurélien*, pp. 80–8, 245–56, 414–31.

48    *Le Phare de Neuilly*, [1933] no. 1, p. 72.

49    Ibid., [1933] no. 2, p. 88.

50    Ibid., no. 1, p. 72.

51    Criel, *Swing*.

52    Ibid., p. 19.

53    Jeffrey H. Jackson cites among them Gustave Fréjaville, Jacques Janin, André Mauprey, Georges Pioch and René Wisner—all writers who in one way or

another evoke jazz as a civilisation-destroying force. 'Making enemies: jazz in inter-war Paris', pp. 192–4.

54   Huddleston, *Back to Montparnasse*, p. 286.
55   See Mauclair, *Mallarmé chez lui*, passim.
56   Jackson ('Making enemies') makes this point particularly well.
57   Quoted by Coeuroy, *Histoire générale du jazz: strette, hot, swing*, p. 8.
58   Matthew F. Jordan gives an excellent array of examples in his Jazz Changes, p. 69 ff.
59   Ibid., pp. 79–83.
60   André Hoérée, 'Le jazz', in *Revue musicale*, octobre 1927, p. 237.
61   André Schaeffner, 'Réflexions sur la musique: le jazz', in *Revue musicale*, (novembre 1927), p. 74. For a more detailed discussion of Schaeffner's reflections on jazz, see Jordan, '*Amphibiologie*', pp. 166–71. See also Clifford, *The Predicament of Culture*, pp. 131–2.
62   Hoérée, 'Le jazz', p. 216.
63   *Le Phare de Neuilly*, no. 1, p. 72.
64   Matisse, *Jazz*, pp. 141–6.
65   Riva Castleman, 'Introduction', in Matisse, *Jazz*, p. xxii.
66   Matisse, *Jazz*, pp. 30–9.

## Chapter 6: Making Crocodiles Daydream

1   Enzo Cormann, 'Comment cette chose est entrée en nous', *Europe* (août-septembre 1997), no. 820–821, p. 41.
2   Yannick Séité, 'Ce que le jazz pense de la littérature', *Europe* (août-septembre 1997), no. 820–821, p. 7.
3   'La plus grande guerre du monde'. 'Jazz', in Drieu La Rochelle, *Fond de cantine*. See Carine Trévisan, 'Jazz martial: Note sur un poème de Drieu La Rochelle', *Europe* (août-septembre 1997), no. 820–821, pp. 58–61.
4   Céline was born Louis-Ferdinand Destouches in 1892. He died in 1961. The title of this chapter, 'Making Crocodiles Daydream', is borrowed from Céline's *Guignol's band*.
5   De Roux et al. (eds), *Louis-Ferdinand Céline*, p. 114.
6   Morand, *Magie noire*, pp. 7–8.
7   This refers to artificial studio light favoured by academic painters, as distinct from the open-air practice of the impressionists.
8   Céline, *Guignol's band*, p. 10.
9   See Donley, *Céline musicien*.
10   Céline dedicated *Voyage au bout de la nuit* to his mistress of the late 1920s, the American dancer Elizabeth Craig. The character of Lili was modelled on his later wife, Lucette Almanzor.
11   For example: 'Il avait l'esprit dans les doigts . . . Des mains de fées! . . . des papillons sur les ivoires . . . Il virevoltait aux harmonies! . . . piquait l'une et l'autre . . . un dièze! . . . songes et toquades! . . . guirlandes . . . détours . . . fredaines prestes

... Possédé! ... pas autre chose à dire! ... par vingt petits diables dans les doigts! ...... Un coup d'accords! dièze! C'est gagné! ... Le charme enchaîne ... C'est la rengaine digne et ficelle ... Jamais venue ... jamais finie! ...' The text, begun some pages earlier, continues for several more (*Guignol's band*, p. 158).

12 Letter to Hindus, 12 June 1947, in de Roux et al., *Louis-Ferdinand Céline*, p. 115.

13 Letter to Hindus, 16 April 1947, ibid., p. 111.

14 Yannick Séité, 'Robert Desnos, "Critique de disques"', *Europe* (août-septembre 1997), no. 820–821, pp. 62–7.

15 Clifford, *The Predicament of Culture*, p. 173.

16 In *Les Temps modernes* (juin 1948), no. 33, cited in *Le Monde, Sélection hebdomadaire*, 17–23 avril 1980, p. 14.

17 De Beauvoir, *Mémoires d'une jeune fille rangée*, pp. 468–9.

18 Sartre, *Écrits de jeunesse*, p. 360.

19 Sartre, 'Nick's Bar, New York City', pp. 680–2.

20 Quoted in Sicard, *Essais sur Sartre*, p. 306.

21 See ibid., p. 298.

22 Various commentators have noted that there are other jazz tunes evoked in *La Nausée*: as well as 'Some of these Days', Roquentin alludes to 'Blue Sky' (*sic*—no doubt intended to be the 1927 Irving Berlin tune 'Blue Skies'), and to another song identified only by two lines: 'When the low moon begins to beam / Every night I dream a little dream.' The latter is in fact a slightly deformed version of the Gershwin song 'The Man I Love' ('low' should read 'mellow'), also recorded by Sophie Tucker (1928).

23 Jean-Louis Pautrot gives a thorough account of critical analyses of the 'Some of these Days' motif in *La Musique oubliée*, passim, but especially pp. 43–5.

24 In order to explain Céline's anti-Semitism, for example, Sartre quite falsely accused him of being in the pay of the Nazis.

25 We know that Sartre owned recordings of Sophie Tucker. Simone de Beauvoir reports on their 1929 jazz-listening sessions in *Mémoires d'une jeune fille rangée*, p. 335.

26 'Illusions', *L'Édition musicale vivante*, no. 4 (avril 1928), p. 22.

27 Cf. Zimmerman, '"Some of these days": Sartre's petite phrase'.

28 Ernest Ansermet had a similar experience in Switzerland: 'I remember travelling by train between Berne and Lausanne with a group of young Americans. One of them started to hum a piece of rag music. They all immediately joined in, beating the rhythm with their hands on the wood of the seats ...': *Revue suisse romande*, p. 171.

29 'Pataphysics was invented by Alfred Jarry at the end of the nineteenth century as 'the science of the realm beyond metaphysics'. Seeking to challenge the limits of humans' conceptual powers, Jarry defined 'Pataphysics as the 'science of imaginary solutions'. His absurdist approach marks him as a precursor of dada, surrealism and the OuLiPo.

30 Queneau, *Bâtons, chiffres et lettres*, pp. 150–5.

31  The OuLiPo began its activities in 1960. Perhaps the two most famous of the OuLiPo writers are Georges Perec and the Italian Umberto Eco. Perec is celebrated, for instance, for having written an entire novel—*La disparition*—without using the letter 'e'. OuLiPo writers often test themselves against existing rhetorical devices such as acrostics or mesostics, as well as playing—with great seriousness—with numerological possibilities.

32  Many of Vian's prolific writings have been collected in his *Chroniques de jazz* and *Autres écrits sur le jazz*.

33  Vian also purported to be the translator of a series of works by a black American writer, 'Vernon Sullivan', material which he in fact wrote. The most famous of these was *J'irai cracher sur vos tombes* (1946, *I Shall Spit on your Graves*), a bitter indictment of the oppressions of American racism.

34  Vian, *Autres écrits sur le jazz*, p. 331.

35  *Été indien* (1963) and *Outback ou l'arrière-monde* (1995).

36  Franck Médioni, 'Les Ravages du jazz dans la littérature contemporaine', *Jazz Magazine* (février 1998), no. 478, p. 10.

37  Ibid., p. 7.

38  Perec, 'La Chose', *Magazine littéraire* (1993) 316, décembre, pp. 55–64. The text is believed to date from 1967, the year that Perec joined the OuLiPo.

39  Both published in Paris by Les Éditions de Minuit.

40  Franck Médioni, 'Les Ravages du jazz dans la littérature contemporaine', *Jazz Magazine*, no. 473 (septembre 1997), p. 23; also, personal interview with the author, 21 May 1997, at L'Écluse in Paris.

41  Echenoz's novels are: *Le Méridien de Greenwich* (1979), *Cherokee* (1983, Prix Médicis), *L'Équipée malaise* (1986), *Lac* (1989), *Nous trois* (1992), *Les grandes blondes* (1995), *Un an* (1997), *Je m'en vais* (1999, Prix Goncourt). All are published in Paris, Les Éditions de Minuit.

42  Personal interview with the author, 21 May 1997.

43  Ibid.

44  Ibid.

45  He became a regular contributor to *Jazz Magazine* in 1963, and has remained so for more than thirty years. Ongoing reflections on jazz are scattered across his published work, the most representative of which are found in *L'Improviste: une lecture du jazz* (1990).

46  Réda, 'Propos sur l'actualité du jazz', *Europe*, août-septembre 1997, pp. 23–9.

47  Ibid., p. 28.

48  Ibid., p. 25.

49  Ibid., p. 29.

## Chapter 7: Dancing with De Beauvoir

1   De Beauvoir, *Les Mandarins*, p. 21.

2   See Cazalis, *Les mémoires d'une Anne*, p. 202.

3    We can note the pun in the title of her autobiography, which evokes the memories of an Anne, but also those of an ass—'l'âne' in French.

4    Doelnitz, *La fête à Saint-Germain-des-Prés*, pp. 161–8.

5    *Samedi Soir*, 3 mai 1947, pp. 1, 6.

6    Cazalis, *Les mémoires d'une Anne*, p. 83.

7    Ibid., p. 54.

8    See Cohen-Solal, *Sartre 1905–1980*, p. 156 ff.

9    De Beauvoir, *L'Invitée*, p. 33.

10    See de Beauvoir, *La Force des choses*, p. 157 ff.

11    Cazalis, *Les mémoires d'une Anne*, pp. 50, 53.

12    Already a significant figure in pre-war journalism, Hélène Lazareff, during her American exile (1940–45) worked as an assistant editor at both *Harper's Bazaar* and *The New York Times*. With her husband Pierre, who built the *France-Soir* empire after the war, she was a major force in the reconstruction of the French press after the Liberation.

13    Cazalis, *Les mémoires d'une Anne*, p. 181. She complains, plausibly, that it was taken over and popularised by Guillaume Hanoteau, editor of *Marie-Claire*.

14    Other than recording it in her memoirs and her newspaper reports; though she did publish a late novel about the 1960s, *La décennie* (Fayard, Paris, 1972).

15    De Beauvoir, *Mémoires d'une jeune fille rangée*, pp. 94–5. Cf. Bair, *Simone de Beauvoir: A Biography*, p. 64.

16    In *Mémoires d'une jeune fille rangée* (p. 129), she recounts the scandal provoked by Zaza at a teacher's piano concert when Zaza, undertaking a difficult piece, not only succeeds in playing it perfectly, but pokes out her tongue at her mother in a gesture of triumph, something de Beauvoir would never dream of doing. She is embarrassed by her sister's fine singing voice when performing together in a musical play (pp. 141–2); and expresses general admiration for Zaza's musical talent and accomplishment on piano and violin (p. 155.)

17    Ibid., pp. 336–71.

18    Ibid., p. 425.

19    Ibid., p. 336.

20    Ibid., p. 366.

21    Ibid., p. 269.

22    De Beauvoir, *La Force de l'âge*, p. 343. See Chapter 2 of this book.

23    Ibid., p. 401.

24    Ibid., pp. 484–5.

25    Ibid., pp. 160–1.

26    Ibid., p. 401.

27    See de Beauvoir, *Journal de guerre*, p. 68 (3/2/40); *Lettres à Sartre*, p. 107 (9/3/40); *Tous les hommes sont mortels*, p. 38; *L'Amérique au jour le jour*, p. 37 (3/2/47).

28    For de Beauvoir's relationship with Algren, see for instance Bair, *Simone de Beauvoir: A Biography*, p. 333 ff., and passim.

29 Sartre's adventure with Dolorès Vanetti began during his first trip to New York after the war. She was working in the French program of the Voice of America. See Cohen-Solal, *Sartre 1905-1980*, p. 313 ff.

30 De Beauvoir, *Le deuxième sexe*, vol. 1, p. 27.

31 *Pour une morale de l'ambiguïté*, p. 56.

32 Michèle Le Doeuff's distinction between Sartre's systematic philosophy and de Beauvoir's more flexible 'viewpoint' or 'perspective' is particularly enlightening in the context of the argument developed below. See *L'Étude et le rouet*, pp. 106–7.

33 For instance, during her autumn 1947 visit, Algren explicitly encouraged her to develop her essay on women into a book-length work. Cf. Bair, *Simone de Beauvoir: A Biography*, p. 353.

34 De Beauvoir, *La Force des choses*, II, pp. 399–400.

35 De Beauvoir, *La Cérémonie des adieux*, p. 301.

36 Michèle Le Doeuff (op. cit., p. 138ff) tells a splendid story of a discussion, at the wake after de Beauvoir's funeral, with a group of women friends about what *Le deuxième sexe* meant to them. And it is clear that this book, whatever its limitations or shortcomings, continues to be widely accepted as a pioneering, and indeed a foundational document.

37 Doelnitz, *La Fête à Saint-Germain-des-Prés*, p. 175 ff.

38 Sagan, *Un certain sourire*, p. 85.

39 Ibid.

40 Sagan, *Avec mon meilleur souvenir*, p. 95.

**Chapter 8: 'In One Word: Emotion'**

1 Davis, *Miles: the Autobiography*, p. 217. He is referring to Louis Malle's *Ascenseur pour l'échafaud*, discussed below.

2 De Beauvoir, *Mémoires d'une jeune fille rangée*, p. 425; and *La Force de l'âge*, pp. 59, 162.

3 Leiris, *Zébrage*, pp. 24–5.

4 The title of this chapter is Samuel Fuller's definition of cinema in Jean-Luc Godard's *Pierrot le fou* (1965).

5 See, for instance, Maltby, *Hollywood Cinema* and Miller et al., *Global Hollywood*.

6 Claude Heymann's *L'amour à l'américaine* (1932), Jean Renoir's *Chotard et compagnie* (1933), Julien Duvivier's *Pépé le Moko* (1936), Augusto Genina's *Naples au baiser de feu* (1937), and Pierre Chenal's *L'alibi* (1937). This list is from Hippenmeyer, *Jazz sur films*.

7 Gautier, *Jazz au cinéma*, p. 17.

8 Clair, *Réflexion faite*, p. 144 ff.

9 Bazin, 'Beauté du hasard: Le film scientifique', in *Le cinéma français de la Libération à la Nouvelle Vague (1945-1958)*, pp. 220–2. Originally published in *L'écran français*, 21 octobre 1947. I am grateful to Gilles Mouëllic for drawing my attention to this connection.

10 Hippenmeyer, *Jazz sur films*.

11 Malle won the prize again in 1987, for *Au revoir les enfants*.

12 Malle, *Jazz Hot* (juin 1960), no. 155, p. 14.

13 French, *Malle on Malle*, p. 19. Also, Malle, *Jazz Hot*, ibid.

14 Davis, *Miles: the Autobiography*, p. 217.

15 French, *Malle on Malle*, p. 19.

16 Malle, *Jazz Hot* (juin 1960), no. 155, p. 15.

17 See, for instance, Frodon, *L'âge moderne du cinéma français*, pp. 106–8, and 270–2.

18 Pascal Mérigeau, 'La mort de Louis Malle, cinéaste des passions', *Le Monde*, lundi 27 novembre 1995.

19 Pierre Billard rightly underscores the emotional autobiographical content in *Les amants* and *Le feu follet*. See *Louis Malle: le rebelle solitaire*, p. 241.

20 See Nettelbeck,' 'Getting the Story Right'.

21 French, *Malle on Malle*, p. 104.

22 *Atlantic City USA* (1980), *My Dinner with André* (1981), *Crackers* (1983), *Alamo Bay* (1985), *God's Country* (1986), *And the Pursuit of Happiness* (1987).

23 Mallecot (ed.), *Louis Malle par Louis Malle*, p. 75. Malle also uses Scott Joplin and the original Dixieland Jazz Band in the film.

24 In *Le souffle au coeur*, Laurent discusses with a school friend the relative merits of Jelly Roll Morton and Charlie Parker: his preferences clearly go towards the latter and Dizzy Gillespie. Cf. also Malle, *Jazz Hot* (juin 1960), no. 155, p. 14.

25 Jacques Julliard, 'Louis Malle en mai', *Le Nouvel Observateur*, 25-31 janvier 1990, p. 60. See also, for Malle's professional engagement with the events of May 1968, Billard, *Louis Malle: le rebelle solitaire*, pp. 292–303.

26 French, *Malle on Malle*, p. 196.

27 He uses the term himself in his interview with Jacques Julliard ('Louis Malle en mai'). See also Billard, *Louis Malle: le rebelle solitaire*, p. 493.

28 French, *Malle on Malle*, p. 210.

29 See Thierry Jousse, 'Godard à l'oreille' (pp. 40–3), and Jacques Aumont, 'Lumière de la musique' (pp. 46–8), in *Cahiers du Cinéma* (novembre 1990), supplément au no. 437—'Numéro spécial Godard'.

30 'Entretien avec Antoine Duhamel', ibid., p. 49.

31 See Raspiengeas, *Bertrand Tavernier*, pp. 302–4.

32 On the covernotes of the soundtrack.

33 See for instance, Stovall, *Paris Noir*, pp. xiv–xvi; Blake, *Le Tumulte Noir*.

34 Postif, *Les grands interviews de* Jazz Hot, pp. 183–4.

35 Ken Burns, *Jazz: A History of America's Music*, Florentine Films production, 2000, no. 8, 'Risk'.

## Chapter 9: Non-stop at Le Jockey

1 Quignard, *Les Ombres errantes*, p. 123.

2 Richard Pells, *Not Like Us*, p. 85.

3 For instance, Coeuroy, *Histoire générale du jazz*, pp. 24–30.

4 Collier, *The Reception of Jazz in America: A New View*.

5    Burns, *Jazz*, no. 8 'Risk'.

6    Harvey Levenstein gives a lively account of American tourism in France in *Seductive Journey: American Tourists in France from Jefferson to the Jazz Age*, pp. 233–56 and passim.

7    Shack, *Harlem in Montmartre*, p. 77 ff. Cf. also Jackson, *Making Jazz French*, p. 143 ff.

8    Hansen, *Expatriate Paris*, p. 24.

9    Marès and Milza (eds), *Le Paris des étrangers depuis 1945*, pp. 247–62.

10   Collier, *The Reception of Jazz in America*, p. 46.

11   Hansen, *Expatriate Paris*, p. 88.

12   Man Ray's real name was Emmanuel Radnitsky. He was the child of Jewish Russian immigrants.

13   See Baldwin, *Man Ray: American Artist*, p. 100.

14   In Paris today, just off the Champs Élysées, an exclusive club–bar–restaurant, co-founded by Johnny Depp, bears Man Ray's name and is decorated with his work. It features nightly live jazz in many styles. Coincidentally on the same site, which was once a cinema, Boris Vian in 1959 suffered the premonitory signs of the heart attack that would kill him. He was watching the premiere of the film made from his celebrated *J'irai cracher sur vos tombes*.

15   Rose, *Jazz Cleopatra*, p. 181 ff.

16   Shack, *Harlem in Montmartre*, pp. 36–7.

17   A. E. Hotchner, *Papa Hemingway*, pp. 52–3, cited in Robert E. Gajdusek, *Hemingway's Paris*, p. 124.

18   See Nettelbeck, *Forever French: Exile in the United States 1939–1945*, passim.

19   See Pells, *Not Like Us*, especially Chapter 3.

20   See Sylvain Siclier, 'Le duo Ornette Coleman-Jacques Derrida fait des vagues', *Le Monde*, 3 juillet 1997, p. 25.

21   A journalist from *L'Humanité* reproached them for their intolerance, underlining the paradox of their adulation of Ornette Coleman's radical originality and their simultaneous refusal to experience it in this particular way ('Steve Coleman jazze de Paris à Nice', *L'Humanité*, 7 juillet 1997).

22   In Thierry Jousse, 'La langue de l'autre', *Les Inrockuptibles* (20 août-2 septembre 1997) 115, pp. 37–42, at p. 42.

23   Ibid., p. 40.

24   Gioia, *The History of Jazz*, p. 394.

# Chronology

1900    John Philip Sousa plays ragtime on his French tour.
1902    André Gide publishes his archetypal modernist novel, *L'Immoraliste*.
        The Nouveau Cirque in Paris introduces French audiences to the cakewalk.
1908    Composition of Debussy's 'Golliwog's Cake-Walk', inspired by ragtime music.
1913    Proust publishes the first volume of *A la recherche du temps perdu*.
1916    15th New York Infantry Regiment formed in Harlem.
        Dadaist revolt initiated by Tristan Tzara and Hans Arp in Zurich.
1917    In New York, The Original Dixieland Jazz Band makes the first recordings explicitly linking the word 'jazz' to a particular form of music. (January)
        Death of master ragtime composer and pianist, Scott Joplin. (1 April)
        US entry into World War I. (6 April)
        *Parade* is performed in Paris, with Satie's *Rag-time du paquebot*. (May)
        15th US Infantry Regiment arrives in France. (December)
        African-American musicians, including Louis Mitchell, begin to play in Paris music halls.
1918    Jean Cocteau publishes *Le coq et l'harlequin*.
        James Reese Europe's Military Band performs in the Théâtre Graslin in Nantes. (12 February)
        Europe's band tours provincial France, including four weeks in the American Army rest and recreation leave area in Chambéry–Aix-les-Bains. (February–March)
1919    Ernest Ansermet's article 'Sur un orchestre nègre' appears in *La Revue Romande*.
1920    André Breton and Philippe Soupault publish the key surrealist text *Les Champs magnétiques*.
        Drieu La Rochelle publishes his poem 'Jazz'.
1921    Man Ray arrives in Paris.
        Ernest Hemingway settles in Paris for a seven-year stay.
1922    Parisian bar, 'Le Boeuf sur le toit' (formerly the 'Gaya'), opens. (January)
1923    Louis Mitchell's band begins its long residency at Le Perroquet.
        Ada Louise Smith ('Bricktop') becomes leading female manager in the Paris jazz scene.
        French Prime Minister Poincaré declares the absolute right of 'people of colour to receive equal treatment to whites'.
        First performance of Milhaud's *La création du monde*.
1924    Satie composes jazz-inspired background music for surrealist film *Entr'acte*.
1925    Creation of regular radio jazz programs in France.
        Maurice Ravel composes *L'Enfant et les sortiléges*.
        First production of Marcel Pagnol's play *Jazz*.

*La Revue Nègre*, starring Josephine Baker and Sidney Bechet, is performed in Paris. (2 October–19 November)

1926    André Schaeffner and André Coeuroy publish the first jazz history, *Le Jazz*.
        Paul Whiteman's orchestra performs 'symphonic jazz' at the Théâtre des Champs-Elysées. (July)

1927    Jack Hylton's English jazz orchestra performs at the Théâtre de l'Empire.
        First sound film produced in Hollywood, *The Jazz Singer*.

1928    Launch of monthly magazine, *Jazz: l'Actualité intellectuelle*.
        Paul Morand publishes his jazz-influenced collection of stories, *Magie noire*.

1929    First release of Louis Armstrong's work in France.
        Bechet deported for using a firearm while in Paris.
        Simone de Beauvoir meets Jean-Paul Sartre.
        *Revue de Jazz* is founded.

1930    First issue of *Jazz Tango* magazine. (October).

1932    Robert Goffin publishes his essay *Aux frontières du jazz*.
        Publication of Louis Ferdinand Céline's *Voyage au bout de la nuit*.
        Hugues Panassié creates the Hot Club of France.

1933    Duke Ellington's first Paris concert at the Salle Pleyel. (July 27)

1934    Django Reinhardt meets Stéphane Grappelli. (January)
        Major political riots in France. (February)
        Louis Armstrong plays at the Salle Pleyel.
        First public concert of the Quintet of the Hot Club of France. (December)

1935    *Jazz Hot*, the first magazine in the world devoted exclusively to jazz, is launched in France. (May)

1936    Coleman Hawkins plays at the Salle Pleyel.

1937    Charles Delaunay creates the jazz recording company, Swing.
        First edition of Charles Delaunay's *Hot discography* appears.
        Universal Exhibition opens in Paris. (June)
        New York Cotton Club review at the Moulin Rouge. (11 June–23 July)

1938    French *chanson* revolutionised by swing-influenced performances of Jean Sablon, Charles Trenet and Johnny Hess.
        Jean-Paul Sartre publishes his first novel, *La Nausée*.

1939    Quintet of the Hot Club of France tours England. (August)
        World War II declared. (September)

1941    USA enters World War II.
        Emergence of 'zazou' movement in France.
        Claude Abadie band forms from Lyon student group, including trumpeter, Boris Vian.

1942    Quintet of the Hot Club of France tours Belgium and the north of France. (April)

1943    Publication of Simone de Beauvoir's first novel, *L'invitée*.
        Django Reinhardt performs at the Salle Pleyel. (September)

| 1944 | Allied invasion of Normandy. (June) |
|---|---|
| | Liberation of Paris. (August) |
| 1945 | Stéphane Grappelli returns to Paris from London. |
| 1946 | Claude Luter's band begins playing at the Lorientais. |
| | Be-bop music is discovered by jazz musicians in France. |
| | Rift between Panassié and Delaunay: the French 'Jazz War'. |
| | Boris Vian becomes jazz critic for *Jazz Hot*, *Jazz News* and *Combat* and publishes *Vercoquin de et plancton*. |
| | Simone de Beauvoir meets Boris Vian. |
| 1947 | Hubert Fol creates the Be-Bop Minstrels. |
| | André Hodeir becomes editor-in-chief of *Jazz Hot*. |
| | Production of Henri Matisse's mixed media work, *Jazz*. |
| | Publication of Raymond Queneau's *Exercises de style* and Boris Vian's *L'Ecume des jours*. |
| | Popular weekly *Samedi Soir* launches Saint-Germain as a socio-cultural phenomenon. |
| 1948 | Collège de 'Pataphysique founded. |
| | Boris Vian broadcasts for New York radio station WNEW. |
| | Dizzy Gillespie plays in Paris at the Salle Pleyel. |
| | Panassié organises the world's first international jazz festival in Nice. (February) |
| 1949 | Sidney Bechet returns to France. |
| | Simone de Beauvoir publishes her foundational feminist text, *Le deuxième sexe*. |
| | Delaunay organises the first formal International Paris Jazz Festival. (May) |
| | Miles Davis meets Juliette Gréco. (May) |
| 1950 | Benny Goodman plays at the Théâtre de Chaillot. (June) |
| 1953 | Django Reinhardt dies. (May) |
| 1954 | French defeated in Indochina; beginning of Algerian War of Independence. |
| | Hodeir creates the Jazz Groupe de Paris. |
| | Academy of Jazz founded in Paris. |
| | Publication of Françoise Sagan's scandalous first novel, *Bonjour Tristesse*. |
| | Count Basie performs in Paris, Lyon, Bordeaux and Lille. (March–April) |
| | First American jazz festival, in Newport. (July) |
| 1955 | Olympia concert celebrating the sale of Bechet's millionth record. (October) |
| 1956 | Modern Jazz Quartet makes its first trip to France. |
| | Bud Powell begins residency with Kenny Clarke and Pierre Michelot at the Club Saint-Germain. |
| 1957 | Miles Davis performs at the Club Saint-Germain and composes the music score for Malle's *Ascenseur pour l'échafaud*. |
| 1958 | Sidney Bechet's last public appearance. (December) |
| 1959 | Publication of Queneau's novel *Zazie dans le métro*. |
| | Beginning of French cinema's New Wave'. |

Lester Young dies. (March)

Thelonious Monk plays at the Club Saint-Germain. (April)

Sidney Bechet dies. (May)

Boris Vian dies at age 39. (June)

1960     Ornette Coleman launches 'free' jazz with an eponymous recording.

Release of François Truffaut's *Tirez sur le pianiste* and Jean-Luc Godard's *À bout de souffle*.

1962     Martial Solal's Big Band performs at the Club Saint-Germain.

End of Algerian War.

1963     Don Cherry and Sonny Rollins play free jazz in Paris.

Death of Jean Cocteau.

1965     Release of Godard's *Pierrot le fou*.

1966     French 'free' musicians give a concert for peace in Vietnam at the Mutualité. (May)

1967     Barney Wilen, France's fusion pioneer, forms his 'Free Rock Group'. (November)

1968     Student and trade union demonstrations lead to major social and political upheaval. (May)

1969     Miles Davis releases *Bitches Brew*.

1975     Josephine Baker is given a state funeral.

1977     'Jazz in Marciac' festival begins. (August)

1978     Publication of Georges Perec's masterpiece, *La vie: mode d'emploi*.

1981     Jack Lang appointed Minister for Culture under the Mitterrand presidency.

Simone de Beauvoir publishes *La cérémonie des adieux*.

1983     Publication of Jean Echenoz's *Cherokee*.

1985     Jazz is first taught at the Paris Conservatorium by Michel Portal.

1986     Release of Bertrand Tavernier's *Round Midnight*.

National Jazz Orchestra established at La Villette in Paris.

The Bibliothèque Nationale de France organises a week of jazz to celebrate the donation of the Delaunay collection. (May)

1989     Release of Malle's *Milou en mai*.

1992     Jazz Department is created at the Paris Conservatorium.

1993     Jean-Christophe Averty's television series *Jazzband: Une histoire du jazz français*.

Pianist Michel Petrucciani returns to France after ten years in the United States.

1995     Death of Louis Malle.

Publication of Christian Gailly's jazz novel, *Be-Bop*.

1997     Ornette Coleman and Jacques Derrida perform an improvised jazz–text music duo at the Paris La Villette jazz festival. (July)

1999     Michel Petrucciani dies in New York. (January)

2000     Televised history of jazz produced in America by Ken Burns.

# Bibliography

**Académie du cirque et du music-hall,** *Histoire du music-hall,* Éditions de Paris, Paris, 1954.

**Anderson, Alexandra and Sattusz Carol** (eds), *Jean Cocteau and the French Scene,* Abbeville Press, New York, 1984.

**Ansermet, Ernest,** 'Sur un orchestre nègre', *Revue suisse romande,* 15 octobre 1919, reprinted in *Écrits sur la musique,* à la Baconnière, Neuchâtel, 1983, pp. 171–8.

**Aragon, Louis,** *Aurélien,* Gallimard, Paris, 1944.

**Badger, R. Reid,** *A Life in Ragtime: A Biography of James Reese Europe,* Oxford University Press, New York/Oxford, 1995.

**Bair, Deidre,** *Simone de Beauvoir: A Biography,* Jonathan Cape, London, 1990.

**Baldwin, Neil,** *Man Ray: American Artist,* Clarkson N. Potter, New York, 1988.

**Barrot, Olivier and Ory, Pascal** (eds), *Entre-deux-guerres, la création française,* François Bourrin, Paris, 1990.

**Baudelaire, Charles,** *Oeuvres,* Gallimard, Bibliothèque de la Pléiade, Paris, 1954.

**Bazin, André,** 'Beauté du hasard: Le film scientifique', in *Le Cinéma français de la Libération à la Nouvelle Vague (1945-1958),* Éditions de l'Étoile, Paris, 1983, pp. 220–2. Originally published in *L'Écran français,* 21 octobre 1947.

**Beauvoir, Simone de,** *L'Invitée,* Gallimard, Paris, 1943.

—— *Tous les hommes sont mortels,* Gallimard, Paris, 1946.

—— *Pour une morale de l'ambiguïté,* Gallimard, Paris, 1947.

—— *L'Amérique au jour le jour,* Morihien, Paris, 1948.

—— *Le deuxième sexe,* tome 1, Gallimard, coll. Idées, Paris, 1949.

—— *Les mandarins,* Gallimard, Paris, 1954.

—— *Mémoires d'une jeune fille rangée,* Gallimard, Paris, 1958.

—— *La Force de l'âge,* Gallimard, Paris, 1960.

—— *La Force des choses,* Gallimard, Paris, 1964.

—— *La Cérémonie des adieux, suivi de: Entretiens avec Jean-Paul Sartre août-septembre 1974,* Gallimard, Paris, 1981.

—— *Journal de guerre, septembre 1939-janvier 1941,* Gallimard, Paris, 1990.

—— *Lettres à Sartre I: 1930-1939; II: 1940-1963,* Gallimard, Paris, 1990.

**Bechet, Sidney,** *Treat it Gentle,* Da Capo Press, New York, 1975.

**Berlin, Edward A.,** *Ragtime: A Musical and Cultural History,* University of California Press, Berkeley, 1980.

**Berliner, Brett,** 'Dancing Dangerously: Colonizing the Exotic at the Bal Nègre in the Inter-war Years', *French Cultural Studies,* vol. 1, part 1, no. 34, February 2001, pp. 59–75.

**Berman, Art,** *Preface to Modernism,* University of Illinois Press, Urbana, 1994.

**Bernanos, Georges,** *Le crépuscule des vieux,* Gallimard, Paris, 1956.

**Billard, Pierre,** *Louis Malle: le rebelle solitaire,* Plon, Paris, 2003.

Bisland, Elizabeth, *The Life and Letters of Lafcadio Hearn*, Archibald Constable & Co., London, 1906.

Blake, Jody, *Le Tumulte Noir: Modernist Art and Populist Entertainment in Jazz-Age Paris 1900–1930*, The Penn State University Press, University Park, Pennsylvania, 1999.

Blesh, Rudy, *Shining Trumpets: A History of Jazz*, Cassell, London, 1949.

Bricktop, with James Haskins, *Bricktop*, Atheneum, New York, 1983.

Brierre, Jean-Dominique, *Le jazz français de 1900 à aujourd'hui*, Éditions Hors Collection, Paris, 2000.

Büchman-Møller, Frank, *You Just Fight for your Life: The Story of Lester Young*, Praeger, New York, 1990.

Buss, Robin, *French Film Noir*, Marion Boyars, London/New York, 1994.

Carpenter, Humphrey, *Geniuses Together: American Writers in Paris in the 1920s*, Unwin Hyman, London, 1987.

Cau, Jean, *Croquis de mémoire*, Julliard, Paris, 1985.

Cazalis, Anne-Marie, *Les mémoires d'une Anne*, Stock, Paris, 1976.

Céline, Louis-Ferdinand, *Voyage au bout de la nuit*, Denoël, Paris, 1932.

—— *Mort à crédit*, Denoël, Paris, 1936.

—— *Guignol's band I*, Denoël, Paris, 1944.

—— *Guignol's band II (Le pont de Londres)*, Gallimard, Paris, 1964.

Clair, René, *Réflexion faite*, Gallimard, Paris, 1951.

Clifford, James, *The Predicament of Culture: Twentieth-Century Ethnography, Literature and Art*, Harvard University Press, Cambridge, Massachusetts/London, 1988.

Cocteau, Jean, *Le Coq et l'Arlequin* (Préface de Georges Auric), Stock/Musique, Paris, 1979.

Coeuroy, André, *Histoire générale du jazz: strette, hot, swing*, Éditions Denoël, Paris, 1942.

Coeuroy, André and Schaeffner, André, *Le jazz*, Éditions Claude Aveline, Paris, 1926.

Cohen-Solal, Annie, *Sartre 1905-1980*, Gallimard, Paris, 1985.

Coleman, Bill, *Trumpet Story*, Macmillan, London, 1990; Northeastern University Press, Boston, 1991.

Collier, James Lincoln, *The Making of Jazz: A Comprehensive History*, Houghton Mifflin, Boston, 1978.

—— *The Reception of Jazz in America: A New View*, Institute for Studies in American Music, Brooklyn College of the City University of New York, Brooklyn, 1988.

Conte, Gérard, 'Jim Europe et les Hellfighters', *Jazz Hot*, (octobre 1968), pp. 8–9.

—— 'Les Mitchell's Jazz Kings', *Jazz Hot*, (novembre 1968), pp. 34–6.

Cooke, Mervyn, *The Chronicle of Jazz*, Thames & Hudson, London, 1997.

Criel, Gaston, *Swing*, Éditions Universitaires Françaises, Paris, 1948.

Cronin, Vincent, *Paris: City of Light 1919–1939*, Harper Collins, London, 1994.

Cunard, Nancy, *Black Man and White Ladyship: An Anniversary*, Utopia Press, London, 1921.

**Danius, Sara,** *The Senses of Modernism: Technology, Perception and Aesthetics*, Cornell University Press, New York, 2002.

**Daven, André,** 'Bonjour Joséphine', *Nouvelles littéraires*, 28 mai 1959, pp. 1, 10.

**Davis, Miles,** with Quincy Troupe, *Miles: The Autobiography*, Simon and Schuster, New York, 1989.

**De Beauvoir, Simone,** *Les Mandarins*, Gallimard, Paris, vol. 1, 1954.

**Delaunay, Charles,** *De la vie et du jazz*, Éditions Hot Jazz, Paris, 1941.

—— *Django mon frère*, Éric Losfeld, Paris, 1968.

—— *Delaunay's dilemma: de la peinture au jazz*, W, Mâcon, 1985.

**Delong, Thomas A.,** *Pops: Paul Whiteman, King of Jazz*, New Century Publishers Inc., Piscataway, New Jersey, 1983.

**De Roux, Dominique** et al. (eds), *Louis-Ferdinand Céline*, L'Herne, Paris, 1972.

**Désormière,** 'Une séance de musique moderne', *Courrier musical*, 1 janvier 1922.

**Dewitte, Philippe,** *Les mouvements nègres en France 1919-1939*, Éditions de l'Harmattan, Paris, 1985.

**Doelnitz, Marc,** *La Fête à Saint-Germain-des-Prés*, Robert Laffont, Paris, 1979.

**Donley, Michael,** *Céline musicien*, Nizet, Saint-Genouph, 2000.

**Dorigné, Michel,** *La Guerre du jazz*, E. Buckner, Paris, 1948.

—— *Jazz, culture et société*, Éditions Ouvrières, Paris, 1966.

—— *Jazz: les origines du jazz, le style Nouvelle Orléans et ses prolongements*, L'École des loisirs, Paris, 1968.

**Drew, Bettina,** *Nelson Algren: A Life on the Wild Side*, Bloomsbury, London, 1991.

**Drieu La Rochelle, Pierre,** *Fond de cantine*, NRF, Paris, 1920.

**Duroselle, Jean-Baptiste,** *La France de la 'Belle Époque'*, (2nd edn), Presse de la Fondation Nationale des Sciences Politiques, Paris, 1992.

**Dutton, Jacqueline and Nettelbeck, Colin** (eds), *Jazz Adventures in French Culture*, special number of *Nottingham French Studies*, vol. 43, no. 1 (Spring 2004).

**Echenoz, Jean,** *Cherokee*, Minuit, Paris, 1983.

—— *Les grandes blondes*, Minuit, Paris, 1995.

**Francis, André,** *Jazz*, Seuil, Paris, 1958.

**Fréjaville, Gustave,** *Au Music-Hall*, Aux Éditions du Monde Nouveau, Paris, 1923.

**French, Phillip** (ed.), *Malle on Malle*, Faber & Faber, London, 1993.

**Frodon, Jean-Michel,** *L'âge moderne du cinéma français: de la Nouvelle Vague à nos jours*, Flammarion, Paris, 1995.

**Gailly, Christian,** *Be-Bop*, Minuit, Paris, 1995.

—— *Un soir au club*, Minuit, Paris, 2001.

**Gajdusek, Robert E.,** *Hemingway's Paris*, Charles Scribner's Sons, New York, 1978.

**Gautier, Henri,** *Jazz au cinéma*, Premier Plan, no. 11, Serdoc, Lyon, 1960.

**Gillmore, Alan M.,** *Erik Satie*, Twayne Publishers, Boston, 1988.

**Gioia, Ted,** *The Imperfect Art: Reflections on Jazz and Modern Culture*, Oxford University Press, New York/Oxford, 1988.

—— *The History of Jazz*, Oxford University Press, New York, 1997.

**Goddard, Chris,** *Jazz away from Home*, Paddington Press, New York/London, 1979.

**Goffin, Robert,** *Aux frontières du jazz*, Sagittaire, Paris, 1932.

**Gréco, Juliette,** *Jujube*, Stock, Paris, 1982.

**Halls, W. D.,** *Politics, Society and Christianity in Vichy France*, Berg, Oxford/ Providence, 1995.

**Hansen, Arlen J.,** *Expatriate Paris: A Cultural and Literary Guide to Paris of the 1920s*, Arcade, New York, 1990.

**Hasse, John,** *Beyond Category: The Life and Genius of Duke Ellington*, Simon & Schuster, New York, 1993.

—— *Jazz: the First Century*, William Morrow, New York, 2000.

**Heimermann, Benoît,** *Titaÿna, 1897-1966*, Flammarion, Paris, 1994.

**Hélian, Jacques,** *Les grands orchestres de music-hall en France: souvenirs et témoignages*, Filipacchi, Paris, 1984.

**Hewitt, Nicholas,** 'The Changing Landscape of Montmartre', *Australian Universitites Modern Languages Association*, no. 96 (November 2001), pp. 1–18.

**Hippenmeyer, Jean-Roland,** *Jazz sur films*, Éditions de la Thièle, Yverdon, Switzerland, 1973.

**Hodeir, André,** *Introduction à la musique de jazz*, Larousse, Paris, 1948.

—— *Hommes et problèmes du jazz*, Flammarion, Paris, 1954 (English translation: Grove Press, New York, 1956).

—— *Toward Jazz*, Grove Press, New York, 1962.

—— *Les mondes du jazz*, UGE, Paris, 1970.

**Hotchner, A. E.,** *Papa Hemingway*, Random House, New York, 1966.

**Huddleston, Sisley,** *Paris Salons, Cafés, Studios*, Blue Ribbon Books, New York, 1928.

—— *Back to Montparnasse*, George Harrap, London, 1931.

**Jackson, Jeffrey H.,** *Making Jazz French: Music and Modern Life in Inter-war Paris*, Duke University Press, Durham/London, 2003.

—— 'Making Enemies: Jazz in Inter-war Paris', *French Cultural Studies*, vol. 10, part 2, no. 29 (June 1999), pp. 179–99.

**Jasen, David A. and Tichenor, Trebor Jay,** *Rags and Ragtime: A Musical History*, Seabury Press, New York, 1978.

**Jordan, Matthew F.,** Jazz Changes: A History of French Discourse on Jazz From Ragtime to Be-Bop, PhD dissertation, The Claremont Graduate University, 1998.

—— '*Amphibiologie*: Ethnographic Surrealism in French Discourse on Jazz', *Journal of European Studies* XXXI (2001), pp. 157–96.

**Karl, Frederick,** *Modern and Modernism: The Sovereignty of the Artist 1885–1925*, Athaneum, New York, 1985.

**Kenney, William H. III,** '*Le Hot*: the Assimilation of American Jazz in France, 1917–1940', *American Studies*, vol. 25, no. I (1984), pp. 5–24.

**Kern, Stephen,** *The Culture of Time and Space 1880–1918*, Harvard University Press, Cambridge, Massachusetts, 1983.

Klein, Jean-Claude, 'La Revue Nègre', in Olivier Barrot and Pascal Ory (eds), *Entre-deux-guerres, la création française*, François Bourrin, Paris, 1990, pp. 365–77.

Kimball, Robert, *Reminiscing with Sissle and Blake*, Viking, New York, 1973.

Lapprand, Marc, *Boris Vian: la vie contre*, Nizet, Paris, 1993.

Le Boterf, Hervé, *Harry Bauer*, Pigmalian/Gérard Watelet, Paris, 1995.

Lebovic, Herman, *True France: The Wars over Cultural Identity 1900–1945*, Cornell University Press, Ithaca/London, 1992.

Le Doeuff, Michèle, *L'Étude et le rouet*, tome 1, Seuil, Paris, 1989.

Leiris, Michel, *L'Âge d'homme*, Gallimard, Paris, 1939.

—— *Langage Tangage, ou ce que les mots me disent*, Gallimard, Paris, 1985.

—— *Zébrage*, Gallimard, Paris, 1992.

Levenstein, Harvey, *Seductive Journey: American Tourists in France from Jefferson to the Jazz Age*, The University of Chicago Press, Chicago/London, 1998.

Levinson, André, 'Paris ou New York', *Comoedia*, 12 octobre 1925, p. 2.

Little, Arthur W., *From Harlem to the Rhine: The Story of New York's Colored Volunteers*, Covici Friede, New York, 1936.

Lomax, Alan, *Mr Jelly Roll: The Fortunes of Jelly Roll Morton, New Orleans Creole and Inventor of Jazz* (2nd edn), University of California Press, Berkeley, 1973.

Lottman, Herbert, *The Left Bank: Writers in Paris from the Popular Front to the Cold War*, Heinemann, London, 1982.

McCarthy, Albert, *The Dance Band Era: The Dancing Decades from Ragtime to Swing 1910–1950*, Spring Books, London, 1971.

Mallecot, Jacques (ed.). *Louis Malle par Louis Malle*. France, Éditions de l'Athenor, 1979.

Malson, Lucien, *Histoire du jazz moderne*, La Table Ronde, Paris, 1961.

Maltby, Richard, *Hollywood Cinema*, Blackwell Publishing, Malden, Massachusetts, 2003.

Marès, Antoine and Milza, Pierre (eds), *Le Paris des étrangers depuis 1945*, Publications de la Sorbonne, Paris, 1994.

Marrus, Michaël R. and Paxton, Robert O., *Vichy et les juifs*, Calmann-Lévy, Paris, 1981.

Martin, Denis-Constant and Roueff, Olivier, *La France du jazz: musique, modernité et identité dans la première moitié du XX^e siècle*, Éditions Parenthèses, Marseille, 2002.

Matisse, Henri, *Jazz*, George Braziller Inc., New York, 1983.

Mauclair, Camille, *Mallarmé chez lui*, Grasset, Paris, 1935.

Merriam, Alan P. and Garner, Fradley H., 'Jazz: The Word', *Ethnomusicology*, no. 12 (1968), pp. 373–96.

Miller, Judith Graves, *Françoise Sagan*, Twayne Publishers, Boston, 1988.

Miller, Toby et al., *Global Hollywood*, BFI Publishing, London, 2001.

Morand, Paul, *Magie noire*, Grasset, Paris, 1928.

Mouëllic, Gilles, *Jazz et cinéma*, Éditions Cahiers du Cinéma, coll. Essais, Paris, 2000.

——— *Le jazz: une esthétique du XX<sup>e</sup> siècle*, Presses Universitaires de Rennes, Rennes, 2000.

**Mouly, Raymond,** *Sidney Bechet: notre ami*, La Table Ronde, Paris, 1959.

**Murray, Paul,** *A Fantastic Journey: The Life and Literature of Lafcadio Hearn*, Japan Library, Kent, 1993.

**Nettelbeck, Colin W.,** 'Getting the Story Right', in Gerhard Hirschfeld and Patrick Marsh (eds), *Collaboration in France: Politics and Culture during the Nazi Occupation 1940–1944*, Berg, Oxford/New York/Munich, 1989, pp. 252–93.

——— *Forever French: Exile in the United States 1939–1945*, Berg, New York/Oxford, 1991.

**Nouailhat, Yves-Henri,** *Les Américains à Nantes et Saint-Nazaire 1917-1919*, Belles-Lettres, Paris, 1972.

**Ollier, Claude,** *Été indien*, Flammarion, Paris, 1963.

——— *Outback ou l'arrière-monde*, P.o.l., Paris, 1995.

**Panassié, Hugues,** *Douze années de jazz (1927-1939): souvenirs*, Corrêa, Paris, 1946.

——— *Cinq mois à New York*, Corrêa, Paris, 1946.

——— *La Musique de jazz et le swing*, Corrêa, Paris, 1943.

——— *La véritable musique de jazz*, Corrêa, Paris, 1946.

**Pautrot, Jean-Louis,** *La Musique oubliée: La Nausée, l'Écume des jours, À la recherche du temps perdu, Moderato cantabile*, Droz, Genève, 1994.

**Pells, Richard,** *Not Like Us: How Europeans Have Loved, Hated, and Transformed American Culture Since World War II*, Basic Books, New York, 1997.

**Perec, Georges,** 'La Chose', *Magazine Littéraire*, no. 316 (déc. 1993), pp. 55–64.

**Pesquinne, Blaise,** 'De l'improvisation dans le jazz', *La Revue musicale*, no. 149 (sept.-oct. 1934), pp. 177–88.

——— 'Le blues, la musique nègre des villes: naissance et avenir du jazz', *La Revue musicale*, (nov. 1934), no. 150 pp. 273–82.

**Pizer, Donald,** *American Expatriate Writing and the Paris Moment: Modernism and Place*, Louisiana State University Press, Baton Rouge/London, 1996.

**Postif, François,** *Les grands interviews de* Jazz Hot, Éditions de l'Instant, Paris, 1989.

**Queneau, Raymond,** *Exercices de style*, Gallimard, Paris, 1947.

——— *Zazie dans le métro*, Gallimard, Paris, 1959.

——— *Bâtons, chiffres et lettres* (édition revue et augmentée), Gallimard, Paris, 1965.

**Quignard, Pascal,** *Les Ombres errantes*, Grasset, Paris, 2002.

**Raspiengeas, Jean-Claude,** *Bertrand Tavernier*, Flammarion, Paris, 2001.

**Rearick, Charles,** *The French in Love and War: Popular Culture in the Era of the World Wars*, Yale University Press, New Haven/London, 1997.

**Réda, Jacques,** *L'Improviste: une lecture du jazz*, édition revue et définitive, Gallimard, Paris, 1990.

**Renaud, Henri** (ed.), *Jazz classique*, Castermann, Paris, 1979.

——— *Jazz moderne*, Castermann, Paris, 1979.

**Rose, Phyllis,** *Jazz Cleopatra*, Doubleday Press, New York, 1989.

**Russell, Dick,** *Black Genius and the American Experience*, Carrol & Graf, New York, 1998.

**Rye, Howard,** 'The Southern Syncopated Orchestra', in R. E. Lotz and I. Pegg (eds), *Under the Imperial Carpet: Essays in Black History 1780–1950*, Rabbit Press, Crawley, UK, 1986, pp. 217–32.

**Sachs, Maurice,** *Au temps du Boeuf sur le toit*, Éditions Nouvelle Revue Critique, Paris, 1939.

**Sagan, Françoise,** *Bonjour Tristesse*, René Julliard, Paris, 1954.

—— *Un certain sourire*, René Julliard, Paris, 1956.

—— *Avec mon meilleur souvenir*, Gallimard, Paris, 1984.

**Sartre, Jean-Paul,** *La Nausée*, Gallimard, Paris, 1938.

—— 'Nick's Bar, New York City', in Michel Contat and Michel Rybalka, *Les Écrits de Sartre*, Gallimard, Paris, 1970.

—— *Les Carnets de la drôle de guerre Novembre 1939-Mars 1940*, Gallimard, Paris, 1983.

—— *Lettres au Castor I et II*, Gallimard, Paris, 1983.

—— *Écrits de jeunesse*, Gallimard, Paris, 1990.

**Shack, William A.,** *Harlem in Montmartre: A Paris Jazz Story between the Great Wars*, University of California Press, Berkeley, 2001.

**Shattuck, Roger,** *The Banquet Years: The Origins of the Avant-Garde in France 1885 to World War I*, Vintage Books, New York, 1968.

**Sicard, Michel,** *Essais sur Sartre*, Galilée, Paris, 1989.

**Singer, Hal,** *Jazz Roads*, Edition 1, Paris, 1990.

**Soupault, Philippe,** *Le nègre*, Seghers, Paris, 1975 (first published 1927).

**Sowerwine, Charles,** *France Since 1870: Culture, Politics and Society*, Palgrave, New York, 2001.

**Starr, S. Frederick.** *Bamboula! The Life and Times of Louis Moreau Gottschalk*, Oxford University Press, New York/Oxford, 1995.

**Stearns, Marshall and Stearns, Jean,** *Jazz Dance: The Story of American Vernacular Dance*, Schirmer Books, New York, 1968.

**Stovall, Tyler,** *Paris Noir: African Americans in the City of Light*, Houghton Mifflin, Boston/New York, 1996.

**Sullivan, Jack,** *New World Symphonies: The Influence of American Culture on European Music*, Yale University Press, New Haven, 1999.

**Ténot, Frank,** *Boris Vian: le jazz et Saint-Germain*, Du May, Paris, 1973.

**Tirro, Frank,** *Jazz: A History* (2nd edn), W. W. Norton & Co., New York, 1993.

**Tournès, Ludovic,** *New Orleans sur Seine: histoire du jazz en France*, Fayard, Paris, 1999.

**Vian, Boris,** *L'Écume des jours*, Pauvert, coll. 10-18, Paris, 1965.

—— *Textes et chansons*, Julliard, Paris, 1966.

—— *Chroniques de jazz*, La Jeune Parque, Paris, 1967.

—— *Autres écrits sur le jazz*, Christian Bourgois, Paris, 1981.

—— *Jazz in Paris*, Pauvert, Paris, 1997.

**Ward, Geoffrey C. and Burns, Ken,** *Jazz: A History of America's Music*, Pimlico/ Random House, London, 2001.

**Webster, Paul and Powell, Nicholas,** *Saint-Germain-des-Prés*, Constable, London, 1984.

**Wiéner, Jean,** *Allegro appassionato*, Pierre Belfond, Paris, 1978.

**Zimmerman, Eugenia Noik,** ' "Some of these days": Sartre's petite phrase', *Contemporary Literature*, vol. XI, (1970) no. 3, pp. 375–81.

# Index

Abadie, Claude, 62
accordion, 88–9
Action française, 32, 99
Addison, Fred, 56
African-Americans: music of, 5–7, 8, 9, 16–18, 23, 28, 29–30, 61, 197, 198; and racism, 17, 26, 33, 71, 73–4, 155, 195, 199, 201, 216n. 33; stereotypes of, 40, 113; writers in France, 73, 193, 197. *See also* jazz; jazz musicians in France
Alex, Joe, 40
Algren, Nelson, 154, 156, 157, 218n. 32
*Alleluia* (King Vidor), 162
Allier, Pierre, 55
America *See* United States
'années folles, les', 32
Ansermet, Ernest, 11, 29–30, 105
anti-Semitism, 101
Apollinaire, Guillaume, 105, 107
Aragon, Louis: *Aurélien*, 103, 114, 212n. 17
Armstrong, Louis, 2, 37, 47, 49, 190; stature in world of jazz, 66, 194
Arnold, Billy, 36
Arp, Hans, 105
art: avant-garde, 24, 34, 104, 105, 117, 121, 124, 134; demands of, 187; and ethnography, 112; and jazz, 117, 121–2; and modernism, 97, 99, 105; 'nègre', 103; and primitivism, 100–1; and progress, 179; and transcendence, 187–8; and World War I, 104
automatic writing: affinities with jazz, 111
avant-garde *See* art; culture; theatre
Averty, Jean-Christophe, 24, 43
Aznavour, Charles, 88

Bach, J. S., 115
Badger, Reid, 24
Baker, Josephine, 37–41, 48, 70, 194–6, 201
Baldwin, James, 197

Ballets russes, 105, 107
bands and ensembles, 42–3, 45, 50; André Ekyan band, 50; André Réwéliotty band, 69, 70, 166; Australian Dixieland band, 67; Be-Bop Minstrels, 71; Billy Arnold band; Claude Abadie band, 62; Dizzy Gillespie band, 66; Double-Six, 89, 211n. 21; Free Rock Group, 87; 'Gregor and his Gregorians', 43; 'Hellfighters', 8, 28; Jazz Groupe de Paris, 82; Jazz Messengers, 166; Jazz de Paris, Le, 56; Lorientais, the, 63, 66, 69, 70, 166; Louis Mitchell's Jazz Kings, 33, 37, 45, 205n. 37; Maxime Saury band, 70; Michel Portal Unit, 84; Miles Davis quintet, 78; military bands, 8, 16–18, 22–8; Modern Jazz Quartet, 72, 141, 166; Multicolor Feeling, 89; National Jazz Orchestra, 90; New Phonic Art, 84; Original Dixieland Jazz Band, 8, 28; Quintet of the Hot Club de France, 49–51, 52, 53, 55, 66, 173–4, 194; Ray Ventura and his Collegians, 43, 164; Southern Syncopated Orchestra, 28–29; swing, 56; Teddy Hill band, 66; Ted Lewis band, 45
Bataille, Georges, 112
Baudelaire, Charles, 97, 99
Bazin, André, 165
Beauvoir, Simone de: and American culture, 152–4, 162; *Cérémonie des adieux, La*, 157–8; *deuxième sexe, Le*, 154–6, 218n. 35; existentialist perspective of, 155–6, 218n. 31; feminist philosophy of, 146, 150, 154–6, 158–9, 197; *L'Invitée*, 148, 150, 152; interest in jazz and other music, 146, 150–4, 156–8; and Jean-Paul Sartre, 129, 146, 151, 154; *Les Mandarins*, 157; and Nelson Algren, 154, 156, 157; *Pour une morale de l'ambiguïté*, 155–6

be-bop, 2, 64, 66, 70, 87, 109, 117, 140, 157, 181, 183

Bechet, Sidney, 7, 28, 30, 37–8, 39, 41, 61, 67, 73; deported, 41; performs in films, 166; settles in France, 68; status of, 69–70, 92, 194

Becker, Jacques: *Rendez-vous de juillet*, 166

Beiderbecke, Bix, 2, 42

Bell, Graeme, 67

Bellamy, Paul, 20–22

Belle Époque, La, 97, 103, 211n. 3

Belmondo, Jean-Paul, 181

Bergson, Henri, 98, 104

Berlin, Irving, 215n. 22

Bernanos, Georges, 104–5

*Blackbirds* (show), 112

Blake, Jody, 12, 40

Blakey, Art, 166

Blesh, Rudy, 7

blues, 109, 144

Bolden, Buddy, 175

Boulez, Pierre, 81, 85

Brancour, René, 118–19

Braque, Georges, 105

Breillat, Catherine, 161

Breton, André, 111

Bricktop (Ada Louise Smith), 33–4, 194

Briggs, Arthur, 28, 34, 53, 194

Brooks, Shelton: 'Some of these Days', 131

Brown, 'Jasbo', 2

Brubeck, Dave, 2, 191

Brun, Philippe, 36, 43

Bullard, Eugene, 33–4

Bureau, Jacques, 45, 46

Burns, Ken, 12, 187, 198

Butor, Michel, 140

cakewalk *See* dance

Calloway, Cab, 47

Camus, Albert, 148, 197

Canetti, Jacques, 45, 46, 47

Caratini, Patrice, 80

Carné, Marcel: *Tricheurs, Les*, 166

Carradine, Keith, 175

Catholic Church, 58

Cau, Jean, 63

Cazalis, Anne-Marie, 63, 149–50, 216n. 1; and feminism, 147, 150; and jazz culture, 146–8

Céline, Louis-Ferdinand, 124–5, 128–9, 133, 144, 185, 214n. 4; *Guignol's Band*, 126; influence of, 145; *Mort à crédit*, 101–2, 127; reaction to jazz, 126–8; *Voyage au bout de la nuit*, 126–7, 129

censorship, 193

Centre d'Étude de Jazz, 52

Chaillou, Maurice, 37

*Champs magnétiques, Les* (Breton and Soupault), 111

chanson, 52, 88; and jazz, 75, 88

*Chotard et compagnie* (Renoir), 165

Chekhov, Anton, 179

Cherry, Don, 86

Chiboust, Noël, 55

cinema, 103; American, 164, 166–7, 170, 175, 181, 185, 197; beginnings of, 163–4; European tradition in, 164. *See also* French cinema

circuses, 103–4, 121–2

Clair, René, 164

Clarke, Kenny, 61, 70–1, 73

Clifford, James, 129

clubs *See* jazz venues

cocktail epoch, 106–7

Cocteau, Jean, 105–7; *Coq et l'Arlequin, Le*, 106, 107; jazz enthusiast, 106, 128

Coeuroy, André, 58–9

Coleman, Ornette, 78, 87, 141–2, 198–201, 220n. 21

collaborationists, 55, 60

Collier, James Lincoln, 11, 190

colonialism: and interest in African cultures, 101; and racial and cultural stereotypes, 101–2, 112

Coltrane, John, 77, 78, 143

Combelle, Alix, 36, 43, 55, 56

Communist Party, French, 32
composers: 'high culture', 107–9, 121, 184; jazz, 81–3, 165
conservatism, 98, 117–18
Cook, Will Marion, 7, 28, 30
Cotton Club of New York (show), 48–9, 151–2
*Courrier musical, Le*, 119
*Cousins, Les* (Claude Chabrol), 166
Cousteau, Jacques: *Autour d'un récif*, 165; *Monde du silence, Le* 168
Covarrubias, Miguel, 39
Criel, Gaston; *Swing*, 115–17
culture, 24–5, 41; American, 152–5, 181, 186, 191, 197; avant-garde, 10, 107; and commercialism, 199; cultural pluralism, 112. *See also* French culture; jazz culture

dadaism, 105, 111
dance, 6, 196; bal musette, 88; cakewalk, the, 9–10, 100, 104; and femininity, 41; and jazz, 3, 23, 24, 37, 39–41, 48, 51, 62, 63, 76–7, 88, 104, 106–8, 111, 112, 126–7, 140, 152; jitterbug, 148; quadrille, 3; tango, 37
Darzens, Rodolphe, 110
Daven, André, 38–9
Davis, Miles, 67, 73–4, 87, 141; *Bitches Brew*, 79; and Juliette Gréco, 73–5; and soundtrack for *Ascenseur pour l'échafaud* (Malle), 74, 168, 169–70, 218n. 1
Debussy, Claude; 'Golliwog's Cakewalk', 10
decadence, 183–4
de Gaulle, Charles, 86, 174
Delacroix, Eugène, 100–1
Delaunay, Charles, 46, 50, 64–7, 72, 116; donates personal collections, 90; fosters jazz, 56–7
Delaunay, Robert, 105
Derrida, Jacques, 198–201
Deslys, Gaby, 105
Desnos, Robert, 128

Désormière, Roger, 51
Diaghilev, Sergei, 29. *See also* Ballets russes
diversity, 201
*Documents* (journal), 112
Doelnitz, Marc, 147
Dolphy, Eric, 78
Dorigné, Michel, 65
Doucet, Clément, 35
Duchamp, Marcel, 194
Dudley, Caroline, 38
Duhamel, Antoine, 184
Dvořák, Antonin, 7

Echenoz, Jean, 140, 144; *Cherokee*, 141–2; writing in jazz style, 141–3
Eiffel Tower, 98
Ekyan, André, 36, 43, 55, 56
Ellington, Duke, 38, 49, 68, 140
emotion, 169, 180
entertainment: and illusion of spontaneity, 104; new forms of, 103–4, 163
ethnography, 96, 114; and jazz, 112–13
Europe, James Reese, 7, 8, 10, 16–18, 23–8, 191
Evans, Bill, 77
existentialism, 133–4, 137, 139, 150, 155–6, 158; and jazz, 157; misunderstanding of, 149; and youth culture, 134, 147
exoticism, 103

fashionable society, 103, 104
Feather, Leonard, 46
feminism, 146, 148, 150, 154, 158–9; and jazz, 149, 158; and race relations, 154–5
film *See* cinema
film direction, 170
Fol, Hubert, 71
France: anglophobia of, 198; cultural effervescence of, 97, 134; German Occupation of, 52–8, 59, 167; after Liberation, 60, 62, 135, 156, 169, 197; old order challenged, 86, 177; postwar

Jarry, Alfred, 135, 215n. 29

jazz: African element in, 2, 6, 29, 40; arrival in France, 2, 8, 16–18, 100, 120, 197; concepts associated with, 2–3, 106, 108, 117, 118, 125, 126, 129–31, 139, 141, 167, 186, 191; in Britain, 28–30, 42; criticism, 11–12, 35–6, 45, 51, 80, 82, 128, 132, 136, 211n. 11; and cultural renewal, 24–5, 27, 132, 144, 190; definitions of, 2, 24, 30, 46, 49, 117; eclipse of, 77; education, 90–1; as essence, 54, 115, 191; etymologies of, 3–4; in Europe, 11, 40, 42, 190; and high culture, 51–2, 77; history, 11, 12, 24, 29, 38, 40, 43, 45–6, 66, 91, 157, 175–6, 195, 201, 204n. 11; origins of, 1–4, 6–7, 9, 59, 78–9, 99, 108, 112–13, 116, 119, 175–6, 185, 197, 198; popularity of, 45–7, 50, 54–5, 58, 77, 134, 167, 190, 198; reception in France, 1–2, 19–20, 23–4, 28, 30, 34–5, 39–42, 46–7, 90, 99, 107–10, 119, 190–1, 198, 207n. 50, 213n. 53; as response to a painful world, 138–9, 185; spread of, 7–8, 16–18, 43, 113, 115, 120, 124, 132; traditional, 2, 3, 65, 70, 117, 157, 175. *See also* French cinema; jazz culture; literature; modernism(e)

*Jazz, Le* (Coeuroy and Schaeffner), 11–12

*Jazz: l'Actualité intellectuelle* (journal), 110–11

jazz culture, 48–9, 190; divergent tendencies in, 61, 66–7, 72, 77; in France, 12, 33–5, 43, 49–50, 54–8, 61–2, 64–73, 76–92, 117, 130, 134, 147–50, 153–4, 159, 185, 190–1, 193–4; Franco American exchange in, 71–5, 86–7, 187, 190–2, 197–8, 210n. 55; under German Occupation, 54–8; spontaneity in, 77, 133, 142, 169, 197; in United States, 61–2, 74–5, 77–8, 130, 181, 191, 193; and violence, 41, 43. *See also* cinema; jazz; jazz musicians in France; jazz venues; modernism; nightclubs

jazz festivals, 65–7, 79–80, 198

*Jazz Hot* (journal), 10, 11, 47, 56–7

jazz musicians in France, 28, 44, 49–50, 72, 83; American, 2, 7, 8, 16–20, 23, 26, 33–5, 38–42, 53, 64, 68, 70, 71–3, 79–80, 91, 139, 152, 186–7, 191, 197, 200; French, 1, 34–7, 43, 53–8, 71, 75, 80–92, 136, 192. *See also* jazz culture; under individual names

*Jazz Singer, The* (Al Jolson), 151, 162

*Jazz-Tango* (journal), 46

jazz venues, 34; Bal Nègre, Le, 111, 152, 153; bars, 111, 125; Blue Note, 70, 185; 'Boeuf sur le toit, Le', 34; Bricktop's, 34, 111; cabarets, 28, 55; Casino de Paris, 33; Caveau de la Huchette, 70; cellars, 53, 62–3, 140, 147, 166 ; circuses, 104; clubs, 33–4, 159; Club Saint-Germain, 82; concert halls, 55, 185; Gaya bar, 34; Jimmy's, 54; music halls, 28, 55, 103–4; Palais de Chaillot, 47; Perroquet, Le, 33, 34; Salle Pleyel, 47, 66, 140; Tempo Club, 111; theatres, 28; Théâtre des Champs Élysées, 38–9, 42; Zelli's, 33, 34. *See also* nightclubs

Johnson, Freddy, 45

Jonasz, Michel, 88

Jones, Palmer, 34

Jones, Florence, 34

Joplin, Scott, 8

Joyce, James, 141, 193, 194

*Joyeux Nègres, Les* (show), 104

Kandinsky, Wassily, 105

Kirk, Roland, 143

Kitt, Eartha, 68

Klein, Jean-Claude, 41

Kosakievicz, Olga, 148, 151

*Laissez-les tomber!* (show), 105

Laloy, Louis, 111
Lang, Jack, 90
La Rochelle, Drieu, 124
Laubreaux, Alain, 55
Lazareff, Hélène, 217
Legrand, Raymond, 56
Leiris, Michel, 112–14, 117, 125, 162–3, 213n. 43; *L'Afrique fantôme*, 129
Léon, Claude, 62
Levallet, Didier, 80
Levenstein, Harvey, 192
Levinson, André, 41
Lewis, Charlie, 53–4, 208n. 2
Lewis, John, 71–2, 166
Lewis, Ted, 111
Lewis, Willy, 45
Liberation of France, 59, 134
literature, French, 33, 72, 168; and appropriation of jazz, 133–4, 144; and influence of jazz, 123–9, 131, 134–44; and modernism, 124, 128; and the Nouveau Roman, 140; reflecting social and cultural changes, 145; its traditions subverted, 133; transformation of literary language, 125–7, 129, 134
Little, Arthur, 18, 20
Lockwood, Didier, 89
Loisy, Alfred, 97
'lost generation', the, 192–3, 197
Louiss, Eddy, 89
Lowry, Vance, 35
Lumière brothers, 163
Luter, Claude, 63–4, 65, 69, 70, 166

McAlmon, Robert, 194
Mallarmé, Stéphane, 118
Malle, Louis, 67, 74, 171, 178, 180, 219n. 25; American period of, 175; *Ascenseur pour l'échafaud*, 74, 87, 166, 168; *Au revoir les enfants*, 174, 175, 177; autobiographical work of, 171–4; documentaries of, 171, 175; jazz as an inspiration for, 167–8, 172–80, 185; *Lacombe Lucien*, 173; love of literature, 168, 171; *Milou en mai*, 177–9; *Monde du silence, Le* (with Jacques Cousteau), 168; *My Dinner with André*, 179; *Pretty Baby*, 175–7; *Soufle au Coeur, Le*, 171–2, 174; *Vanya on 42nd Street*, 179–80
marginalisation, 199, 200
material progress: artists' views of, 99
Matisse, Henri, 101, 105; *Jazz*, 121–2
Mauclair, Camille, 118
Mehldau, Brad, 179
Méliès, Georges, 163–4
Melville, Jean-Pierre: *Bob le flâneur*, 166, 170; *Deux hommes dans Manhattan*, 83, 166; *Samouraï, Le*, 166
Mezrow, Milton Mezz, 45, 66
Michelot, Pierre, 80
Mikell, Francis Eugene, 18
Milhaud, Darius, 35, 108, 121; *Création du monde, La*, 108, 191
Mills, Florence, 42
Mingus, Charles, 77, 78
Mirò, Joan, 105
Mistinguett, 52
Mitchell, Louis, 28, 33, 35, 194
modernism(e), 97–9, 112; and cinema, 162–3, 184; and colonialism, 211n. 2; conservative opposition to, 98, 117–18; French cultural, 97–8, 105, 121; and jazz, 2, 35, 96–7, 100, 103, 105, 109–15, 117–22, 135, 162, 185; and material progress, 98; and nationalism, 116; paradoxes of, 99; precursors of, 97, 99, 124; and popular culture, 100
Molinaro, Édouard: *Des femmes disparaissent*, 166; *Une fille pour l'été*, 166; *Un témoin dans la ville*, 87, 166
Monet, Claude, 99
Monk, Thelonious, 2, 61, 140, 141, 166; 'Round Midnight', 186
Monnier, Adrienne, 40
Montand, Yves, 88
Montmartre, 33–4, 39, 111, 192

Suarès, André, 47
surrealism, 96, 105, 112; and jazz, 111, 114, 123, 125
swing, 52, 55, 56, 58, 144
synaesthesia: and jazz, 107

tango *See* dance
Tavernier, Bertrand, 185; *Round Midnight*, 80, 185–8
Taylor, Cecil, 78, 87
*Temps modernes, Les* (journal), 137
Ténot, Frank, 203n. 32
Texier, Henri, 80
theatre, 105, 179–80; 'absurdist', 197; avant-garde, 135; and the young, 134
Thompson, E. E., 28
Titaÿna (Elisabeth Sauvy), 110
Tournès, Ludovic, 12, 40, 69
Trenet, Charles, 52, 56, 88
Truffaut, François: *Tirez sur le pianiste*, 166
Trumbauer, Frank, 42
Tucker, Sophie, 131–2
Tusques, François, 87
Tzara, Tristan, 105

United States: entering World War I, 176; French jazz in, 84; and political and cultural hegemony, 198; Prohibition in, 192, 193; social and political conditions, 26, 33, 73, 77, 78, 85, 175–6, 187, 193, 194–6

Vadim, Roger: *Liaisons dangereuses, Les*, 166; *Sait-on jamais?*, 166

Vauchant, Léo, 36–7, 43–4
Vian, Boris, 53, 63, 67, 134, 144, 216n. 33, 220n. 14; *L'Écume des jours*, 137–8; influence of jazz on his writing, 137–40; jazz performer and critic, 62, 66, 136, 157, 185; pessimism of, 139; 'shooting star', 136
Vichy regime, 54–5
Viseur, Gus, 56

Wagner, Christian, 36, 55
Warlop, Michel, 43
Wellmon, W. H., 28, 111–12
Whiteman, Paul, 42, 46
Wiéner, Jean, 34–6
Willen, Barney, 87, 166
women's liberation, 147, 158–9, 161
Wooding, Sam, 45
World War I, 20, 107; impact on national life in France, 102, 104, 105, 113, 120; and spread of jazz, 8, 16–17, 113, 115, 120, 124, 132
World War II, 53, 59, 197. *See also* Occupation of France

xenophobia, 114; and arrival of jazz in Paris, 47

Young, Lester, 187, 210n. 51
youth culture and jazz, 58–9, 134, 147, 150, 159, 166

'zazous', 58, 134, 208n. 15; rebelliousness of, 58, 135